# WHISKEY:
## WHAT TO DRINK NEXT

**STERLING EPICURE**
New York

An Imprint of Sterling Publishing
1166 Avenue of the Americas
New York, NY 10036

Conceived, edited, and designed by
Marshall Editions
The Old Brewery
6 Blundell Street
London N7 9BH
www.marshalleditions.com

The publishers will be grateful for any information that will assist them in keeping
future editions up to date. Although all reasonable care has been taken in the
preparation of this book, neither the publishers nor the author can accept any
liability for any consequence arising from the use thereof, or the information
contained therein.

ISBN 978-1-4549-1572-0

Distributed in Canada by Sterling Publishing
c/o Canadian Manda Group, 664 Annette Street
Toronto, Ontario, Canada M6S 2C8

For information about custom editions, special sales, and premium and
corporate purchases, please contact Sterling Special Sales at 800-805-5489
or specialsales@sterlingpublishing.com.

**Senior Editor** Chelsea Edwards
**Designer** Hugh Schermuly
**Illustrator** Jason Anscomb
**Picture Researcher** Sarah Bell
**Art Director** Caroline Guest
**Creative Director** Moira Clinch
**Publisher** Paul Carslake

Manufactured in China
2  4  6  8  10  9  7  5  3  1

www.sterlingpublishing.com

Cover image: Photography by Sarah Bell

# WHISKEY:
# WHAT TO DRINK NEXT

## CRAFT WHISKEYS, CLASSIC FLAVORS,
## NEW DISTILLERIES, FUTURE TRENDS

**DOMINIC ROSKROW**

STERLING EPICURE
New York

# THE PERIODIC TABLE OF WHISKY

The whiskies are grouped together according to their origins. Columns are arranged to reflect the chapter groupings of the book.

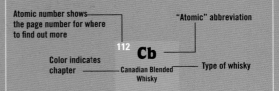

## HOW THE TABLE WORKS

Atomic number shows the page number for where to find out more

"Atomic" abbreviation

112 Cb

Color indicates chapter

Canadian Blended Whisky

Type of whisky

| | | | | | | |
|---|---|---|---|---|---|---|
| **16 Sl**<br>Scotch Single Malt Whisky: Lowlands | | | | | | |
| **18 Sc**<br>Scotch Single Malt Whisky: Campbeltown | **34 Sbc**<br>Scotch Single Malt Whisky: Bourbon Cask | | | | | **108 Sab**<br>South African Blended Whisky |
| **20 She**<br>Scotch Single Malt Whisky: East Highlands | **36 Sni**<br>Scotch Single Malt Whisky: Non-Islay, Peated | **50 Isp**<br>Irish Single Malt Whiskey: Peated | **64 Sa**<br>South African Single Malt Whisky | | **94 Rsb**<br>Rare and Exclusive Scottish Blended Whisky | **110 Spb**<br>Spanish Blended Whisky |
| **22 Sh**<br>Scotch Single Malt Whisky: South Highlands | **38 Shc**<br>Scotch Single Malt Whisky: Sherry Cask | **52 As**<br>American Single Malt Whiskey | **66 Ts**<br>Taiwanese Single Malt Whisky | **78 Fs**<br>French Single Malt Whisky | **96 Sib**<br>Standard Irish Blended Whiskey | **112 Cb**<br>Canadian Blended Whisky |
| **24 Snh**<br>Scotch Single Malt Whisky: Northeast Highlands | **40 Sfp**<br>Scotch Single Malt Whisky: Special Finishes, Port | **54 Js**<br>Japanese Single Malt Whisky | **68 Bs**<br>Belgian Single Malt Whisky | **80 Gs**<br>Germanic Single Malt Whisky | **98 Pbi**<br>Premium Blended Irish Whiskey | **118 Fbm**<br>Fruity Blended Malt Whiskies |
| **26 Ssb**<br>Scotch Single Malt Whisky: Speyside—Bourbon Cask | **42 Sfr**<br>Scotch Single Malt Whisky: Special Finishes, Rum | **56 Jsp**<br>Japanese Single Malt Whisky: Peated | **70 Ds**<br>Danish Single Malt Whisky | **82 Ms**<br>Mediterranean Single Malt Whisky | **100 Sjb**<br>Standard Japanese Blended Whisky | **120 Sb**<br>Spicy Blended Malt Whiskies |
| **28 Ssc**<br>Scotch Single Malt Whisky: Speyside—Sherry Cask | **44 Sfm**<br>Scotch Single Malt Whisky: Special Finishes, Madeira | **58 Asm**<br>Australian Single Malt Whisky | **72 Dus**<br>Dutch Single Malt Whisky | **84 Sws**<br>Swedish Single Malt Whisky | **102 Pjb**<br>Premium Japanese Blended Whisky | **122 Smp**<br>Smoky and Peaty Blended Malt Whiskies |
| **30 Si**<br>Scotch Single Malt Whisky: Islands | **46 Sfw**<br>Scotch Single Malt Whisky: Special Finishes, Wine | **60 Ism**<br>Indian Single Malt Whisky | **74 Es**<br>English Single Malt Whisky | **90 Stb**<br>Standard Scottish Blended Whisky | **104 Fb**<br>French Blended Whisky | **124 Jb**<br>Japanese Blended Malt Whiskies |
| **32 Sy**<br>Scotch Single Malt Whisky: Islay | **48 Is**<br>Irish Single Malt Whiskey | **62 Nz**<br>New Zealand Single Malt Whisky | **76 Ws**<br>Welsh Single Malt Whisky | **92 Psb**<br>Premium Scottish Blended Whisky | **106 Ibw**<br>Indian Blended Whisky | **126 Eh**<br>European Hybrid Blended Malt Whisky |

# KEY TO THE COLOR CODING
## The pages in each chapter also follow these colors

| | | | | | | 206 **Fsi** Flavored Whiskies—Scotland and Ireland |
|---|---|---|---|---|---|---|
| | | 162 **Dr** Dutch Rye Whisky | 178 **Ips** Irish Pot Still and Malt Whiskey | 194 **Afg** American Four-Grain Whiskey | 208 **Fiw** Fruit-Infused Whiskies |
| 132 **Skb** Standard Kentucky Bourbon | | 152 **Sar** Standard American Rye Whiskey | 164 **Or** Other European Rye Whiskies | 180 **Jg** Japanese Grain Whisky | 196 **Dfg** Dutch Five-Grain Malt Spirit | 210 **Ipn** Irish Poitín |
| 134 **Pkb** Premium Kentucky Bourbon | | 154 **Par** Premium American Rye Whiskey | 170 **Aw** American Wheat Whiskey | 182 **Sag** South African Grain Whisky | 198 **Ow** Oat Whisk(e)y | 212 **Tw** Triticale Whisky |
| 136 **Nkb** Non-Kentucky Bourbon | 142 **Tb** Tennessee Whiskey | 156 **Cr** Canadian Blended Rye Whisky | 172 **Sg** Scottish Grain Whisky | 184 **Eo** European Oat and Other Grain Whiskies | 200 **Qw** Quinoa Whiskey | 214 **Frw** French Rogue Whisky |
| 138 **Nwb** New Wave/Craft Bourbon | 144 **Kc** Kentucky Corn Whiskey | 158 **Sr** Single Malt Rye Whisky | 174 **Ipt** Irish Single Pot Still Whiskey | 190 **Etg** English Three-Grain Whisky | 202 **Sm** Smoked Whisk(e)y | 216 **Sow** Solera Whisky |
| 140 **Bb** Baby Bourbon | 146 **Oc** Other Corn Whiskey/ Moonshine | 160 **Ar** Austrian Rye Whisky | 176 **Ig** Irish Grain Whiskey | 192 **Itg** Italian Three-Grain Whisky | 204 **Fwu** Flavored Whiskeys—USA | 218 **Ym** Young Malt Spirit Drinks |

# INTRODUCTION

Whisky. There is no other spirit, no other drink, quite like it. It invokes passion, it promotes lifelong friendship, and now that we have whisky from all over the world, it has the capacity to take you on a global journey.

Top-grade whisky is all about provenance and heritage, of putting quality before quantity, and of appreciating art in a glass. I've been a drinks writer for nearly 25 years now, but until I became editor of *Whisky Magazine* I never realized that a drink could change my life. But it has. I even ended up launching my own whisky range called Discovery Road and my own whisky and music festival called TRIBE. Exploring and finding new family; that's whisky right there.

As a former newspaper journalist, my instincts are to question everything. And the more you learn about whisky, the more questions there are to answer. It seems to be a complicated drink to understand, but it needn't be. And that's where this book comes in. Through the use of color, the periodic table, and whisky "atoms", this book will take you on a simple path into the most complex regions of whisky. The approach is straightforward, but no other book explores Triticale whiskey, or Italian three-grain whisky, or South African solera whisky, as this book does. And it does so in a fun way.

I hope you enjoy dipping into this as much as I enjoyed writing it. Happy dramming and, as they say in Scotland, sláinte!

Dominic Roskrow

# ABOUT THIS BOOK

Whisky is in vogue right now and there are myriad books that describe in depth the whisky-making process and focus on distilleries around the world.

This book is different. It has taken all the different styles of whisky and grouped them into seven categories, given them seven different colors, and put them into seven different chapters, with the last chapter, "Rebel Whiskies," bringing together all the misfits and oddballs.

Each chapter has a short introduction about the overall category—for example, single malt whisky—followed by a series of spreads covering each style of malt within the genre.

Through the use of color and the easy-to-understand atom illustration, you can quickly and easily navigate around the world of whisky.

**CENTRAL RING**
This ring contains the names of the distilleries or whiskies that best represent each style.

At the top of the page there is a guide identifying the countries that produce each style of whisky, the range of alcoholic strengths from minimum to maximum, and the grains used in its production.

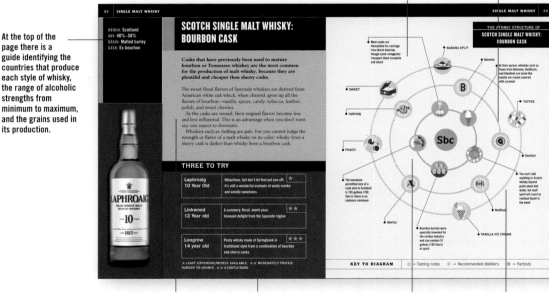

The main body of text explains a little bit of background to the whisky category, its history, how it developed as it has, and anecdotal commentary on its position in the world of whisky.

Where there are numerous whiskies within a particular genre, we have picked three that we recommend you to try. In most cases, these will be at different price points and different levels of rarity.

**INNER RING**
Featured here are some unusual or surprising facts about each category.

**OUTER RING**
Typically, each atom has a ring with a description of the flavors you would find in each whisky.

# HOW TO TASTE WHISKY

You've no doubt seen or heard all sorts of "experts" telling you how you should and shouldn't drink whisky and it can all get just a little bit overwhelming. So let's get a few things cleared up right from the start.

1. Whisky is an alcoholic drink made and consumed for pleasure. We are not in a science laboratory here.

2. Despite what some people will tell you, there is only one rule about drinking whisky—and that's that you should drink it any way you like.

That said, though, there are guidelines that, if followed, may enhance the pleasure derived from nosing and sipping whisky. You can pick and choose which guidelines to follow and which to ignore, but I think we can all see the foolhardiness of drowning a rare malt whisky in cola, or of trying to appreciate the subtleties of a great bourbon while eating chicken curry or chili dogs.

Here, then, are a few simple guidelines.

## THE GLASS

It always amuses me how many whisky books include information on what glass to use when nosing whisky and then the publisher sticks a picture of a tumbler on the cover. Just as with tasting, the glass you use depends on what you prefer. A tumbler is fine if you want to add ice and cradle it in your hands. Branded whisky glasses from the industry itself come in all shapes and sizes.

But for nosing it is better to use a small glass, preferably a copita glass, stemmed or unstemmed, with a bulbous bottom and a thin tapered neck. This captures the aromas from the whisky and allows you to nose them more easily. The whisky industry itself increasingly uses a specially designed whisky glass with a solid, stubby base. You'll find Glencairn glasses at any good whisky shop. Otherwise, a small red wine glass would suffice.

### GETTING STARTED

Pour your whisky into the glass until it is one-quarter to one-third full. Get a small jug of cool but not over-chilled mineral water, just in case it's needed. That's it. You're good to go.

### NOSING

Bring your nose slowly to the rim of the glass. Breathe in gently for a short time, then move the glass away. Be careful—whisky is a strong alcohol. Return and approach again. Try both nostrils individually and see if you recognize any aromas. Then taste.

### TASTING

Put a small amount of whisky into the mouth. Be careful, because it might be at a very high strength. When you're comfortable, taste a little more. Move the whisky around your entire mouth and try to identify flavors. Then either spit or swallow. If you're doing this for fun, swallow. But remember, your palate will get weary very quickly. Enjoy.

### WATER OR NO WATER?

Despite what you hear, a small amount of water is good for whisky. It unlocks aromas. So once you have tasted it neat, add water to suit your personal palate. A few drops should suffice, so it's a good idea to use a pipette. There is no right or wrong here—professional blenders will normally make the mix half-and-half so that they can nose around 20% ABV (alcohol by volume).

## TASTING NOTES

Tasting comes with practice. Most of us aren't particularly naturally gifted, so the more you taste the better at it you will become. And remember, tasting notes aren't really for anyone but you. Make them as personal as you like and keep them as a reminder for you of what you did and didn't like.

## A WORLD OF DIFFERENCE

To me, saying you don't like the taste of whisky is a little like saying you don't like curry. Both terms are generic, and there are dozens of different types within each category.

This is important, because when people say they don't like the taste of whisky they normally mean blended Scotch, and invariably at a young age they had a blended Scotch as a chaser after too much beer and it made them ill.

The mere fact that you're reading this suggests you've overcome that hurdle, but it's really important to remember that different whiskies from different countries are MEANT to taste different from Scottish single malt whiskies. Bourbon is as different from most single malts as olives are different from grapes.

Increasingly we're seeing the development of national whisky identities, just as we have regional styles in Scotland. The whole point of this book is to guide you into previously unchartered waters—and it may be that your perfect whisky is an Australian rye whisky that tastes like nothing else you've ever experienced. So it's good you found it, isn't it?

You're about to start on a great adventure, one that will lead you to pretty distilleries in some of the world's loveliest locations. You're going to make new friends and be adopted by a global family. And you're going to taste some of the finest spirits on the planet. Frankly, it just doesn't get better than that. Enjoy.

# SINGLE MALT WHISKY

# CHAPTER ONE

Single malt whisky is a simple drink consisting of just three ingredients—malted barley, yeast, and water—and yet it provides a complex, sophisticated, and flavorsome spirit that can be quite sublime.

For most whisky enthusiasts, single malt is where it all begins and ends. Not just any old single malt: Scottish single malt, made with malted barley. Other grains can be malted, and in theory can therefore claim to be single malts, but for the purpose of simplicity, and because this book is all about associating flavors, these are dealt with elsewhere.

As for the "Scottish" bit, it's true that the vast majority of single malts are Scottish, and that Scotland leads the world in their production. But as we shall see, many other nations produce excellent single malt whiskies.

So what do we mean by single malt whisky? The word "single" refers to the fact that the whisky comes from just one distillery. Unless the label tells you that you are drinking a single cask whisky, the contents of your bottle will be made up of lots of barrels of different ages and styles.

It is the magic of malt whisky that no matter how much we learn about its production, we'll never be able to fully control what happens to the spirit during maturation. Every cask matures whisky spirit differently. And because whisky is produced in batches, once the makers have chosen their casks to create the recognized flavor of the whisky in question, the whole process has to start again from scratch.

Single malt whisky is spirit distilled from beer and then matured for a minimum of three years in an oak barrel. It is made by taking barley, malting it (letting it start to grow), and then halting that process by drying.

Malting allows the kernel of the grain to be broken, thus accessing all the compounds needed to make alcohol. During the drying period, peat fires may be used, and it is from their smoke that the smoky-flavored whiskies get their taste—not, as is often thought, from the water used in the process.

Once the malted barley is dried, it is ground into flour and hot water is added to it, normally two or three times. The husks are then removed, and yeast is added to the sweet, dark liquid that remains. The yeast feeds on the sugars in the wash, creating carbon dioxide and alcohol—distiller's beer.

Distillation is the process of separating alcohol from water. This is done in a pot still—a large copper kettle. During the first distillation, all the alcohol spirit is re-condensed and collected.

In the second distillation, the first alcohols to come off, the strongest ones, are foul-tasting and poisonous. These are collected in a tank until the distillers reach the point where they want to start collecting the body of the spirit. This is collected in a different container. The process continues until the alcohols are weak and bland, and these "tails" are collected separately. The "heads" from the first part of the distillation and the tails at the end are mixed and kept ready for the next distillation.

The middle part of the run, the "body," has water added to it to bring it to the ideal strength for casking. It is then put into oak barrels that would probably have previously contained bourbon or sherry—malt spirit is too delicate to mature in spicy, tannin-rich, virgin oak casks. Then the cask is stored, and the magic begins...

**ORIGIN:** Scotland
**ABV:** 40%–60%
**GRAIN:** Malted barley
**CASK:** Mainly ex-bourbon, some ex-sherry

# SCOTCH SINGLE MALT WHISKY: LOWLANDS

**Traditionally, whiskies from Lowland distilleries are light and floral, in contrast to their Highland counterparts, which are heavier and oilier. There is a very good historical reason for this distinction.**

Lowland stills are bigger than Highland stills, because their proximity to Edinburgh and Glasgow made them the most accessible and therefore the most popular Scottish whiskies. The bigger the still, the lighter the whisky. This is because as the spirit passes over copper, impurities and flavor compounds are removed. The further the spirit travels, the more its heaviest components fall to the bottom of the still.

This reflux process means that only the lightest and most floral spirits make it to the condensation stage. As a result, Lowland whiskies are lighter and may not be able to mature in a wooden cask for as long as a Highland one might.

## THREE TO TRY

| | | |
|---|---|---|
| **Bladnoch**<br>**10 Year Old** | Delightfully refreshing and zesty. Lemon and lime starburst with a sprinkling of savory spice | ★ |
| **Auchentoshan**<br>**21 Year Old** | Pronounced "ok-en-tosh-en," this is the distillery's malt at its peak. Lots of honey, vanilla and fruit, and traces of milk chocolate | ★★ |
| **Rosebank**<br>**12 year old** | This product of a now defunct distillery defines the region's floral heritage | ★★★ |

★ LEAST EXPENSIVE/WIDELY AVAILABLE ★★ MODERATELY PRICED/HARDER TO SOURCE ★★★ COSTLY/RARE

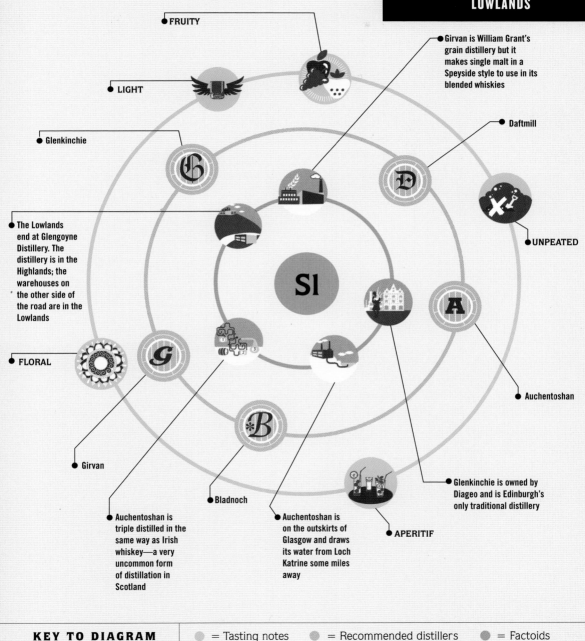

● FRUITY

● LIGHT

Girvan is William Grant's grain distillery but it makes single malt in a Speyside style to use in its blended whiskies

● Daftmill

● Glenkinchie

● UNPEATED

The Lowlands end at Glengoyne Distillery. The distillery is in the Highlands; the warehouses on the other side of the road are in the Lowlands

Sl

● FLORAL

● Auchentoshan

● Girvan

Auchentoshan is triple distilled in the same way as Irish whiskey—a very uncommon form of distillation in Scotland

● Bladnoch

Auchentoshan is on the outskirts of Glasgow and draws its water from Loch Katrine some miles away

Glenkinchie is owned by Diageo and is Edinburgh's only traditional distillery

● APERITIF

**KEY TO DIAGRAM**   ● = Tasting notes   ● = Recommended distillers   ● = Factoids

**ORIGIN:** Scotland
**ABV:** 46%–58%
**GRAIN:** Malted barley
**CASK:** Ex-bourbon, ex-sherry

# SCOTCH SINGLE MALT WHISKY: CAMPBELTOWN

**Campbeltown has only recently been acknowledged as a distinct whisky region. This recognition was long overdue, because it never made sense to class its full-flavored, gutsy products with light and floral Lowlands whiskies.**

This long finger of land in southwestern Scotland doesn't offer a great deal in the way of whiskies, but those it does produce are well worth seeking out. J & A Mitchell and Company can take much of the credit for keeping whisky traditions alive in the area, although the folk at Glen Scotia have played their part, too.

The styles may vary, but there is a distinctive Campbeltown flavor and a waxy, briny quality to all the local produce. Peat may be used in production, and in the case of Longrow, it's the main characteristic.

## THREE TO TRY

| | | |
|---|---|---|
| **Hazelburn 8 Year Old** | Not typical of the region, this is a triple-distilled sweet and clean whisky with a honeycomb heart | ★ |
| **Longrow 14 Year Old** | Lots of peat, oak, salt, and spice make this a savory whisky lover's idea of heaven | ★★ |
| **Springbank 18 Year Old** | A big whisky, with unripe banana, cocoa, licorice, and sugarcane as well as delicate smoke | ★★★ |

★ LEAST EXPENSIVE/WIDELY AVAILABLE  ★★ MODERATELY PRICED/ HARDER TO SOURCE  ★★★ COSTLY/RARE

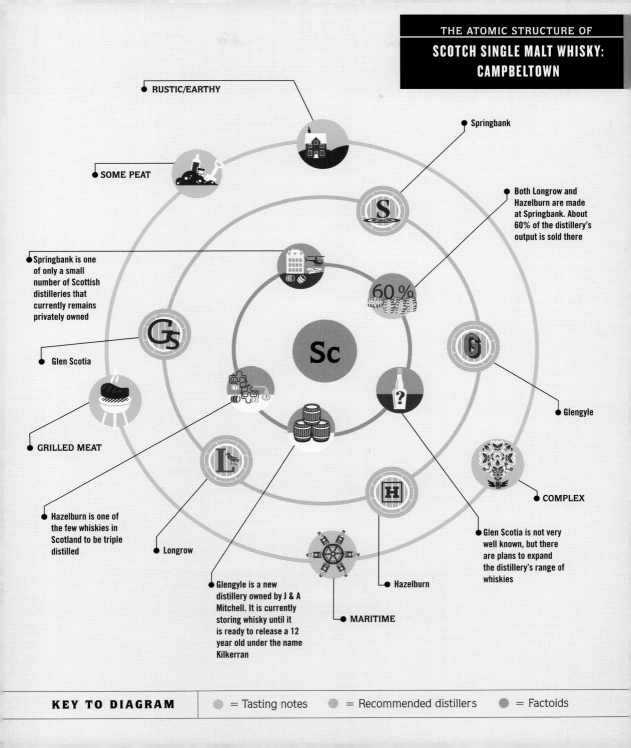

THE ATOMIC STRUCTURE OF
# SCOTCH SINGLE MALT WHISKY: CAMPBELTOWN

RUSTIC/EARTHY

SOME PEAT

Springbank

Both Longrow and Hazelburn are made at Springbank. About 60% of the distillery's output is sold there

Springbank is one of only a small number of Scottish distilleries that currently remains privately owned

**S**

**60%**

**Sc**

**Gs**

Glen Scotia

**G**

Glengyle

GRILLED MEAT

?

Hazelburn is one of the few whiskies in Scotland to be triple distilled

**L**

**H**

COMPLEX

Longrow

Glen Scotia is not very well known, but there are plans to expand the distillery's range of whiskies

Glengyle is a new distillery owned by J & A Mitchell. It is currently storing whisky until it is ready to release a 12 year old under the name Kilkerran

Hazelburn

MARITIME

**ORIGIN:** Scotland
**ABV:** 40%–60%
**GRAIN:** Malted barley
**CASK:** Ex-bourbon,
ex-sherry

# SCOTCH SINGLE MALT WHISKY: EAST HIGHLANDS

**The distilleries of this region, which forms an arc around Aberdeen, are widely separated, but are well worth making long journeys between them.**

The whiskies produced here are of three main types: the rich, honeyed sugar-and-spice delights of Aberfeldy and Dalwhinnie; the fully paid-up members of Scotch whisky's misfit squad, feisty and challenging creations such as Fettercairn, Glencadam, and Glen Garioch; and plain-talking "tourist" whiskies—Royal Lochnagar, Edradour, and Blair Athol.

There is a sweetness to these whiskies. The honeycomb center of Dalwhinnie and Aberfeldy contrasts starkly with esoteric Glen Garioch and earthy, rootsy Fettercairn. Edradour explores heavily peated whiskies and a large number of special cask finishes as well as more traditional Highland styles.

## THREE TO TRY

| | | |
|---|---|---|
| **Glen Garioch Founder's Reserve** | Excellent introduction to the magic, with some chocolate and nut, chewy barley and rich fruit | ★ |
| **Dalwhinnie 25 Year Old** | One of the original classic malts, with a rich honeycomb heart bouncing off a smoky base and yellow and tropical fruits cuddling up to peat reek | ★★ |
| **Aberfeldy 21 Year Old** | Everything a Highland whisky should be. Honey, liquorice, orange, and a touch of peat and oak | ★★★ |

★ LEAST EXPENSIVE/WIDELY AVAILABLE  ★★ MODERATELY PRICED/ HARDER TO SOURCE  ★★★ COSTLY/RARE

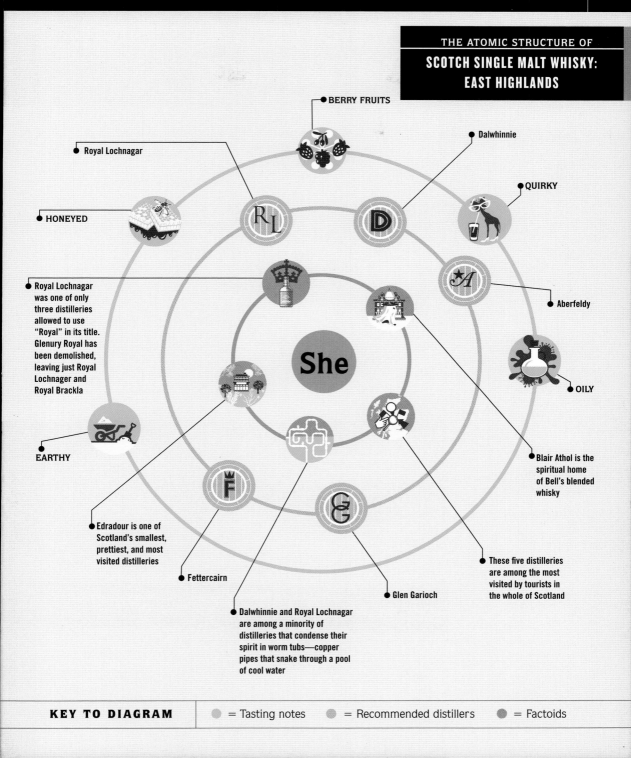

BERRY FRUITS

Royal Lochnagar

Dalwhinnie

QUIRKY

HONEYED

Royal Lochnagar
was one of only
three distilleries
allowed to use
"Royal" in its title.
Glenury Royal has
been demolished,
leaving just Royal
Lochnager and
Royal Brackla

She

Aberfeldy

OILY

EARTHY

Blair Athol is the
spiritual home
of Bell's blended
whisky

Edradour is one of
Scotland's smallest,
prettiest, and most
visited distilleries

Fettercairn

These five distilleries
are among the most
visited by tourists in
the whole of Scotland

Glen Garioch

Dalwhinnie and Royal Lochnagar
are among a minority of
distilleries that condense their
spirit in worm tubs—copper
pipes that snake through a pool
of cool water

**KEY TO DIAGRAM**   ● = Tasting notes   ● = Recommended distillers   ● = Factoids

**ORIGIN:** Scotland
**ABV:** 40%–60%
**GRAIN:** Malted barley
**CASK:** Ex-bourbon, ex-sherry

# SCOTCH SINGLE MALT WHISKY: SOUTH HIGHLANDS

**The five distilleries in this region are all mid-league players. Ignoring Loch Lomond to the west, which is a complex multi-malt-making plant, the other four are linked by their no-nonsense, easy-to-drink whiskies.**

Glengoyne has a delightful waterfall. It's proud of its peat-free whisky, which in its most juvenile form is an unspectacular malt. But its sherry-casked special bottlings are meaty, big, and feisty.

Deanston is an old cotton mill with a waterwheel that generates electricity. Its visitor facilities have been upgraded in recent years. The whisky has improved, too.

Tullibardine makes a wide range of whiskies and is one of Scotland's most visited distilleries.

Although overshadowed by the on-site Famous Grouse Experience—a celebration of the blend—Glenturret is lovely and as traditional as tartan.

## THREE TO TRY

| | | |
|---|---|---|
| **Deanston 12 Year Old** | Longer, fuller and richer than of old, with orange and ginger barley delivered in unfussy and clean style | ★ |
| **Glengoyne 18 year Old** | Some badass sherry casks and the odd drift of sulfur, but plenty of butterscotch maple and vanilla | ★★ |
| **Tullibardine Vintage Release** | Some of these date to the early 1960s and they're Christmas cake, chocolate, candy and oak all rolled in to one | ★★★ |

★ LEAST EXPENSIVE/WIDELY AVAILABLE  ★★ MODERATELY PRICED/ HARDER TO SOURCE  ★★★ COSTLY/RARE

THE ATOMIC STRUCTURE OF

# SCOTCH SINGLE MALT WHISKY: SOUTH HIGHLANDS

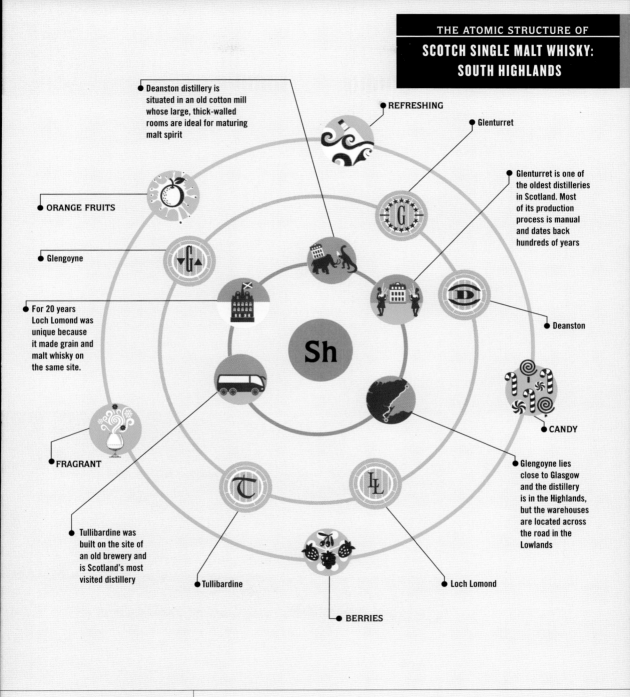

Deanston distillery is situated in an old cotton mill whose large, thick-walled rooms are ideal for maturing malt spirit

REFRESHING

Glenturret

ORANGE FRUITS

Glengoyne

Glenturret is one of the oldest distilleries in Scotland. Most of its production process is manual and dates back hundreds of years

For 20 years Loch Lomond was unique because it made grain and malt whisky on the same site.

Sh

Deanston

CANDY

FRAGRANT

Glengoyne lies close to Glasgow and the distillery is in the Highlands, but the warehouses are located across the road in the Lowlands

Tullibardine was built on the site of an old brewery and is Scotland's most visited distillery

Tullibardine

Loch Lomond

BERRIES

**KEY TO DIAGRAM** ● = Tasting notes ● = Recommended distillers ● = Factoids

**ORIGIN:** Scotland
**ABV:** 40%–58%
**GRAIN:** Malted barley
**CASK:** Ex-bourbon, ex-sherry, ex-port pipes, French wine casks

# SCOTCH SINGLE MALT WHISKY: NORTHEAST HIGHLANDS

**Although sometimes known as the forgotten coastline, the eastern shore of Scotland to the north of Loch Ness is the location of some of the nation's most iconic distilleries.**

The distilleries of the Northeast Highlands effectively rebut the notion that each region produces just a single style of whisky. The output here is richly varied, from the full-flavored, traditional, and rich Dalmore, through the very fruity Balblair and Glenmorangie, to the salty and citrusy Old Pulteney. Yet they all share the strong, rich flavors of a good Highland malt and a clean and fresh taste. Additionally, they almost all place a low emphasis on peat—the sole exception to this general rule is the iconic and now defunct Brora, which was the sister distillery to Clynelish.

## THREE TO TRY

| | | |
|---|---|---|
| **Glenmorangie Traditional** | Rhymes with "orangey," which partly describes its taste. There is also honey, fresh clean malt, and a little nuttiness | ★ |
| **Dalmore 15 Year Old** | Big, bold, and spicy, with oaky tannins punching above their weight, satsumas, vanilla, cinnamon, and floral polish | ★★ |
| **Brora 30 Year Old** | If it's a proprietary bottling, it'll be fabulous. Buckets of fruit and spice and peat: whisky perfection? | ★★★ |

★ LEAST EXPENSIVE/WIDELY AVAILABLE  ★★ MODERATELY PRICED/ HARDER TO SOURCE  ★★★COSTLY/RARE

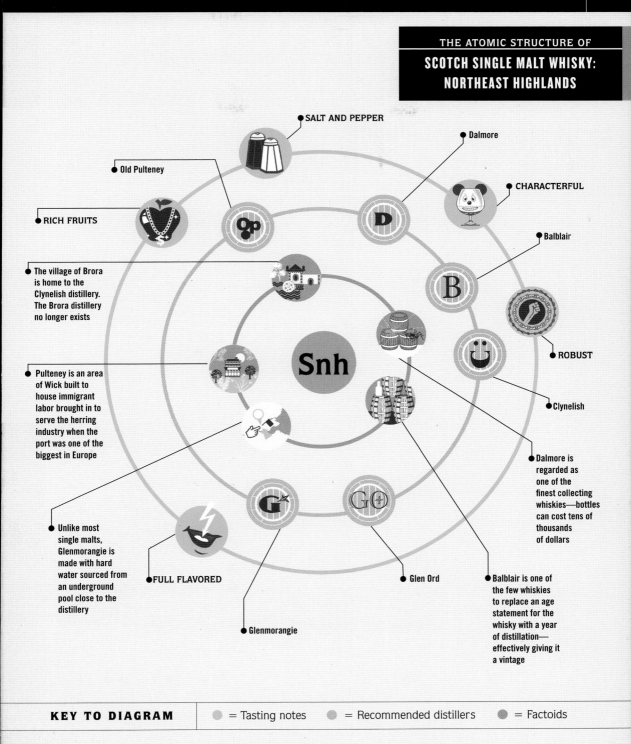

THE ATOMIC STRUCTURE OF
# SCOTCH SINGLE MALT WHISKY: NORTHEAST HIGHLANDS

SALT AND PEPPER

Dalmore

Old Pulteney

CHARACTERFUL

RICH FRUITS

Balblair

The village of Brora is home to the Clynelish distillery. The Brora distillery no longer exists

**Snh**

ROBUST

Pulteney is an area of Wick built to house immigrant labor brought in to serve the herring industry when the port was one of the biggest in Europe

Clynelish

Dalmore is regarded as one of the finest collecting whiskies—bottles can cost tens of thousands of dollars

Unlike most single malts, Glenmorangie is made with hard water sourced from an underground pool close to the distillery

FULL FLAVORED

Glen Ord

Balblair is one of the few whiskies to replace an age statement for the whisky with a year of distillation—effectively giving it a vintage

Glenmorangie

**KEY TO DIAGRAM** ● = Tasting notes ● = Recommended distillers ● = Factoids

ORIGIN: Scotland
ABV: 40%–60%
GRAIN: Malted barley
CASK: Ex-bourbon

# SCOTCH SINGLE MALT WHISKY: SPEYSIDE—BOURBON CASK

Under U.S. law, a barrel may be used for whisky only once. After that it must be sold on. Consequently there is a ready source of good-quality bourbon and Tennessee whiskey casks that are ideally suited to enriching Scottish malt.

During maturation, changes in temperature cause the spirit to move in the cask and expand and contract. The color of the whisky comes as a result of this process. A host of flavors that we may identify as fruity, nutty, or spicy have in fact been created by a chemical reaction between the alcohol and the wood. Oxidization of the spirit also occurs at this time.

American white oak barrels that are redolent of the whiskey they once contained can add attractive, sweet, dessert-like qualities to the new product.

## THREE TO TRY

| | | |
|---|---|---|
| BenRiach 12 Year Old | Vanilla, butterscotch, and yellow fruits make this a perfect entry-level whisky | ★ |
| Glenlivet Nadurra 16 Year Old | Bourbon cask whisky at its very finest. Rich, creamy, and with tropical fruits | ★★ |
| The Balvenie 14 Year Old Golden Cask | All Balvenie bourbon cask whiskies are great, but this glows with yellow fruits, pineapple, and cream | ★★★ |

★ LEAST EXPENSIVE/WIDELY AVAILABLE   ★★ MODERATELY PRICED/ HARDER TO SOURCE   ★★★ COSTLY/RARE

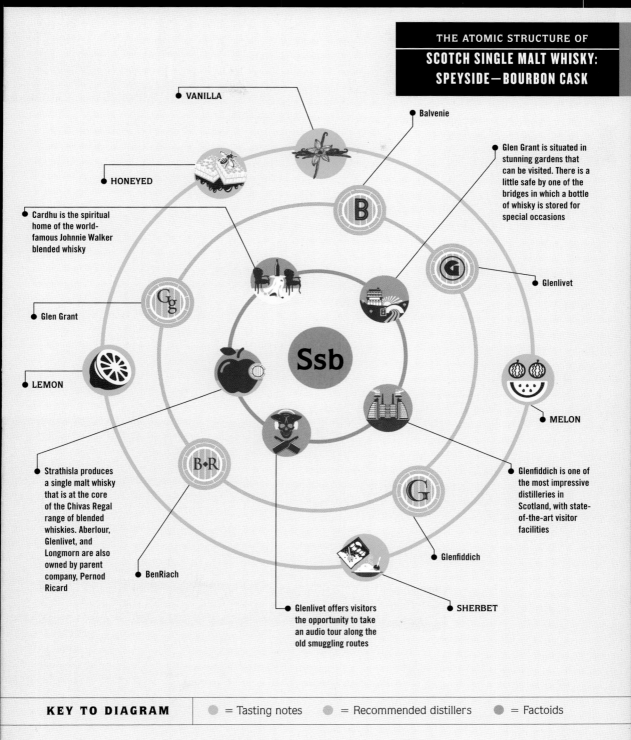

THE ATOMIC STRUCTURE OF

# SCOTCH SINGLE MALT WHISKY: SPEYSIDE—BOURBON CASK

VANILLA

Balvenie

HONEYED

Glen Grant is situated in stunning gardens that can be visited. There is a little safe by one of the bridges in which a bottle of whisky is stored for special occasions

Cardhu is the spiritual home of the world-famous Johnnie Walker blended whisky

B

G

Glenlivet

Gg

Glen Grant

Ssb

LEMON

MELON

Strathisla produces a single malt whisky that is at the core of the Chivas Regal range of blended whiskies. Aberlour, Glenlivet, and Longmorn are also owned by parent company, Pernod Ricard

B•R

G

Glenfiddich is one of the most impressive distilleries in Scotland, with state-of-the-art visitor facilities

BenRiach

Glenfiddich

Glenlivet offers visitors the opportunity to take an audio tour along the old smuggling routes

SHERBET

**KEY TO DIAGRAM**    ● = Tasting notes    ● = Recommended distillers    ● = Factoids

ORIGIN: Scotland
ABV: 40%–58%
GRAIN: Malted barley
CASK: Ex-sherry casks

# SCOTCH SINGLE MALT WHISKY: SPEYSIDE—SHERRY CASK

**Between one half and two-thirds of all Scotland's distilleries are located in the Speyside region. They're there because the water of the Spey River and its tributaries is plentiful and perfect for distillation.**

Speyside was a hotbed of smuggling until 1824, when the Excise Act reduced government tax on whisky and encouraged the growth of legal distilleries. The first whisky-maker to set up in the region was Glenlivet's George Smith; his success encouraged many others to set up their own businesses nearby.

Speyside whisky tends to be clean, sweet, and fruity. Sherried whiskies—those matured in casks that have previously been used to hold sherry—tend to be rich in red berry flavors and orange fruits. They may taste like Christmas cake and have feisty, earthy tones.

## THREE TO TRY

| | | |
|---|---|---|
| **Glenfarclas 105** | Classic, full-strength portion of sherried loveliness that is widely regarded as the last word in whiskies of this style | ★ |
| **Glendronach 15 Year Old** | Some object to the sulfur meaty notes, but most adore the underlying orange and red fruits | ★★ |
| **Macallan 25 Year Old** | Oloroso sherry dominates, with tannin and spice in supporting roles. There are distinctive orange and raisin notes, too | ★★★ |

★ LEAST EXPENSIVE/WIDELY AVAILABLE  ★★ MODERATELY PRICED/ HARDER TO SOURCE  ★★★ COSTLY/RARE

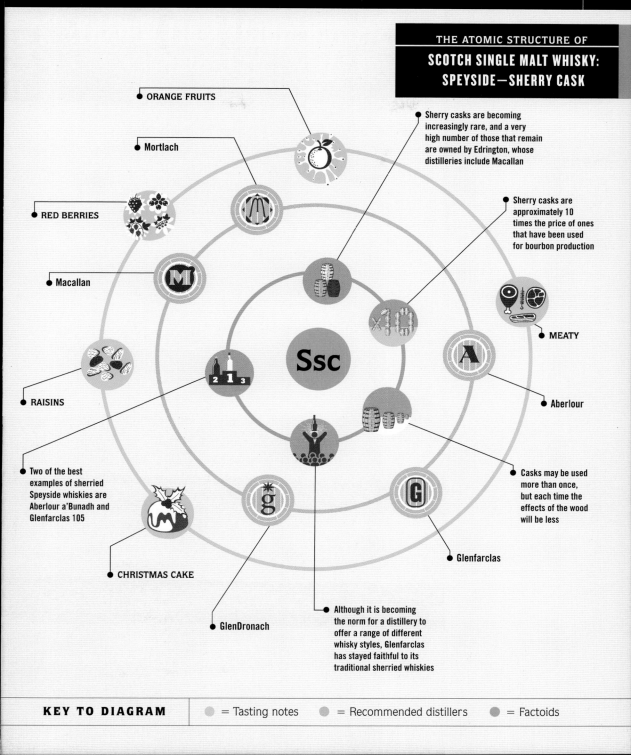

THE ATOMIC STRUCTURE OF
# SCOTCH SINGLE MALT WHISKY: SPEYSIDE—SHERRY CASK

ORANGE FRUITS

Mortlach

Sherry casks are becoming increasingly rare, and a very high number of those that remain are owned by Edrington, whose distilleries include Macallan

RED BERRIES

Sherry casks are approximately 10 times the price of ones that have been used for bourbon production

Macallan

**Ssc**

MEATY

RAISINS

Aberlour

Two of the best examples of sherried Speyside whiskies are Aberlour a'Bunadh and Glenfarclas 105

Casks may be used more than once, but each time the effects of the wood will be less

CHRISTMAS CAKE

Glenfarclas

GlenDronach

Although it is becoming the norm for a distillery to offer a range of different whisky styles, Glenfarclas has stayed faithful to its traditional sherried whiskies

**KEY TO DIAGRAM** ● = Tasting notes ● = Recommended distillers ● = Factoids

ORIGIN: Scotland
ABV: 43%–60%
GRAIN: Malted barley
CASK: Ex-bourbon,
ex-sherry, ex-wine, rum,
Madeira, port

# SCOTCH SINGLE MALT WHISKY: ISLANDS

**The Scottish islands extend over a great distance, from Arran in the southwest to the Orkneys in the northeast, so it is unsurprising that they produce a broad range of whisky styles, from heavily peated to spicy and salty.**

On the islands, most whiskies are made by the traditional method of drying barley over peat fires—the coal that became readily available in mainland Scotland during the Industrial Revolution was little in evidence here. But not all island whiskies have a smoky flavor. Scapa in the Orkneys doesn't use peat and the original and principal styles of whiskies from Jura, Arran, and Tobermory are all peat-lite.

It's a triumph that distilleries on remote islands are still operating commercially when many mainland distilleries have been taken over or closed down. No region better illustrates the diversity of Scotch.

## THREE TO TRY

| | | |
|---|---|---|
| **Tobermory 10 Year Old** | They have upped the strength of this and don't filter it. Tasty, nutty, fruity, and peat-light | ★ |
| **Talisker 57 North** | Throws raw peat and brine onto the brittle peat and pepper for which the distillery is known | ★★ |
| **Highland Park 18 Year Old** | Seen by many as the best all-round malt, with honey, fruit, spice, peat, and oak in perfect balance | ★★★ |

★ LEAST EXPENSIVE/WIDELY AVAILABLE  ★★ MODERATELY PRICED/ HARDER TO SOURCE  ★★★ COSTLY/RARE

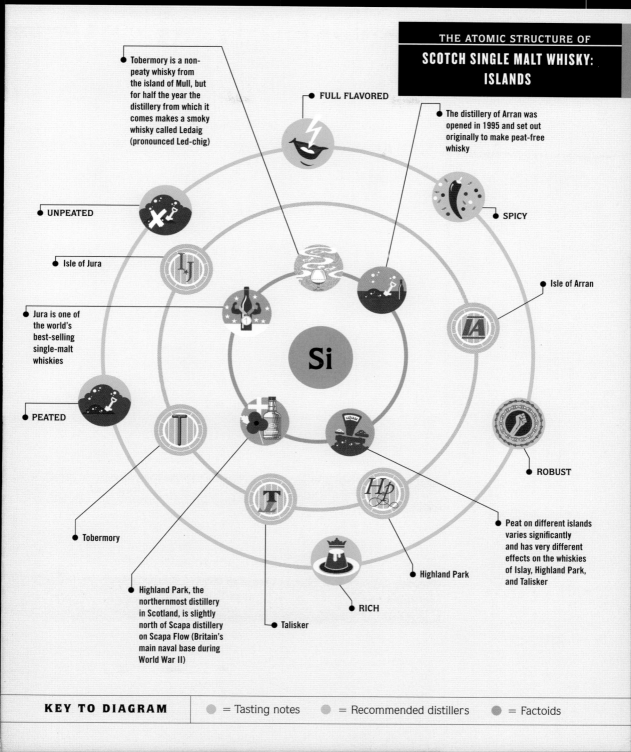

THE ATOMIC STRUCTURE OF

# SCOTCH SINGLE MALT WHISKY: ISLANDS

Tobermory is a non-peaty whisky from the island of Mull, but for half the year the distillery from which it comes makes a smoky whisky called Ledaig (pronounced Led-chig)

FULL FLAVORED

The distillery of Arran was opened in 1995 and set out originally to make peat-free whisky

UNPEATED

SPICY

Isle of Jura

Isle of Arran

Jura is one of the world's best-selling single-malt whiskies

Si

PEATED

ROBUST

Tobermory

Peat on different islands varies significantly and has very different effects on the whiskies of Islay, Highland Park, and Talisker

Highland Park

Highland Park, the northernmost distillery in Scotland, is slightly north of Scapa distillery on Scapa Flow (Britain's main naval base during World War II)

RICH

Talisker

**KEY TO DIAGRAM** ● = Tasting notes ● = Recommended distillers ● = Factoids

**ORIGIN:** Scotland
**ABV:** 43%–58%
**GRAIN:** Malted barley
**CASK:** Ex-bourbon, some ex-sherry

# SCOTCH SINGLE MALT WHISKY: ISLAY

**With eight working distilleries and more on the way, Islay—pronounced "eye-la"—is a paradise for whisky lovers, particularly those with a penchant for peaty and smoky varieties.**

In the south of the island are Ardbeg, Lagavulin, and Laphroaig—the holy trinity of peaty whiskies. Close behind them are Bowmore and Kilchoman. Caol Ila, one of Diageo's biggest distilleries, makes peaty whiskies and an unpeated malt; the latter is mainly for blending purposes.
    The principal malts from the other two distilleries—Bunnahabhain (pronounced "boona-ha-ven") and Bruichladdich ("brook-laddie")—have little or no peat, although both have respectable peated malts, too.
    Islay enjoys a status unmatched anywhere in the world, with the possible exception of Speyside, which has more distilleries.

## THREE TO TRY

| | | |
|---|---|---|
| **Laphroaig 10 Year Old** | Multidimensional and flavorful, with masses of bonfire smoke and barbecued meats | ★ |
| **Lagavulin 16 Year Old** | A true classic with big, bold wine notes, rich, mouth-coating oils, and wave after wave of smoke | ★★ |
| **Ardbeg Corryvreckan** | Hits you like a hammer blow and then unleashes a string of wonderful flavors, from chili spice to dark chocolate and puréed fruit | ★★★ |

★ LEAST EXPENSIVE/WIDELY AVAILABLE ★★ MODERATELY PRICED/ HARDER TO SOURCE ★★★COSTLY/RARE

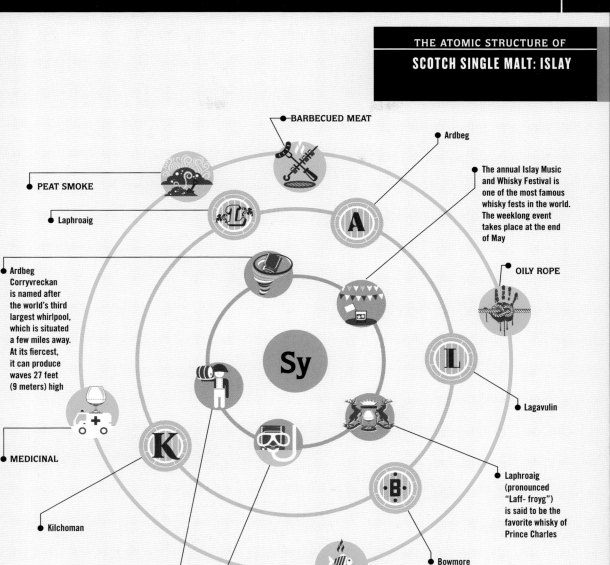

BARBECUED MEAT

Ardbeg

PEAT SMOKE

The annual Islay Music and Whisky Festival is one of the most famous whisky fests in the world. The weeklong event takes place at the end of May

Laphroaig

OILY ROPE

Ardbeg Corryvreckan is named after the world's third largest whirlpool, which is situated a few miles away. At its fiercest, it can produce waves 27 feet (9 meters) high

**Sy**

Lagavulin

MEDICINAL

Laphroaig (pronounced "Laff- froyg") is said to be the favorite whisky of Prince Charles

Kilchoman

Bowmore

The island's latest, and smallest, distillery is called Gartbreck and it is owned by a Frenchman

The excess heat produced when making Bowmore is used to heat the swimming pool next door

GRILLED FISH

**KEY TO DIAGRAM**      = Tasting notes      = Recommended distillers      = Factoids

**ORIGIN:** Scotland
**ABV:** 40%–58%
**GRAIN:** Malted barley
**CASK:** Ex-bourbon

# SCOTCH SINGLE MALT WHISKY: BOURBON CASK

**Casks that have previously been used to mature bourbon or Tennessee whiskey are the most common for the production of malt whisky, because they are plentiful and cheaper than sherry casks.**

The sweet floral flavors of Speyside whiskies are derived from American white oak which, when charred, gives up all the flavors of bourbon—vanilla, spices, candy, tobacco, leather, polish, and sweet cherries.

As the casks are reused, their original flavors become less and less influential. This is an advantage when you don't want any one aspect to dominate.

Whiskies such as Ardbeg are pale, but you cannot judge the strength or flavor of a malt whisky on its color: whisky from a sherry cask is darker than whisky from a bourbon cask.

## THREE TO TRY

| | | |
|---|---|---|
| **Laphroaig 10 Year Old** | Ubiquitous, but don't let that put you off: it's still a wonderful example of peaty smoke and vanilla sweetness | ★ |
| **Linkwood 12 Year old** | A summery, floral, sweet-pear, honeyed delight from the Speyside region | ★★ |
| **Longrow 14 year old** | Peaty whisky made at Springbank in traditional style from a combination of bourbon and sherry casks | ★★★ |

★ LEAST EXPENSIVE/WIDELY AVAILABLE  ★★ MODERATELY PRICED/ HARDER TO SOURCE  ★★★COSTLY/RARE

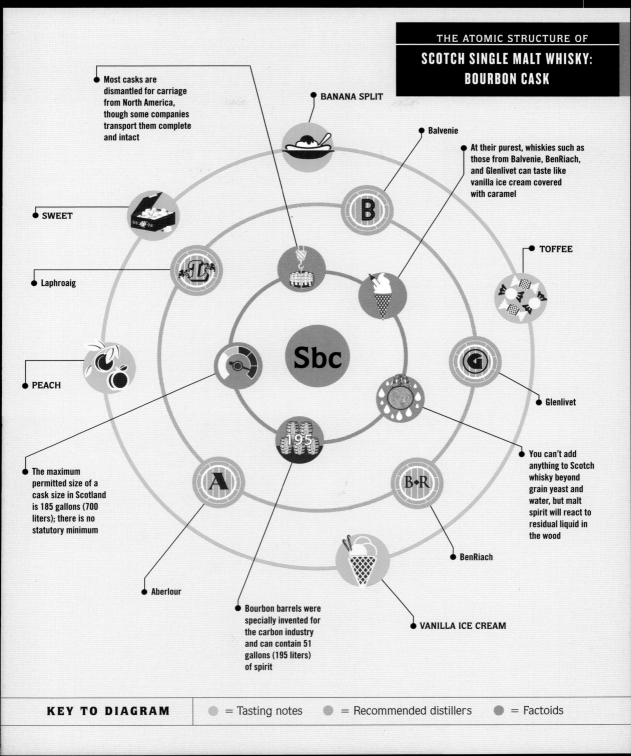

Most casks are dismantled for carriage from North America, though some companies transport them complete and intact

BANANA SPLIT

Balvenie

At their purest, whiskies such as those from Balvenie, BenRiach, and Glenlivet can taste like vanilla ice cream covered with caramel

SWEET

TOFFEE

Laphroaig

Sbc

PEACH

Glenlivet

You can't add anything to Scotch whisky beyond grain yeast and water, but malt spirit will react to residual liquid in the wood

The maximum permitted size of a cask size in Scotland is 185 gallons (700 liters); there is no statutory minimum

195

A

B•R

BenRiach

Aberlour

Bourbon barrels were specially invented for the carbon industry and can contain 51 gallons (195 liters) of spirit

VANILLA ICE CREAM

**KEY TO DIAGRAM** ● = Tasting notes  ● = Recommended distillers  ● = Factoids

**ORIGIN:** Scotland
**ABV:** 43%–48%
**GRAIN:** Malted barley
**CASK:** Ex- bourbon, ex-sherry

# SCOTCH SINGLE MALT WHISKY: NON-ISLAY, PEATED

**Although most whisky distilleries on the Scottish mainland now dry their barley using electricity or gas, some Highland whiskies are still prepared in the old way with a measure of peated barley.**

Even relatively small levels of peated barley help to provide Highland whiskies with their distinctive backbone. Smoke and peat aren't necessarily the dominant flavors here, but the whiskies tend to be less sweet than, for example, those from Speyside. They have an underlayer of flavor that might be described as earthy, rustic, or even grungy.

Some distilleries in areas not normally associated with peat and smoke now make uncompromising whiskies. Among them is BenRiach, which has released a range of heavily peated products because original owners Allied didn't have an Islay distillery.

## THREE TO TRY

| | | |
|---|---|---|
| **Isle of Arran Machrie Moor** | Arran didn't originally intend to make a peated whisky, but when it did it produced this rich, smoky, savory delight | ★ |
| **Jura Prophecy** | A match for many malts from neighboring Islay, this delivers a phenolic, tarry, seaweed, beach barbecue of a whisky | ★★ |
| **BenRiach Authenticus 21 Year Old** | This 21 year old is the perfect combination of oaky age and smoky beauty | ★★★ |

★ LEAST EXPENSIVE/WIDELY AVAILABLE  ★★ MODERATELY PRICED/ HARDER TO SOURCE  ★★★ COSTLY/RARE

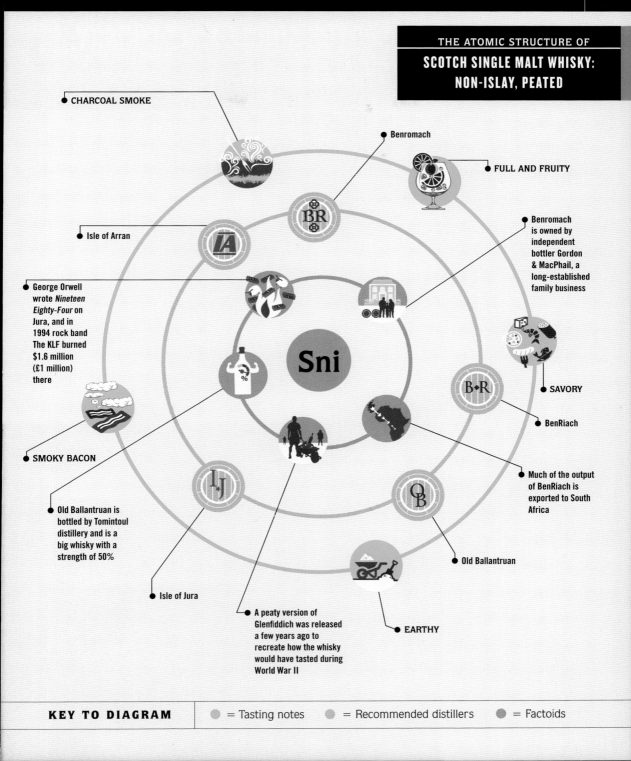

CHARCOAL SMOKE

Benromach

FULL AND FRUITY

BR

Isle of Arran

IA

Benromach
is owned by
independent
bottler Gordon
& MacPhail, a
long-established
family business

George Orwell
wrote *Nineteen
Eighty-Four* on
Jura, and in
1994 rock band
The KLF burned
$1.6 million
(£1 million)
there

Sni

B·R

SAVORY

BenRiach

SMOKY BACON

Old Ballantruan is
bottled by Tomintoul
distillery and is a
big whisky with a
strength of 50%

LJ

OB

Much of the output
of BenRiach is
exported to South
Africa

Old Ballantruan

Isle of Jura

A peaty version of
Glenfiddich was released
a few years ago to
recreate how the whisky
would have tasted during
World War II

EARTHY

**KEY TO DIAGRAM**  ● = Tasting notes  ● = Recommended distillers  ● = Factoids

**ORIGIN:** Scotland
**ABV:** 40%–60%
**GRAIN:** Malted barley
**CASK:** Ex-Oloroso, ex-Pedro Ximenez, ex-Fino casks

# SCOTCH SINGLE MALT WHISKY: SHERRY CASK

**Although whisky consists just of grain, yeast, and water, there are two other important contributors to its quality: peat, which provides smoky flavors, and the cask, which can contribute up to three-quarters of the flavor.**

Most malt spirits are matured in ex-bourbon or ex-Tennessee whiskey casks, but about one in ten of them is matured in casks that previously held sherry.

Sherry casks are bigger than bourbon barrels. This is important because the larger the cask, the less the interaction between spirit and wood and the slower the maturation. The principal casks used are hogsheads and puncheons.

The rules governing Scotch whisky demand that oak be used, but no one would want to use any other material: oak is strong but flexible, porous but waterproof, and allows oxygen to pass through it so that the spirit is oxidized.

## THREE TO TRY

| | | |
|---|---|---|
| **Glenfarclas 10 Year Old** | Honest to goodness, no frills, fully sherried with raisins and orange peel in the mix | ★ |
| **Aberlour A'Bunadh** | Made in small batches, A'Bunadh is never less than a hammer attack of fruitcake sherry and earthy, spent-match loveliness | ★★ |
| **Mortlach 18 Year Old** | Part of the new Mortlach range; shows the rich, complex, and delightfully fruity side to sherry cask whisky | ★★★ |

★ LEAST EXPENSIVE/WIDELY AVAILABLE   ★★ MODERATELY PRICED/ HARDER TO SOURCE   ★★★COSTLY/RARE

ABERLOUR
ESTD 1879
HIGHLAND SINGLE MALT
SCOTCH WHISKY
A'BUNADH
MATURED IN SPANISH OLOROSO SHERRY BUTT
STRAIGHT FROM THE CASK AT   59.6%
CHILL FILTERED   BATCH N° 30

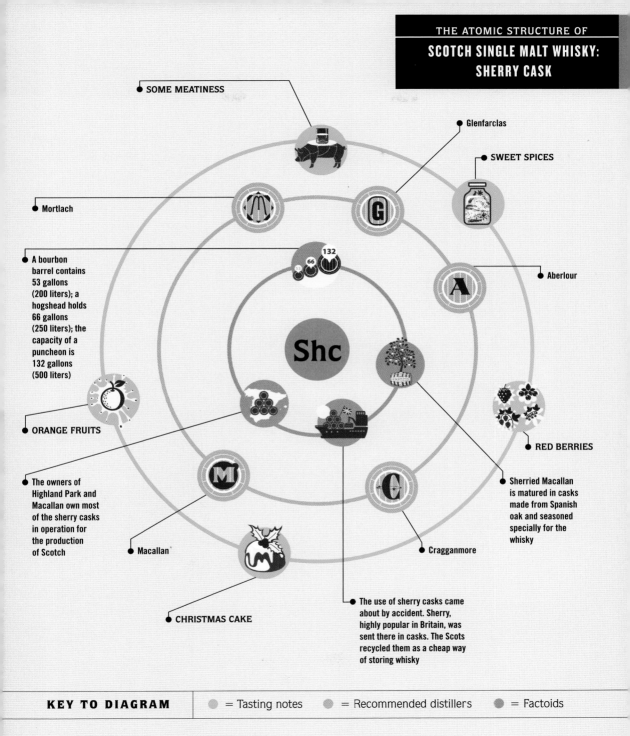

SOME MEATINESS

Glenfarclas

SWEET SPICES

Mortlach

132

66

A bourbon barrel contains 53 gallons (200 liters); a hogshead holds 66 gallons (250 liters); the capacity of a puncheon is 132 gallons (500 liters)

Aberlour

Shc

ORANGE FRUITS

RED BERRIES

The owners of Highland Park and Macallan own most of the sherry casks in operation for the production of Scotch

Macallan

Sherried Macallan is matured in casks made from Spanish oak and seasoned specially for the whisky

Cragganmore

CHRISTMAS CAKE

The use of sherry casks came about by accident. Sherry, highly popular in Britain, was sent there in casks. The Scots recycled them as a cheap way of storing whisky

**KEY TO DIAGRAM**  = Tasting notes  = Recommended distillers  = Factoids

**ORIGIN:** Scotland
**ABV:** 40%–48%
**GRAIN:** Malted barley
**CASK:** Ex-bourbon, ex-port pipes

# SCOTCH SINGLE MALT WHISKY: SPECIAL FINISHES, PORT

**The rules governing Scotch whisky are very clear—you can't add anything to the liquid except some unflavored coloring. So there were some raised eyebrows a few years back when pink whiskies started appearing.**

The color was part of a fad for "finishing" whisky in a different style by putting it in a port or rum cask for the first few months of maturation.

Some saw this merely as a clumsy attempt to conceal faults in inferior whiskies. But when carried out successfully, special finishes can be extraordinary.

Port is a big-flavored drink and may be used as a battering ram in whiskies, notably in those from Australia and India. Penderyn in Wales has also produced some amazing port-matured whiskies. In Scotland, the use of port has been more nuanced, adding a sprinkling of flavor.

## THREE TO TRY

| | | |
|---|---|---|
| **Glenmorangie Quinta Ruban** | Dark, rich, and beautiful, this whisky has orange, dark chocolate, and fruit jello at its core | ★ |
| **BenRiach 15 Year Old Tawny Port** | An oily, full, and winey whisky with tropical fruits and a long sweet finish | ★★ |
| **Balvenie 21 Year Old Portwood** | As fruity as a good brandy, but with dried fruits, some nuttiness, and a velvet chocolate heart—a classic | ★★★ |

★ LEAST EXPENSIVE/WIDELY AVAILABLE  ★★ MODERATELY PRICED/
HARDER TO SOURCE  ★★★COSTLY/RARE

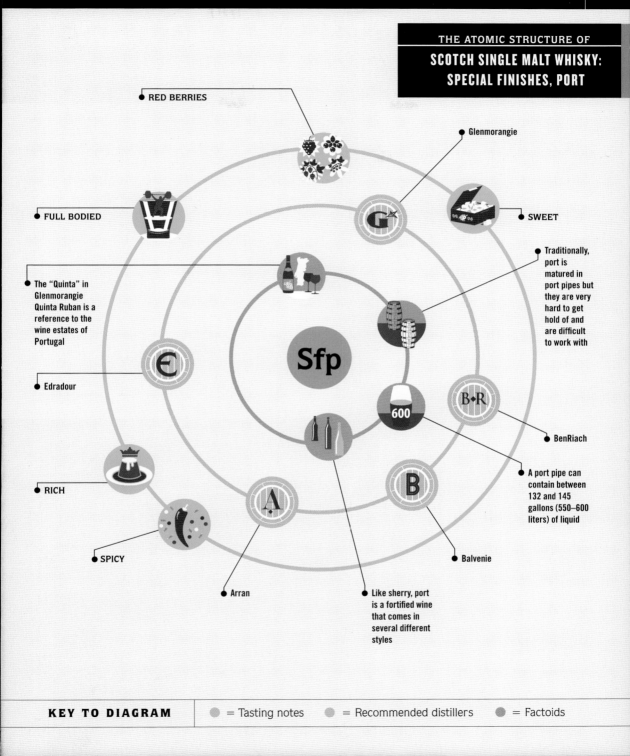

RED BERRIES

Glenmorangie

FULL BODIED

SWEET

Traditionally, port is matured in port pipes but they are very hard to get hold of and are difficult to work with

G

The "Quinta" in Glenmorangie Quinta Ruban is a reference to the wine estates of Portugal

Sfp

E

Edradour

B·R

600

BenRiach

RICH

A port pipe can contain between 132 and 145 gallons (550–600 liters) of liquid

A

B

SPICY

Balvenie

Arran

Like sherry, port is a fortified wine that comes in several different styles

**KEY TO DIAGRAM** ● = Tasting notes ● = Recommended distillers ● = Factoids

ORIGIN: Scotland
ABV: 43%–48%
GRAIN: Malted barley
CASK: Ex-bourbon, ex-rum

# SCOTCH SINGLE MALT WHISKY: SPECIAL FINISHES, RUM

**It really shouldn't work, and you might expect rum casks to bring a level of sweetness to malt whisky that is cloying and sickly. But it's not a bit.**

When a good-quality whisky such as Balvenie is finished in a rum cask, it can make quite an outstanding drink. Some might disparage it as a dessert malt, but anyone who likes the rich, dark fruit and spirity combination of a rum-and-raisin chocolate bar will fall in love with it on their first encounter. The presence of spices is an unexpected additional pleasure.

Although most casks come from Jamaica, a few years ago Bruichladdich released whiskies finished in rum casks from pretty much every Caribbean island and also from mainland Central America.

## THREE TO TRY

| | | |
|---|---|---|
| BenRiach Aromaticus 12 Year | A great name for a great whisky with, unusually, peated barley nuzzling up to vanilla, sweet grape, and honey | ★ |
| Balvenie 17 Year Old Rum Cask | A more grown-up, drier, and less sweet version of a rum finish; beautifully balanced and packed with complex flavors | ★★ |
| Glenfiddich 21 Year Old Gran Reserva | Banana and mango with banoffee pie notes and delightful sweet spices | ★★★ |

★ LEAST EXPENSIVE/WIDELY AVAILABLE  ★★ MODERATELY PRICED/ HARDER TO SOURCE  ★★★ COSTLY/RARE

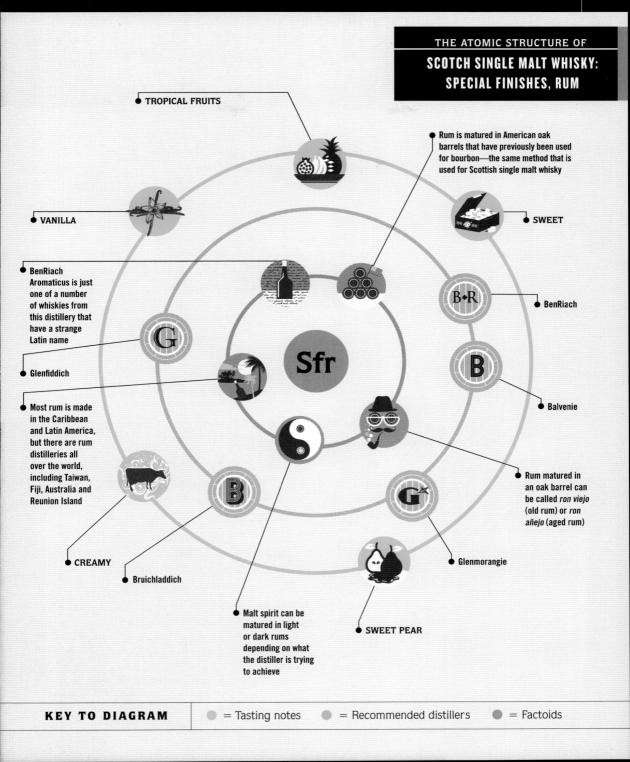

TROPICAL FRUITS

Rum is matured in American oak barrels that have previously been used for bourbon—the same method that is used for Scottish single malt whisky

VANILLA

SWEET

BenRiach Aromaticus is just one of a number of whiskies from this distillery that have a strange Latin name

B•R

BenRiach

G

Sfr

B

Glenfiddich

Balvenie

Most rum is made in the Caribbean and Latin America, but there are rum distilleries all over the world, including Taiwan, Fiji, Australia and Reunion Island

Rum matured in an oak barrel can be called *ron viejo* (old rum) or *ron añejo* (aged rum)

B

G

CREAMY

Bruichladdich

Glenmorangie

Malt spirit can be matured in light or dark rums depending on what the distiller is trying to achieve

SWEET PEAR

**KEY TO DIAGRAM**   ● = Tasting notes   ● = Recommended distillers   ● = Factoids

ORIGIN: Scotland
ABV: 43%–48%
GRAIN: Malted barley
CASK: Ex-bourbon,
ex-Madeira

# SCOTCH SINGLE MALT WHISKY: SPECIAL FINISHES, MADEIRA

**Madeira, a Portuguese island in the Atlantic Ocean, is famous for cake and fortified wine. The latter comes from grapes grown across the island; although we tend to think of them as sweet, that isn't always the case.**

The fortified style was developed from the wines being heated on long sea voyages. The island's unique style is created using three different ways of heating the grapes, from a cheaper factory-like method to a very lengthy natural process.

When Scottish malt whisky is finished in Madeira wine casks, the resulting drink may be sweeter, but the overriding effect is to make the whisky more complex, and to add flavors and spices that are subtle and rewarding.

Most Madeira finishes are fresh and peat free, but, as is often the case, the BenRiach distillery goes rogue with its heavily peated Maderensis Fumosus.

## THREE TO TRY

| | | |
|---|---|---|
| **Benromach Madeira Finish** | With a full four years in Madeira wood, this is a big, bubbly, bouncing whisky bursting with fruity goodness | ★ |
| **Balvenie 17 Year Old Madeira** | Perfectly balanced between sugar and spice, fruit and oak, this is a refreshing, clean, and tasty world-class whisky | ★★ |
| **Glenfiddich Age of Discovery 19 Year Old** | Light, jammy, and subtle malt with orange and citrus notes | ★★★ |

★ LEAST EXPENSIVE/WIDELY AVAILABLE    ★★ MODERATELY PRICED/ HARDER TO SOURCE    ★★★ COSTLY/RARE

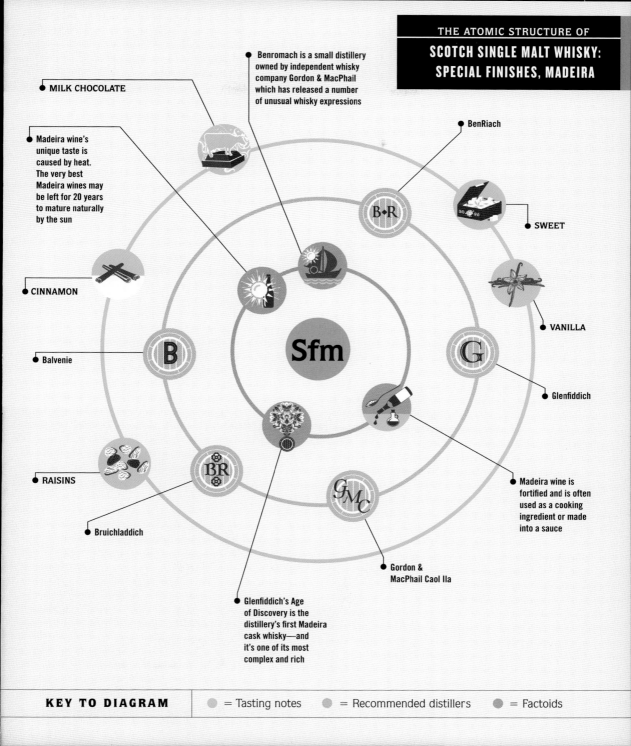

**MILK CHOCOLATE**

Benromach is a small distillery owned by independent whisky company Gordon & MacPhail which has released a number of unusual whisky expressions

BenRiach

Madeira wine's unique taste is caused by heat. The very best Madeira wines may be left for 20 years to mature naturally by the sun

SWEET

B•R

**CINNAMON**

VANILLA

B

Sfm

G

Balvenie

Glenfiddich

RAISINS

Madeira wine is fortified and is often used as a cooking ingredient or made into a sauce

BR

Bruichladdich

GMC

Gordon & MacPhail Caol Ila

Glenfiddich's Age of Discovery is the distillery's first Madeira cask whisky—and it's one of its most complex and rich

**KEY TO DIAGRAM**  ● = Tasting notes  ● = Recommended distillers  ● = Factoids

**ORIGIN:** Scotland
**ABV:** 40%–48%
**GRAIN:** Malted barley
**CASK:** Ex-bourbon, ex-wine

# SCOTCH SINGLE MALT WHISKY: SPECIAL FINISHES, WINE

There is a reason for the expression, "Never mix grape and grain." There have been some disasters when casks previously used for wine have then been used to mature whisky. Some of the worst have involved heavy red wines.

From time to time, though, something really exciting and unusual can result. All styles of red and white wines have been used for Scotch whisky maturation, but perhaps the most common is sweet white French Sauternes.

Unsurprisingly, whiskies made with Sauternes tend to be sweet but sometimes manage to avoid being cloying through grapefruit and lemon notes, and some oaky spiciness.

But more than most categories, this is very much a case of "Buyer beware." Don't believe the hype and try to taste your whisky before purchasing.

## THREE TO TRY

| | | |
|---|---|---|
| **Glenmorangie Nectar D'Or** | Sweet pear and apple crisp with custard, subtle spices, and a rounded and balanced finish; this is excellent whisky making | ★ |
| **BenRiach 16 Year Old Sauternes finish** | Big, bold, and sweet, with lots of juicy, grapy goodness and some soft banana notes | ★★ |
| **Glenmorangie Companta** | Juicy raisins, mixed fruit jello, subtle spices, and a lovely balance. A very special whisky | ★★★ |

★ LEAST EXPENSIVE/WIDELY AVAILABLE  ★★ MODERATELY PRICED/ HARDER TO SOURCE  ★★★ COSTLY/RARE

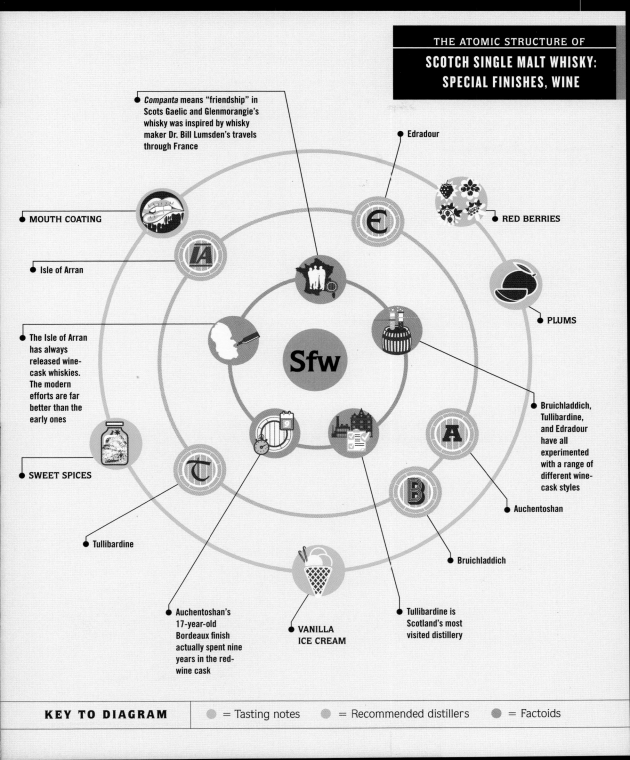

THE ATOMIC STRUCTURE OF
# SCOTCH SINGLE MALT WHISKY: SPECIAL FINISHES, WINE

*Companta* means "friendship" in Scots Gaelic and Glenmorangie's whisky was inspired by whisky maker Dr. Bill Lumsden's travels through France

Edradour

MOUTH COATING

RED BERRIES

Isle of Arran

PLUMS

The Isle of Arran has always released wine-cask whiskies. The modern efforts are far better than the early ones

Bruichladdich, Tullibardine, and Edradour have all experimented with a range of different wine-cask styles

SWEET SPICES

Sfw

Auchentoshan

Tullibardine

Bruichladdich

Auchentoshan's 17-year-old Bordeaux finish actually spent nine years in the red-wine cask

VANILLA ICE CREAM

Tullibardine is Scotland's most visited distillery

KEY TO DIAGRAM     = Tasting notes     = Recommended distillers     = Factoids

**ORIGIN:** Ireland
**ABV:** 40%–58%
**GRAIN:** Malted barley
**CASK:** Ex-bourbon, ex-sherry

# IRISH SINGLE MALT WHISKEY

**Ireland is in the grips of a whiskey revolution, and after years of being confined pretty much to sweet, non-peaty, triple-distilled blends, the new Irish distillers aren't being bound by convention.**

To be fair, one of the country's oldest distilleries doesn't fit this description. Bushmill's has always made single malt whiskeys. But with the arrival of Cooley and its brands such as Connemara and Tyrconnell, single malts became firmly established in the Emerald Isle. Cooley's founders, Jack and Stephen Teeling, now have their own company and in 2013 launched 26-year-old and 30-year-old single malts.

The most noteworthy of the new creators of single malt is Dingle, whose whiskey was described by one distiller in England as the best he had ever tasted.

## THREE TO TRY

| | | |
|---|---|---|
| **Connemara 10 Year Old** | Crisp and fresh with apple and pear notes and a vanilla heart | ★ |
| **Bushmills 16 Year Old** | The best of a strong portfolio; clean, sweet, and refreshing with enough spice and oak to keep the malt in shape | ★★ |
| **Tyrconnell Port finish 10 Year Old** | Rare, but worth seeking; all plum jelly, fat raisins, and a trace of oak | ★★★ |

★ LEAST EXPENSIVE/WIDELY AVAILABLE   ★★ MODERATELY PRICED/ HARDER TO SOURCE   ★★★ COSTLY/RARE

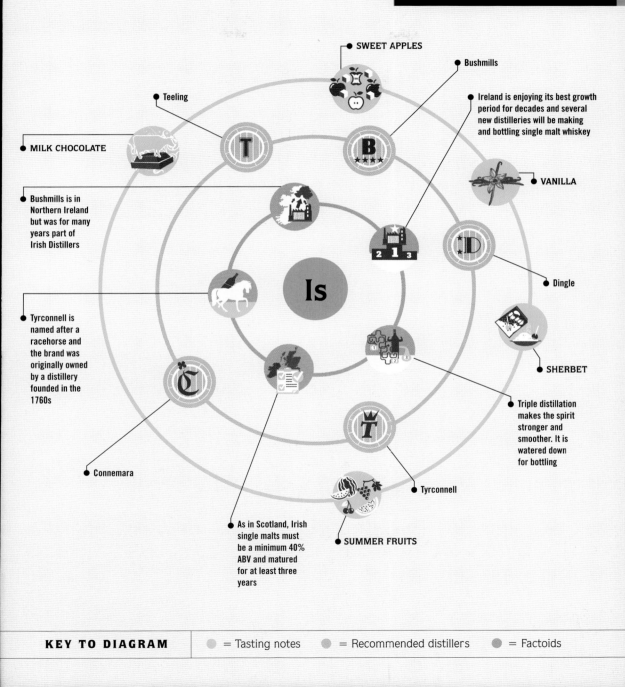

SWEET APPLES

Bushmills

Teeling

Ireland is enjoying its best growth period for decades and several new distilleries will be making and bottling single malt whiskey

MILK CHOCOLATE

VANILLA

Bushmills is in Northern Ireland but was for many years part of Irish Distillers

Dingle

**Is**

SHERBET

Tyrconnell is named after a racehorse and the brand was originally owned by a distillery founded in the 1760s

Triple distillation makes the spirit stronger and smoother. It is watered down for bottling

Connemara

Tyrconnell

As in Scotland, Irish single malts must be a minimum 40% ABV and matured for at least three years

SUMMER FRUITS

**KEY TO DIAGRAM**   ● = Tasting notes   ● = Recommended distillers   ● = Factoids

**ORIGIN:** Ireland
**ABV:** 43%–46%
**GRAIN:** Malted barley
**CASK:** Ex-bourbon

# IRISH SINGLE MALT WHISKEY: PEATED

**On certain Irish distillery tours, chances are they'll tell you that the principal difference between Scotland and Ireland is that Scottish whiskies are made using peaty barley (not always true) and that Irish whiskeys are not (definitely not true).**

These statements are myths that sought to differentiate Irish whiskey from Scotch to ensure the former's survival. It doesn't take much research to find that, back in the day, Ireland had scores of distilleries and that they dried their barley over peat-fueled fires.

Whiskeys in this category are hard to find and are considered oddballs, mainly because the smokiness mixed with sweet fruity malt is unlike any other whiskey, with the possible exception of some of Bladnoch's whiskies in southwest Scotland.

## THREE TO TRY

| Connemara | Superb whiskey with dusty smoke and an earthy peat under a sweet citrus and green fruit carpet | ★ |
| --- | --- | --- |
| Connemara Cask Strength | A heavyweight boxer of a whiskey, great dollops of gloomy fruit raging against billowing smoke | ★★ |
| Connemara Turf Mor | Once described as "an explosion in prophylactic factory," Turf Mor means "big turf." A must for peat fans | ★★★ |

★ LEAST EXPENSIVE/WIDELY AVAILABLE ★★ MODERATELY PRICED/ HARDER TO SOURCE ★★★COSTLY/RARE

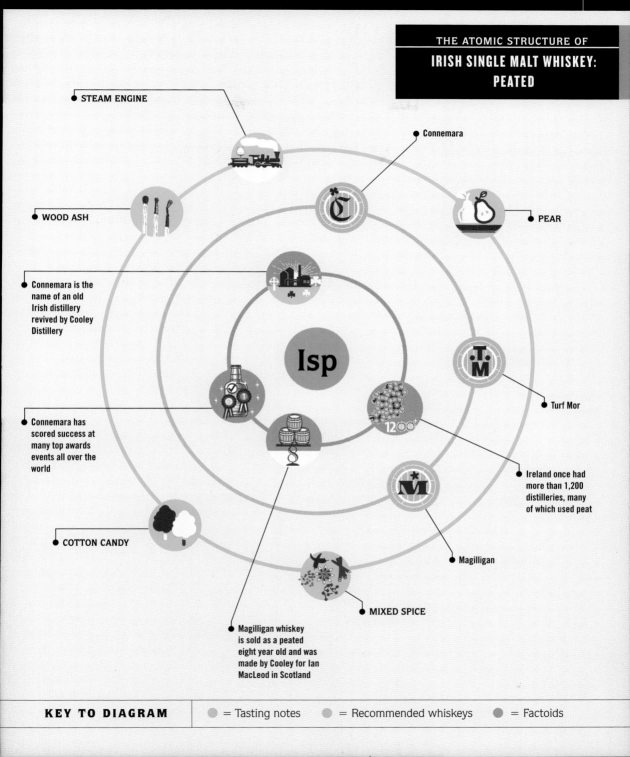

THE ATOMIC STRUCTURE OF
# IRISH SINGLE MALT WHISKEY: PEATED

STEAM ENGINE

Connemara

WOOD ASH

PEAR

Connemara is the name of an old Irish distillery revived by Cooley Distillery

Isp

Turf Mor

Connemara has scored success at many top awards events all over the world

Ireland once had more than 1,200 distilleries, many of which used peat

COTTON CANDY

Magilligan

Mixed Spice

Magilligan whiskey is sold as a peated eight year old and was made by Cooley for Ian MacLeod in Scotland

**KEY TO DIAGRAM**  ● = Tasting notes  ● = Recommended whiskeys  ● = Factoids

**ORIGIN:** USA
**ABV:** 40%–60%
**GRAIN:** Malted barley
**CASK:** Ex-bourbon, virgin oak

# AMERICAN SINGLE MALT WHISKEY

**Single malt whiskey from the United States is nothing new—St. George's Distillery in Alameda, California, has been producing such spirit since the 1980s and formed the vanguard of a legion of craft distillers who are increasingly turning to barley.**

St. George's calls itself the original craft distillery and it pretty much is. It's now been followed by some 800 craft distilleries, some of which make single malt.

The creation of this drink cannot be hurried, so beware: some U.S. products are sappy because they have neither been casked in the best wood nor given long enough to mature.

Among the exceptions are Balcones, which won World's Best Non-Traditional Single Malt for 2014 in my Wizards of Whisky Awards, and Corsair, which is doing some very clever stuff with different woods and drying methods.

## THREE TO TRY

| | | |
|---|---|---|
| **St George's Single Malt** | Spicy, oily, and packed with fruitiness, this goes up through the gears as malt gives way to spice | ★ |
| **Corsair Triple Smoke** | Made with barley, dried by peat, cherry wood, and beech; a big, exciting whiskey | ★★ |
| **Balcones Texas Single Malt** | Slightly smoky maltiness and rich milk chocolate notes make this a delight. Surprisingly full and rich for one so young | ★★★ |

★ LEAST EXPENSIVE/WIDELY AVAILABLE  ★★ MODERATELY PRICED/HARDER TO SOURCE  ★★★ COSTLY/RARE

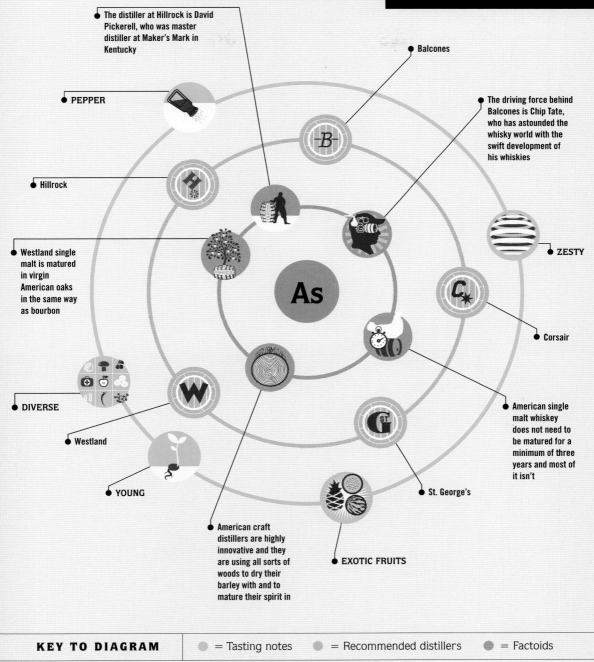

The distiller at Hillrock is David Pickerell, who was master distiller at Maker's Mark in Kentucky

PEPPER

Balcones

The driving force behind Balcones is Chip Tate, who has astounded the whisky world with the swift development of his whiskies

Hillrock

ZESTY

Westland single malt is matured in virgin American oaks in the same way as bourbon

As

Corsair

DIVERSE

American single malt whiskey does not need to be matured for a minimum of three years and most of it isn't

Westland

YOUNG

St. George's

American craft distillers are highly innovative and they are using all sorts of woods to dry their barley with and to mature their spirit in

EXOTIC FRUITS

**KEY TO DIAGRAM**    = Tasting notes    = Recommended distillers    = Factoids

**ORIGIN:** Japan
**ABV:** 43%–60%
**GRAIN:** Malted barley
**CASK:** Ex-bourbon, ex-sherry, Mizunawa oak

# JAPANESE SINGLE MALT WHISKY

**The concept of Japanese whisky is still a novelty for many, but it has a history stretching back nearly 100 years, and it has been the darling of whisky aficionados for some 20 years or so.**

Japanese whisky drinkers adore Scottish malts, so it is not surprising that their distillers have sought to emulate the great distilleries of Scotland.

But there are two factors that set Japanese malts apart from the spirits that inspired them. One is the flavors, all of which are turned up to 11. The other is the maturation method, especially the use of Japanese oak, which gives their whiskies a distinctive and irresistible taste. The oldest are the best, but they're expensive because not enough stock was put aside 25 years ago to meet the huge, and unforeseen, escalation in demand.

## THREE TO TRY

| | | |
|---|---|---|
| **Yoichi 10 Year Old** | A rollercoaster ride, with sherry, toffee, peat, and vanilla rising and falling before finishing safely | ★ |
| **Chichibu Port Pipe** | Young whisky from Japan's newest distillery. The port adds richness and complexity; the sugar and barley are rich, vibrant, and chewy | ★★ |
| **Yamazaki 25 Year Old** | Full, rich, and sherried, with raisins, berries, plum chutney, orange rind, and a pleasant dusty mustiness | ★★★ |

★ LEAST EXPENSIVE/WIDELY AVAILABLE  ★★ MODERATELY PRICED/HARDER TO SOURCE  ★★★ COSTLY/RARE

THE ATOMIC STRUCTURE OF
# JAPANESE SINGLE MALT WHISKY

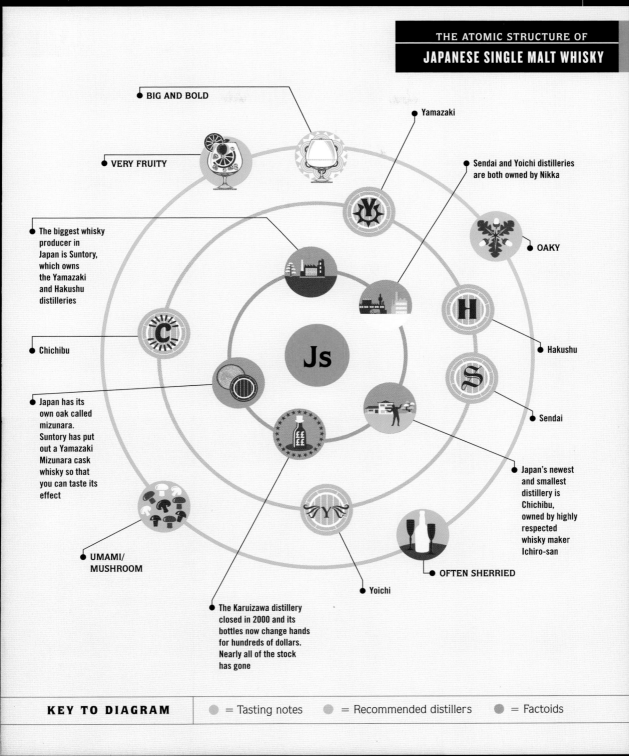

BIG AND BOLD

VERY FRUITY

Yamazaki

Sendai and Yoichi distilleries
are both owned by Nikka

The biggest whisky
producer in
Japan is Suntory,
which owns
the Yamazaki
and Hakushu
distilleries

OAKY

Chichibu

Hakushu

Js

Japan has its
own oak called
mizunara.
Suntory has put
out a Yamazaki
Mizunara cask
whisky so that
you can taste its
effect

Sendai

Japan's newest
and smallest
distillery is
Chichibu,
owned by highly
respected
whisky maker
Ichiro-san

UMAMI/
MUSHROOM

OFTEN SHERRIED

Yoichi

The Karuizawa distillery
closed in 2000 and its
bottles now change hands
for hundreds of dollars.
Nearly all of the stock
has gone

**KEY TO DIAGRAM** | ● = Tasting notes ● = Recommended distillers ● = Factoids

**ORIGIN:** Japan
**ABV:** 43%–62%
**GRAIN:** Malted barley
**CASK:** Ex-bourbon,
ex-sherry, Mizunawa oak

# JAPANESE SINGLE MALT WHISKY: PEATED

**Most Japanese distillers seem to be of the view that if you're going to have a flavor you might as well make sure that people can taste it properly. Their whiskies are forthright and uncompromising.**

When it comes to peaty whiskies, the likes of Chichibu and Yoichi make sure you know what you're drinking. Some even announce themselves by name: one is subtitled "Heavily Peated," another "Salty and Peaty."
Distilleries in Japan are among the most advanced in the world, with the largest ones using several yeasts, many wood types, and both pot stills and Coffey stills to create a range of different flavors with enough variety to create quality blends. Peated barley is part of that complicated distillery make-up, and Japanese whiskies with peaty barley have a personality of their own.

## THREE TO TRY

| Chichibu Heavily Peated | Young, feisty, sweet, and smoky, this whisky is alcohol-laced popping candy | ★ |
|---|---|---|
| Hakushu Heavily Peated | Beautifully made, with berries and green fruit in the mix as well as peat, making a refreshing and stimulating whisky | ★★ |
| Yoichi Salty and Peaty | A savory delight that does just what it says on the bottle. Balanced and ballsy | ★★★ |

★ LEAST EXPENSIVE/WIDELY AVAILABLE   ★★ MODERATELY PRICED/
HARDER TO SOURCE   ★★★ COSTLY/RARE

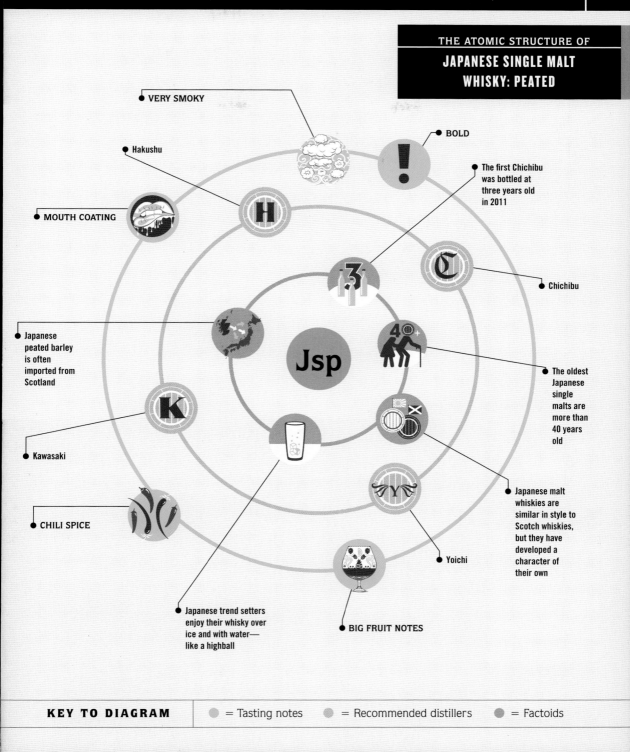

THE ATOMIC STRUCTURE OF
# JAPANESE SINGLE MALT WHISKY: PEATED

VERY SMOKY

BOLD

Hakushu

The first Chichibu was bottled at three years old in 2011

MOUTH COATING

Chichibu

Japanese peated barley is often imported from Scotland

The oldest Japanese single malts are more than 40 years old

Kawasaki

Japanese malt whiskies are similar in style to Scotch whiskies, but they have developed a character of their own

CHILI SPICE

Yoichi

Japanese trend setters enjoy their whisky over ice and with water— like a highball

BIG FRUIT NOTES

**KEY TO DIAGRAM**   = Tasting notes    = Recommended distillers    = Factoids

ORIGIN: Australia
ABV: 40%–62%
GRAIN: Malted barley
CASK: Ex-bourbon,
ex-sherry, ex-port pipes

# AUSTRALIAN SINGLE MALT WHISKY

**Australia is evolving rapidly as a whisky-making nation. The current speed of progress suggests that their distilleries will soon follow their vineyards to fame and fortune all over the world.**

Early efforts were ordinary, designed merely to offer cheap alternatives to imported Scotch. Now there are some stunning whiskies bursting with flavor and a personality all of their own.

Australia can be divided into two: Tasmania, where eight or nine distilleries operate, and the mainland, where activity is centered in the state of Victoria.

Tasmania took the lead when Bill Lark overturned outdated prohibition laws and started a whisky boom. One of his innovations was the use of quarter casks made of wood previously used for port, because sherry casks were scarce. His products are outstandingly big, brash, and peaty.

## THREE TO TRY

| | | |
|---|---|---|
| **Bakery Hill Peated Malt Cask Strength** | Sharp, stinging peat, and spice over a gorgeous sweet, malty whisky | ★ |
| **Limeburners Single Malt Whisky** | No distillery has made such rapid progress. Each batch takes another step forward | ★★ |
| **Overeem Port Cask Matured Cask Strength** | Now part of the Lark operation, this is as fruity and full as whisky gets, with a spicy follow-up to die for | ★★★ |

★ LEAST EXPENSIVE/WIDELY AVAILABLE  ★★ MODERATELY PRICED/ HARDER TO SOURCE  ★★★COSTLY/RARE

THE ATOMIC STRUCTURE OF
# AUSTRALIAN SINGLE MALT WHISKY

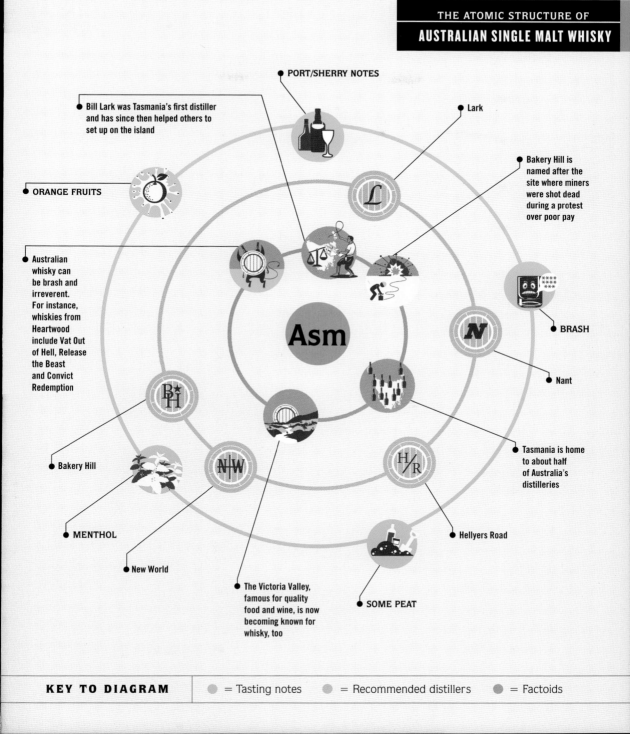

PORT/SHERRY NOTES

Bill Lark was Tasmania's first distiller and has since then helped others to set up on the island

Lark

Bakery Hill is named after the site where miners were shot dead during a protest over poor pay

ORANGE FRUITS

Australian whisky can be brash and irreverent. For instance, whiskies from Heartwood include Vat Out of Hell, Release the Beast and Convict Redemption

Asm

BRASH

Nant

Bakery Hill

Tasmania is home to about half of Australia's distilleries

MENTHOL

New World

Hellyers Road

The Victoria Valley, famous for quality food and wine, is now becoming known for whisky, too

SOME PEAT

**KEY TO DIAGRAM** ● = Tasting notes ● = Recommended distillers ● = Factoids

**ORIGIN:** India
**ABV:** 32%–62%
**GRAIN:** Scottish malted barley, Indian malted barley, molasses (not grain)
**CASK:** Ex-bourbon, ex-sherry, ex-port pipes

# INDIAN SINGLE MALT WHISKY

**India has more whisky brands than anywhere else in the world, but many of these are made with molasses and are therefore not defined as whisky in Europe or North America.**

Indian single malts cover a range of styles and may be both peaty and nonpeaty. Whiskies made with molasses—sugar cane—tend to be sweet, flabby, and two-dimensional, but taste like the real thing when added with a mixer. These are unworthy of serious consideration, but a tiny amount of single malt whisky has found its way from India onto world markets and it is very good indeed. At present, Amrut and Paul John distilleries lead the way and are picking up heaps of awards. A third, as yet unnamed, distillery is close to bottling its first whisky: from the quality of the 18-month spirit, the signs are encouraging.

## THREE TO TRY

| | | |
|---|---|---|
| **Amrut Fusion** | Fruit-and-nut chocolate meets wispy smoke and earthy peat | ★ |
| **Paul John Single Casks** | Big, bold, and richly fruited, John Distillery's single casks 163 and 164 were sublime. Watch for new releases | ★★ |
| **Amrut Portonova** | A light show of a whisky, evolving through spices, fruits, and tannins | ★★★ |

★ LEAST EXPENSIVE/WIDELY AVAILABLE   ★★ MODERATELY PRICED/ HARDER TO SOURCE   ★★★ COSTLY/RARE

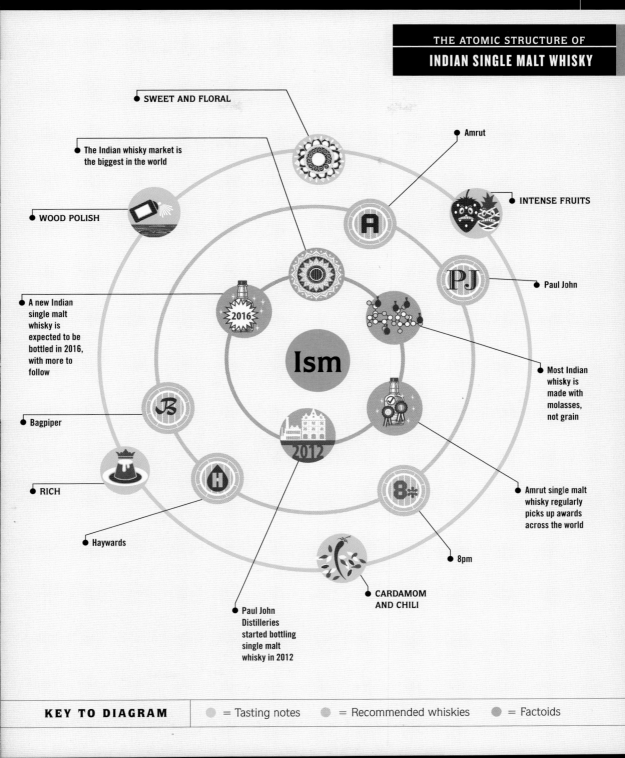

SWEET AND FLORAL

Amrut

The Indian whisky market is the biggest in the world

INTENSE FRUITS

WOOD POLISH

Paul John

A new Indian single malt whisky is expected to be bottled in 2016, with more to follow

Ism

Most Indian whisky is made with molasses, not grain

Bagpiper

RICH

Amrut single malt whisky regularly picks up awards across the world

Haywards

8pm

CARDAMOM AND CHILI

Paul John Distilleries started bottling single malt whisky in 2012

**KEY TO DIAGRAM**    = Tasting notes    = Recommended whiskies    = Factoids

**ORIGIN:** New Zealand
**ABV:** 40%–58%
**GRAIN:** Malted barley
**CASK:** Ex-bourbon, ex-New Zealand red wine

# NEW ZEALAND SINGLE MALT WHISKY

**The South Island of New Zealand bears an uncanny resemblance to Scotland. The Highlands feature mountains and lakes, and a high proportion of the population is of Scottish descent. Dunedin is an amalgam of Dundee and Edinburgh.**

Yet the history of whisky here is a patchy one. Partly because of the small population and the cost of distillation, and partly because the Scottish descendants look to the old country for whisky, the industry has not been sustainable. The one major distillery, Willowbank, which produced the likes of Milford's, Lammerlaw, and Coaster, is long gone. But now the Australian-owned New Zealand Whisky Company is re-casking the considerable remaining stocks and turning them into something quite special. New distilleries are opening, and they promise a bright future for whisky.

## THREE TO TRY

| | | |
|---|---|---|
| **NZ Whisky Co South Island 18 Year Old** | Big citrus flavors and a salt and pepper attack, with menthol and hickory notes | ★ |
| **NZ Whisky Co 1993 Single Cask** | Sweet fruits, menthol, and hickory with floral notes up front and a late burst of earthy peat | ★★ |
| **NZ Whisky Co 1989 Single Cask** | Clean and stylish, with manuka honey, sweet grapefruit and lemon, and a tidal wave of peat late on | ★★★ |

★ LEAST EXPENSIVE/WIDELY AVAILABLE ★★ MODERATELY PRICED/ HARDER TO SOURCE ★★★ COSTLY/RARE

THE ATOMIC STRUCTURE OF

# NEW ZEALAND SINGLE MALT WHISKY

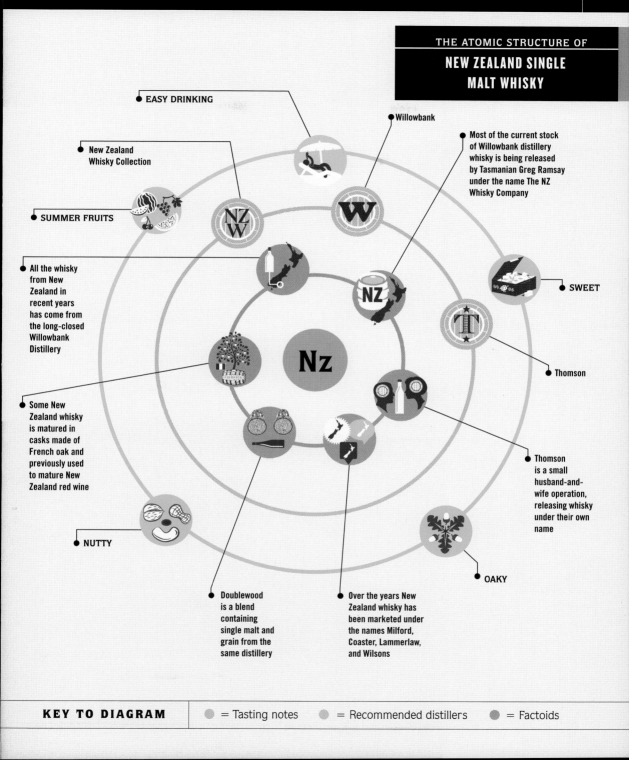

EASY DRINKING

Willowbank

Most of the current stock of Willowbank distillery whisky is being released by Tasmanian Greg Ramsay under the name The NZ Whisky Company

New Zealand Whisky Collection

SUMMER FRUITS

All the whisky from New Zealand in recent years has come from the long-closed Willowbank Distillery

Nz

SWEET

Thomson

Some New Zealand whisky is matured in casks made of French oak and previously used to mature New Zealand red wine

Thomson is a small husband-and-wife operation, releasing whisky under their own name

NUTTY

OAKY

Doublewood is a blend containing single malt and grain from the same distillery

Over the years New Zealand whisky has been marketed under the names Milford, Coaster, Lammerlaw, and Wilsons

**KEY TO DIAGRAM**   ● = Tasting notes   ● = Recommended distillers   ● = Factoids

**ORIGIN:** South Africa
**ABV:** 40%–48%
**GRAIN:** Malted barley
**CASK:** Ex-bourbon, ex-sherry

# SOUTH AFRICAN SINGLE MALT WHISKY

**South Africa doesn't have much of a whisky pedigree, but the whisky that is made there is of a high quality and, in the case of small producer Drayman's, highly innovative.**

The James Sedgwick Distillery is owned by wine and spirits giant Distell, which in 2013 purchased Burn Stewart, owner of three Scottish distilleries. Sedgwick's whiskies are close in style to those of Scotland. Single malt is gaining popularity with the country's emerging black middle class.

South Africa's only other producer is Moritz Kallmeyer, a top craft brewer who makes Drayman's whisky. He has introduced a solera system (a process that involves constantly refilling a cask from the top and drawing liquid from the bottom) into its production and encourages customers to buy a small cask and refill it as a "living" cask in their homes.

## THREE TO TRY

| | | |
|---|---|---|
| Three Ships 10 Year Old | Gutsy and challenging. This has a Highland-style oak and smoke undercarpet that crashes against the fruity center | ★ |
| Three Ships Bourbon Cask | As above only calmer, sweeter, and fruitier with bourbon candy vanilla bringing sophistication | ★★ |
| Drayman's Solera | Varies a lot but can be sherried, with orange fruits, toasted oak, and even coconut | ★★★ |

★ LEAST EXPENSIVE/WIDELY AVAILABLE  ★★ MODERATELY PRICED/HARDER TO SOURCE  ★★★ COSTLY/RARE

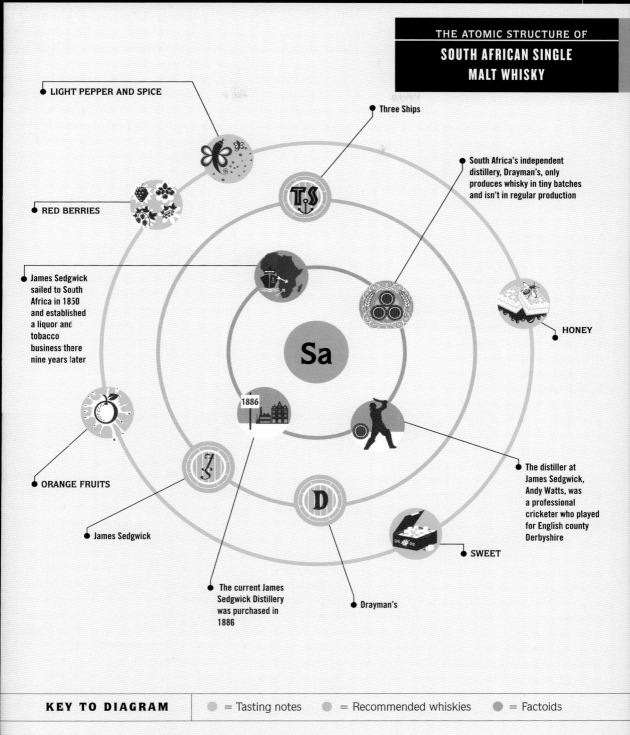

LIGHT PEPPER AND SPICE

Three Ships

South Africa's independent distillery, Drayman's, only produces whisky in tiny batches and isn't in regular production

RED BERRIES

James Sedgwick sailed to South Africa in 1850 and established a liquor and tobacco business there nine years later

HONEY

**Sa**

ORANGE FRUITS

1886

James Sedgwick

The distiller at James Sedgwick, Andy Watts, was a professional cricketer who played for English county Derbyshire

**D**

SWEET

The current James Sedgwick Distillery was purchased in 1886

Drayman's

KEY TO DIAGRAM       ● = Tasting notes       ● = Recommended whiskies       ● = Factoids

**ORIGIN:** Taiwan
**ABV:** 40%–50%
**GRAIN:** Malted barley
**CASK:** Ex-bourbon, ex-sherry, ex-port pipes

# TAIWANESE SINGLE MALT WHISKY

**While the concept of Taiwanese whisky might look odd to Western eyes, the island's Kavalan distillery is no ramshackle set-up at the bottom of someone's garden; it is a serious business that makes an outstanding product.**

Kavalan is a full-scale operation funded by Taiwanese food and drinks giant King Car, which has invested heavily to ensure that everything works in high heat and humidity. Scottish troubleshooter Dr. Jim Swan is part of the supervisory team.

With all this support, it is no surprise that the resulting whisky is great. What is remarkable is the speed with which it is produced. At just two years, both sherried and bourbon styles were outstanding, and in less than a decade Kavalan whisky's reputation has grown to the point where some of the Solist bottlings are regarded as world beaters.

## THREE TO TRY

| | | |
|---|---|---|
| **Kavalan Solist Fino Sherry** | This is all about the interplay between sugar and spice, with a dollop of oak thrown in | ★ |
| **Kavalan Vinho Barrique** | Plummy, jammy, and spicy, this is more of an autumnal offering; like Japanese whisky, it doesn't hold anything back | ★★ |
| **Kavalan Solist Bourbon Cask Cask Strength** | As yellow as whisky gets, with bananas, tropical fruits, vanilla ice cream, and maple syrup. Amazing | ★★★ |

★ LEAST EXPENSIVE/WIDELY AVAILABLE  ★★ MODERATELY PRICED/ HARDER TO SOURCE  ★★★ COSTLY/RARE

THE ATOMIC STRUCTURE OF
# TAIWANESE SINGLE MALT WHISKY

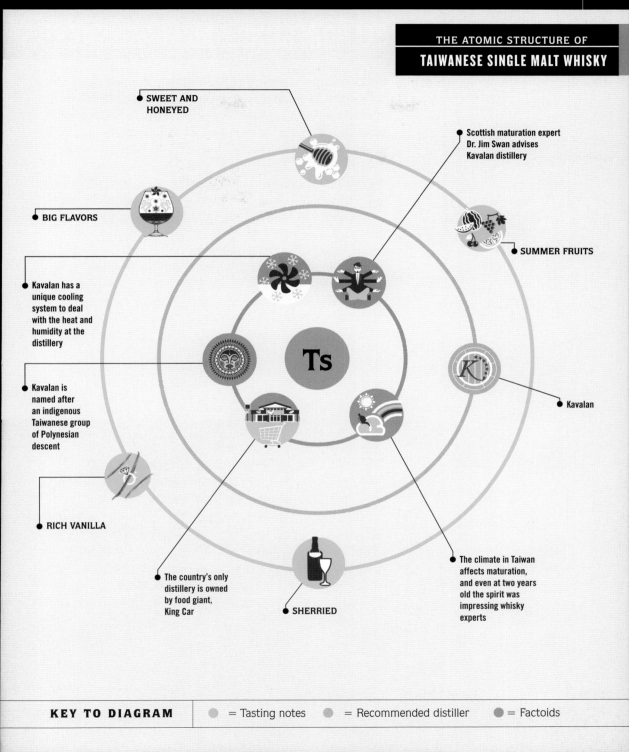

SWEET AND HONEYED

Scottish maturation expert Dr. Jim Swan advises Kavalan distillery

BIG FLAVORS

SUMMER FRUITS

Kavalan has a unique cooling system to deal with the heat and humidity at the distillery

**Ts**

Kavalan is named after an indigenous Taiwanese group of Polynesian descent

Kavalan

RICH VANILLA

The country's only distillery is owned by food giant, King Car

The climate in Taiwan affects maturation, and even at two years old the spirit was impressing whisky experts

SHERRIED

**KEY TO DIAGRAM**   ● = Tasting notes   ● = Recommended distiller   ● = Factoids

# BELGIAN SINGLE MALT WHISKY

**Belgian Owl owner Etienne Bouillon is a perfectionist; he sought help from the outstanding Bruichladdich master distiller, Jim McEwan, who travels to Belgium from time to time to see how the Belgian Owl whisky is developing.**

Bouillon's first products were distilled in a portable still that originally traveled from vineyard to vineyard where it would be hired to turn wine into brandy. Once distilled, the liquid would be casked and stored in modern storage warehouses. These days, Bouillon has Scottish stills on a permanent site near Liège. It's too early to know how this whisky will change, but for now it is a sweet, fruity dessert drink similar to Irish whiskey. Bouillon's cask-strength whisky can weigh in at over 70% ABV. Only small quantities of Belgian Owl are released in batches at four years old.

## TWO TO TRY

| | | |
|---|---|---|
| **Belgian Owl** | Think sweet apple crisp and custard, soft pink candy, and white pepper spice and you'll get some of the flavor of it | ★ |
| **Belgian Owl cask strength** | Not only stronger but spicier too, with more liquorice and menthol notes to the standard bottling. Needs a lot of water though | ★★ |

★ LEAST EXPENSIVE/WIDELY AVAILABLE  ★★ MODERATELY PRICED/ HARDER TO SOURCE

THE ATOMIC STRUCTURE OF
# BELGIAN SINGLE MALT WHISKY

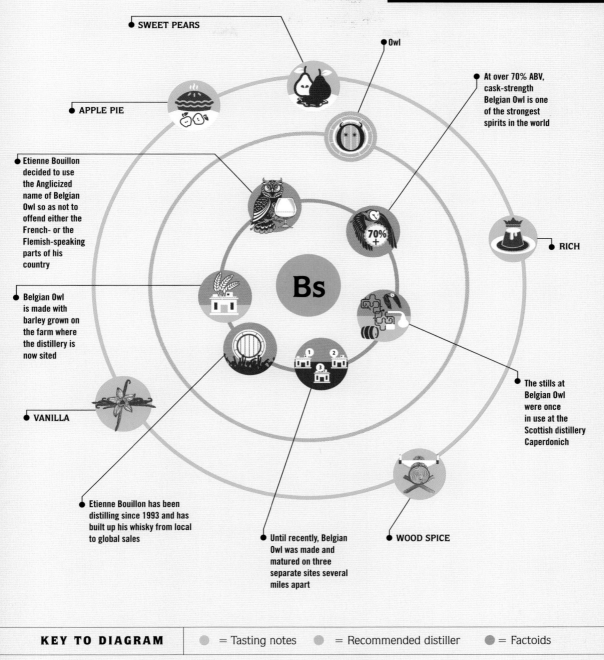

SWEET PEARS

Owl

APPLE PIE

At over 70% ABV, cask-strength Belgian Owl is one of the strongest spirits in the world

Etienne Bouillon decided to use the Anglicized name of Belgian Owl so as not to offend either the French- or the Flemish-speaking parts of his country

RICH

Belgian Owl is made with barley grown on the farm where the distillery is now sited

Bs

The stills at Belgian Owl were once in use at the Scottish distillery Caperdonich

VANILLA

Etienne Bouillon has been distilling since 1993 and has built up his whisky from local to global sales

Until recently, Belgian Owl was made and matured on three separate sites several miles apart

WOOD SPICE

**KEY TO DIAGRAM**   = Tasting notes    = Recommended distiller    = Factoids

**ORIGIN:** Denmark
**ABV:** 43%–58%
**GRAIN:** Malted barley
**CASK:** Ex-bourbon

# DANISH SINGLE MALT WHISKY

**Denmark, like the other Scandinavian countries, looks strongly to Scotland for inspiration. The distillers here are, first and foremost, fans of Scottish single malt whisky and set those standards as their benchmarks.**

As a result, you'll find peaty and non-peaty whisky from this country. But Danish whisky is still in its infancy. Some of the distilleries are extensions of existing breweries. Two have started making their name outside their national borders now, but mainly in Sweden: Braunstein and Stauning. Both make good-quality whiskies, but they're still a way from hitting the peaks of some of the other new world-ranking distillers. Not that they lack ambition, however. The Braunstein brothers have invested heavily in stylish bottles and packaging, and Stauning has already attempted a rye—not easy by any means.

## THREE TO TRY

| | | |
|---|---|---|
| **Stauning Traditional** | Nutty, oily, and undercooked malt, well made with plenty of heart. The sweet barley and notes bode well | ★ |
| **Stauning Peated** | Chocolate and wafting smoke reminiscent of German distillery Blaue Maus, with interesting oily spices | ★★ |
| **Braunstein peated Cask Strength** | Perhaps the best Danish whisky to date; big and bold with plenty of smoke and fruit to hold the attention | ★★★ |

★ LEAST EXPENSIVE/WIDELY AVAILABLE  ★★ MODERATELY PRICED/HARDER TO SOURCE  ★★★ COSTLY/RARE

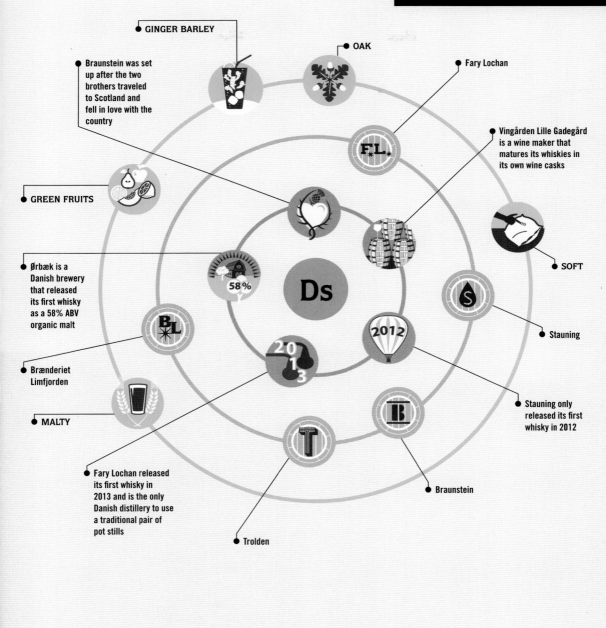

GINGER BARLEY

OAK

Fary Lochan

Braunstein was set up after the two brothers traveled to Scotland and fell in love with the country

Vingården Lille Gadegård is a wine maker that matures its whiskies in its own wine casks

GREEN FRUITS

SOFT

Ørbæk is a Danish brewery that released its first whisky as a 58% ABV organic malt

Stauning

Brænderiet Limfjorden

Stauning only released its first whisky in 2012

MALTY

Braunstein

Fary Lochan released its first whisky in 2013 and is the only Danish distillery to use a traditional pair of pot stills

Trolden

**KEY TO DIAGRAM**    = Tasting notes    = Recommended distillers    = Factoids

**ORIGIN:** Holland
**ABV:** 43%–50%
**GRAIN:** Malted barley
**CASK:** Ex-bourbon, ex-sherry

# DUTCH SINGLE MALT WHISKY

**The Zuidam family distillery on the Belgian–Dutch border makes more than 600 different products. It is a warren of pots and demi jars containing botanicals, liquids, and fruit. No expense is spared to produce top-drawer fruit liqueurs and genevers.**

Unsurprisingly, therefore, Zuidam's whiskies, going under the name Millstone, are of exceptional quality. Its rich sherried whiskies, some 15 years old, would easily pass muster if put up against their equivalents in Speyside, Scotland. Since Zuidam was founded in 1975, its whiskies have been getting better and better. In 1989 the company expanded its premises and introduced a single production line. Such is the family's confidence today that the distillery at Baarle-Nassau has now started bottling its own rye. Its 100 Rye has won awards since its launch.

## THREE TO TRY

| | | |
|---|---|---|
| **Millstone Peated** | Unusual take on the peaty theme, with a lighter smoke, floating on a pleasant fruit and barley base | ★ |
| **Zuidam Millstone 1999 PX Cask** | PX is Pedro Ximenez sherry and in this whisky it manifests itself as dark coffee, bitter cherry, and treacle toffee | ★★ |
| **Millstone Sherry Cask 12 Year Old** | Big-flavored Christmas cake whisky with raisins, dates, berries, and bitter orange | ★★★ |

★ LEAST EXPENSIVE/WIDELY AVAILABLE ★★ MODERATELY PRICED/ HARDER TO SOURCE ★★★ COSTLY/RARE

THE ATOMIC STRUCTURE OF
# DUTCH SINGLE MALT WHISKY

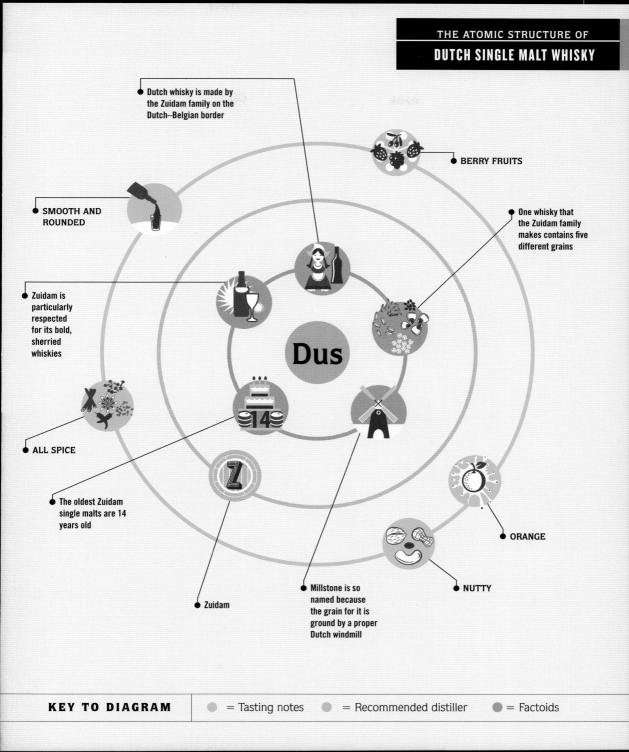

Dutch whisky is made by the Zuidam family on the Dutch–Belgian border

BERRY FRUITS

SMOOTH AND ROUNDED

One whisky that the Zuidam family makes contains five different grains

Zuidam is particularly respected for its bold, sherried whiskies

Dus

ALL SPICE

The oldest Zuidam single malts are 14 years old

ORANGE

Zuidam

Millstone is so named because the grain for it is ground by a proper Dutch windmill

NUTTY

**KEY TO DIAGRAM**    ● = Tasting notes    ● = Recommended distiller    ● = Factoids

**ORIGIN:** England
**ABV:** 43%–58%
**GRAIN:** Malted barley
**CASK:** Ex-bourbon, ex-sherry, ex-white wine, ex-rum, ex-port

# ENGLISH SINGLE MALT WHISKY

**When Norfolk farmers James and Andrew Nelstrop announced that they were opening a whisky distillery, the news was greeted with puzzled amusement. How could they do it in a part of eastern England that had no tradition in this art?**

When they announced that Scottish distilling legend Iain Henderson was heading their team, the laughter stopped. The move was emblematic of the attitude the Nelstrops have brought to whisky. Their malt, both peaty and non-peaty, was drinkable at three years. At eight years, it's fabulous.

Now others are joining the English whisky party. East-coast brewer Adnams is working with virgin oak and mixed grain whisky. Great things are expected of Darren Rook in London, too, and down in Cornwall a partnership between a cider farm and St. Austell Brewery has produced a rich, and very fruity whisky.

## THREE TO TRY

| | | |
|---|---|---|
| **Adnams Single Malt** | Already this three-year-old fizzes with spice and potpourri-style floral and fruity notes. Not there yet, but promising | ★ |
| **St George's Chapter 13** | Banana, toffee, vanilla ice cream, and tinned pears combine in the best release yet from the Norfolk distillers | ★★ |
| **Hicks & Healey Single Malt** | There hasn't been a bottling for a while, but the partners' first release was rich with apple, honey, and a menthol and liquorice combo | ★★★ |

★ LEAST EXPENSIVE/WIDELY AVAILABLE    ★★ MODERATELY PRICED/
HARDER TO SOURCE    ★★★COSTLY/RARE

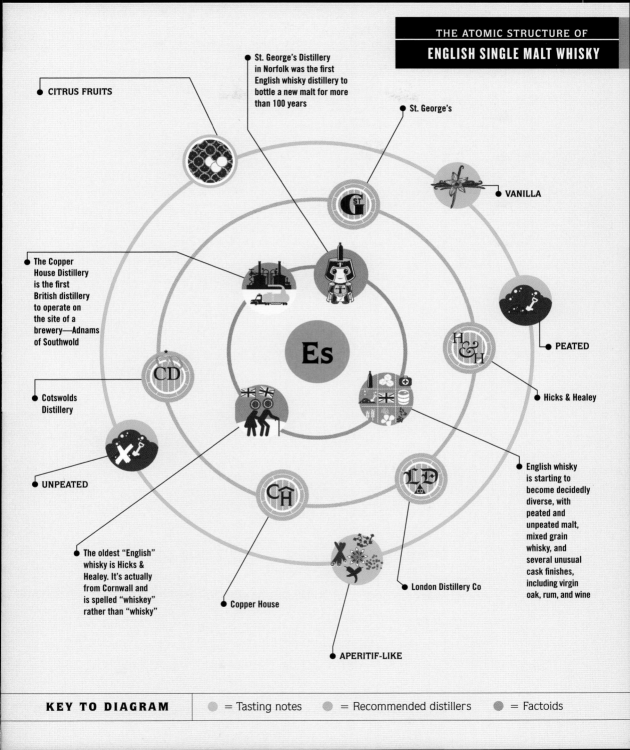

CITRUS FRUITS

St. George's Distillery in Norfolk was the first English whisky distillery to bottle a new malt for more than 100 years

St. George's

VANILLA

The Copper House Distillery is the first British distillery to operate on the site of a brewery—Adnams of Southwold

**Es**

PEATED

Hicks & Healey

Cotswolds Distillery

UNPEATED

English whisky is starting to become decidedly diverse, with peated and unpeated malt, mixed grain whisky, and several unusual cask finishes, including virgin oak, rum, and wine

The oldest "English" whisky is Hicks & Healey. It's actually from Cornwall and is spelled "whiskey" rather than "whisky"

London Distillery Co

Copper House

APERITIF-LIKE

**KEY TO DIAGRAM**   ● = Tasting notes   ● = Recommended distillers   ● = Factoids

**ORIGIN:** Wales
**ABV:** 41%–60%
**GRAIN:** Malted barley
**CASK:** Ex-bourbon,
ex-Scottish malt,
ex-Madeira, ex-sherry

# WELSH SINGLE MALT WHISKY

**The Penderyn distillery may have started the New World whisky boom. It wasn't the first producer from a nontraditional area, but its high profile in Britain, stylish packaging, and unique manufacturing process took small-scale distilling to a new level.**

On the company premises not far from Cardiff, a unique still was developed to make the spirit, and that spirit is matured in Madeira casks, bourbon casks, and casks that have previously held Speyside whisky. The result is a very delicate and sweet malt with its own distinctive character.

The distillery has shown that it can do heavyweight malts, too, if it really wants to. Wales also has a micro-distillery—Dà Mhìle in Llandysul—which is owned by a farmer specializing in organic food.

## THREE TO TRY

| | | |
|---|---|---|
| **Penderyn Madeira** | Made in monthly batches; sweet and grapey with juicy raisins and berry fruits | ★ |
| **Penderyn Portwood** | Shouldn't work because it should be too sweet and cloying, but it does because it's almost like a cassis | ★★ |
| **Penderyn Portwood Cask Strength** | The Scotch Malt Whisky Society doesn't just release Scotch whisky. This is a great whisky bought and released by them. | ★★★ |

★ LEAST EXPENSIVE/WIDELY AVAILABLE   ★★ MODERATELY PRICED/ HARDER TO SOURCE   ★★★COSTLY/RARE

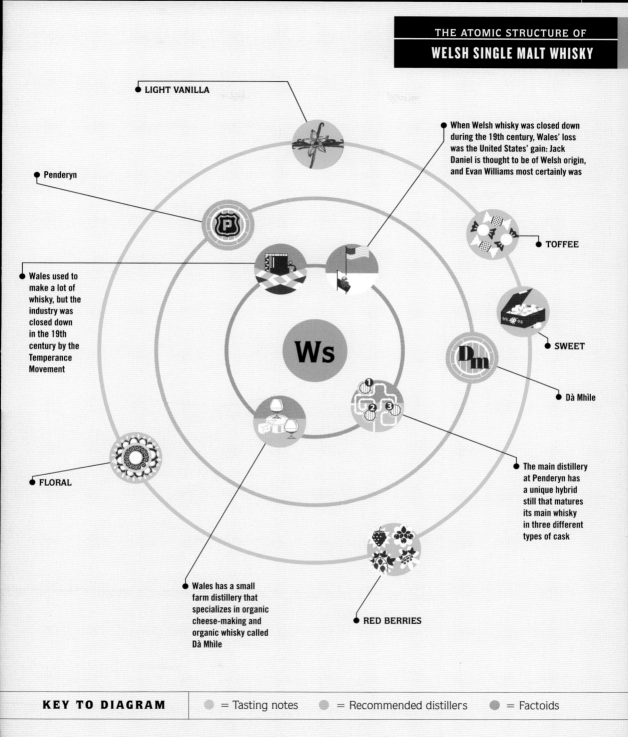

THE ATOMIC STRUCTURE OF
# WELSH SINGLE MALT WHISKY

LIGHT VANILLA

When Welsh whisky was closed down during the 19th century, Wales' loss was the United States' gain: Jack Daniel is thought to be of Welsh origin, and Evan Williams most certainly was

Penderyn

TOFFEE

Wales used to make a lot of whisky, but the industry was closed down in the 19th century by the Temperance Movement

**Ws**

SWEET

**Dm**

Dà Mhìle

FLORAL

The main distillery at Penderyn has a unique hybrid still that matures its main whisky in three different types of cask

Wales has a small farm distillery that specializes in organic cheese-making and organic whisky called Dà Mhìle

RED BERRIES

**KEY TO DIAGRAM**    = Tasting notes    = Recommended distillers    = Factoids

**ORIGIN:** France
**ABV:** 40%–58%
**GRAIN:** Malted barley
**CASK:** Ex-bourbon,
ex-Cognac, ex-sherry,
ex-wine

# FRENCH SINGLE MALT WHISKY

On the face of it, France would not seem to offer much as a whisky-making country. But that is mainly because its spirits have been overshadowed by the marketing initiatives of the nation's wine and cognac producers.

Four of the country's six main distilleries are in Brittany, a northwestern region with a strong cider-making tradition and a range of quality beers. Despite their proximity, these distilleries have little in common with each other and there is no regional style. Glann ar Mor produces Scottish Highland and Island-style whiskies; Distillerie Warenghem has more than a little in common with Speyside; Distillerie des Menhirs is plowing its own furrow with whiskies made with buckwheat; Kaerilis is the newest distillery, founded in 2011. The two main non-Breton whiskies are in the Alsace and Cognac regions, and there are several other non-whisky distilleries which occasionally make a single malt.

## THREE TO TRY

| | | |
|---|---|---|
| **Armorik** | From Distillerie Warenghem, an ever-improving fruity delight; clean, sharp, and balanced | ★ |
| **Brenne** | Nothing like conventional, but delightful. It's from Cognac and tastes like it: light, sweet, liqueur-like, and with a delicate floral taste | ★★ |
| **Glann ar Mor Kornog** | The antithesis of Brenne; a scruffy, peaty delight, with bitter lemon and lime and licorice. Would not be out of place on Islay | ★★★ |

★ LEAST EXPENSIVE/WIDELY AVAILABLE   ★★ MODERATELY PRICED/
HARDER TO SOURCE   ★★★COSTLY/RARE

THE ATOMIC STRUCTURE OF
# FRENCH SINGLE MALT WHISKY

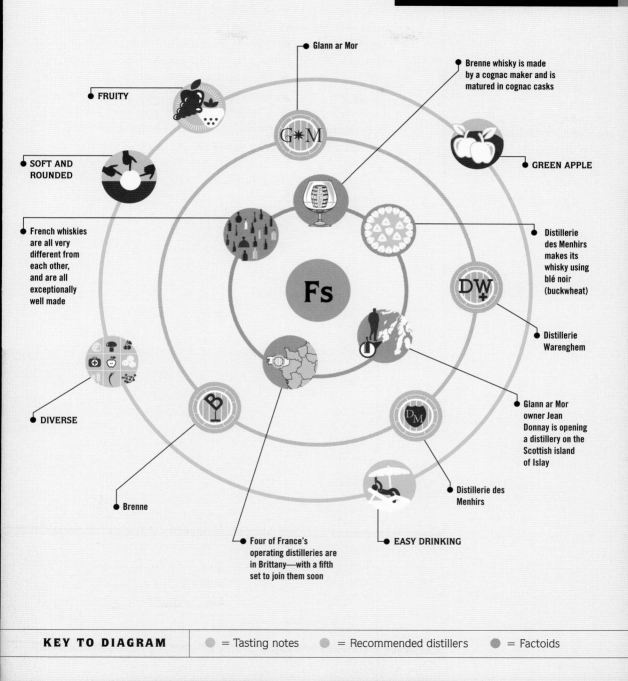

Glann ar Mor

Brenne whisky is made by a cognac maker and is matured in cognac casks

FRUITY

GREEN APPLE

SOFT AND ROUNDED

French whiskies are all very different from each other, and are all exceptionally well made

Distillerie des Menhirs makes its whisky using blé noir (buckwheat)

Fs

DW+

Distillerie Warenghem

DIVERSE

Glann ar Mor owner Jean Donnay is opening a distillery on the Scottish island of Islay

Brenne

Distillerie des Menhirs

Four of France's operating distilleries are in Brittany—with a fifth set to join them soon

EASY DRINKING

**KEY TO DIAGRAM** ● = Tasting notes  ● = Recommended distillers  ● = Factoids

**ORIGIN:** Austria, Germany, Liechtenstein, and Switzerland
**ABV:** 40%–60%
**GRAIN:** Malted barley, wheat, oats, and rye
**CASK:** Ex-bourbon, ex-sherry, ex-wine, ex-beer

# GERMANIC SINGLE MALT WHISKY

**It's a moot point whether so many distilleries across such a large area of Europe should be bracketed together as we have here, but the move is defensible on the grounds that they have a lot in common.**

These distilleries tend to be small—in some cases very small; most of the whisky is consumed within a short radius of the distillery; much of it is not a permanent fixture; much of it is matured in casks used to make the whisky maker's other drinks products—wine, beer, fruit liqueurs; and much of it has a peculiarly intense, oily, and woody taste. There are some fantastic whiskies coming from all four countries (Germany, Austria, Switzerland, and Liechtenstein) and the six distilleries recommended on the facing page are all well worth trying if you can find them.

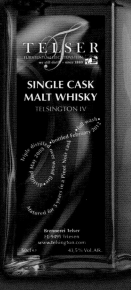

## THREE TO TRY

| | | |
|---|---|---|
| **Blaue Maus Grüner Hund** | Their young whiskies have milk chocolate, honeycomb, and some ginger spice at their heart; their old ones are too woody | ★ |
| **Telsington IV** | Bitter cake from Liechtenstein with amazing spices, delicious chewy fruit, and dark coffee notes | ★★ |
| **Säntis Swiss Highlander Edition** | Locher's Säntis range is world class, but this, with its intense spices and burned bacon taste, can attact a whole new audience | ★★★ |

★ LEAST EXPENSIVE/WIDELY AVAILABLE   ★★ MODERATELY PRICED/ HARDER TO SOURCE   ★★★COSTLY/RARE

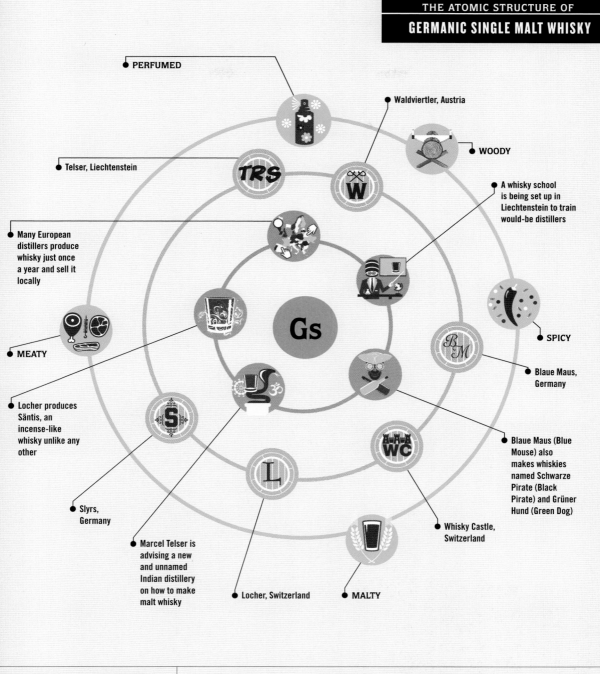

PERFUMED

Waldviertler, Austria

WOODY

Telser, Liechtenstein

A whisky school
is being set up in
Liechtenstein to train
would-be distillers

Many European
distillers produce
whisky just once
a year and sell it
locally

SPICY

MEATY

Blaue Maus,
Germany

Locher produces
Säntis, an
incense-like
whisky unlike any
other

Blaue Maus (Blue
Mouse) also
makes whiskies
named Schwarze
Pirate (Black
Pirate) and Grüner
Hund (Green Dog)

Slyrs,
Germany

Whisky Castle,
Switzerland

Marcel Telser is
advising a new
and unnamed
Indian distillery
on how to make
malt whisky

Locher, Switzerland

MALTY

Gs

TRS

W

BM

S

L

WC

**KEY TO DIAGRAM** ⬤ = Tasting notes ⬤ = Recommended distillers ⬤ = Factoids

**ORIGIN:** Spain and Italy
**ABV:** 40%–60%
**GRAIN:** Malted barley
**CASK:** Ex-bourbon, ex-wine

# MEDITERRANEAN SINGLE MALT WHISKY

**On the face of it, whisky making in Spain and Italy would seem a bit illogical; barley is in short supply, and grapes offer a far easier route into the world of spirits.**

But it's not as odd a proposition as it might first appear. The Spanish love whisky and during the Franco era (1939–75) it made sense to build a distillery, as the dictator did not want to be reliant on a product from another country. Destilerías y Crianza is in an area of Spain with cold, snowy winters. It is owned by Beam Global and for many years it included Laphroaig and Ardmore in its blends. Spanish single malt is now made there. The Italian distillery Puni is in an area annexed from Austria high in the Alps. The industry is very young, but its future looks bright.

## THREE TO TRY

| | | |
|---|---|---|
| **Puni Alba** | Matured for 18 months in Marsala and Pinot Noir wine casks; not real whisky but a spicy, fruity treat | ★ |
| **Embrujo de Granada** | Work in progress; still too thin, but the rich, sweet orange notes bode well | ★★ |
| **DYC Collecion Barricas 10 Year Old** | Firm, fresh, balanced, and deep enough to hold the red berry and spring meadow notes in check; the best Mediterranean release so far | ★★★ |

★ LEAST EXPENSIVE/WIDELY AVAILABLE  ★★ MODERATELY PRICED/ HARDER TO SOURCE  ★★★ COSTLY/RARE

THE ATOMIC STRUCTURE OF
# MEDITERRANEAN SINGLE MALT WHISKY

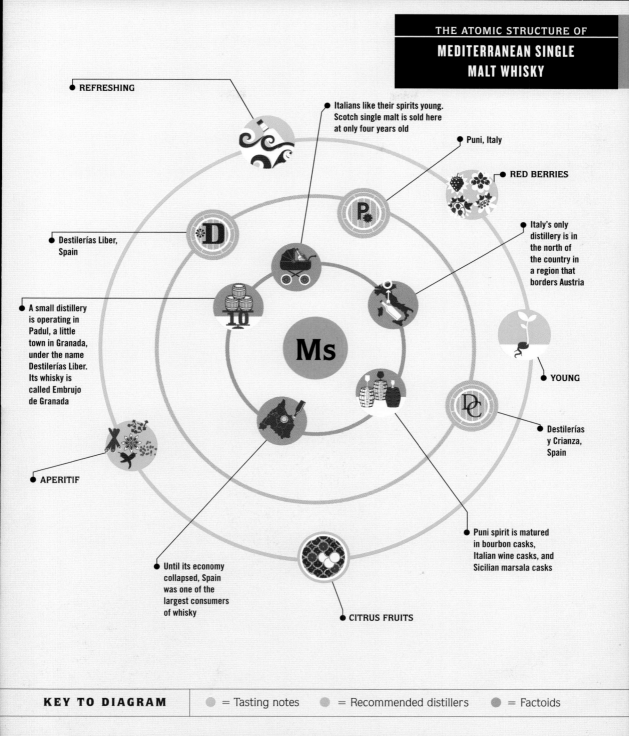

REFRESHING

Italians like their spirits young. Scotch single malt is sold here at only four years old

Puni, Italy

RED BERRIES

Destilerías Liber, Spain

Italy's only distillery is in the north of the country in a region that borders Austria

A small distillery is operating in Padul, a little town in Granada, under the name Destilerías Liber. Its whisky is called Embrujo de Granada

Ms

YOUNG

Destilerías y Crianza, Spain

APERITIF

Puni spirit is matured in bourbon casks, Italian wine casks, and Sicilian marsala casks

Until its economy collapsed, Spain was one of the largest consumers of whisky

CITRUS FRUITS

**KEY TO DIAGRAM**  ● = Tasting notes  ● = Recommended distillers  ● = Factoids

ORIGIN: Sweden
ABV: 43%–60%
GRAIN: Malted barley
CASK: Ex-bourbon,
ex-sherry, ex-port pipes

# SWEDISH SINGLE MALT WHISKY

**Of all the emergent whisky-producing nations around the world, only Australia can match Sweden for the number of new distilleries and the high standard of the spirits produced.**

Mackmyra blazed the trail a few years ago, and Spirit of Hven is now on sale too, with Box set to join them. There are plenty more on the way.

The Swedish are passionate about Scotch whisky and they aim to emulate Scottish single malt's high standards. But they are going further, seeking out barley strains that have long been forgotten and investing in the finest oak. Swedish whisky is also taking on a national identity. The peat comes from under the Baltic Sea and is very salty. The barley is dried with locally sourced juniper twigs.

## THREE TO TRY

| | | |
|---|---|---|
| **Mackmyra Special 10 Year Old** | Entry-level; fruity, sweet, and easy to drink, with the saltiness and pepper held in check | ★ |
| **Spirit of Hven Dubhe** | A sensitive whisky with gentle peat and oak, some vanilla, some honey, and cardamon and cumin | ★★ |
| **Mackmyra Svensk Rök** | The name means "Swedish smoke"; wispy and not as dominant as Mackmyra can be. Some saltiness and nuttiness provide a nice balance | ★★★ |

★ LEAST EXPENSIVE/WIDELY AVAILABLE ★★ MODERATELY PRICED/ HARDER TO SOURCE ★★★COSTLY/RARE

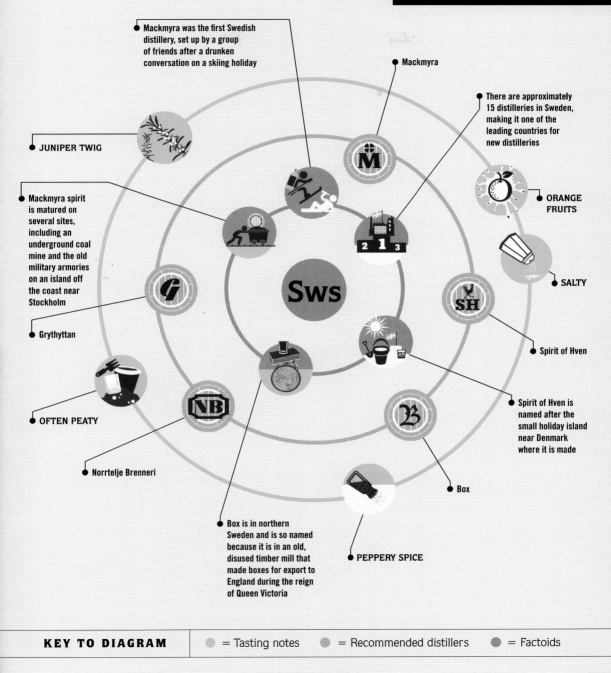

Mackmyra was the first Swedish distillery, set up by a group of friends after a drunken conversation on a skiing holiday

Mackmyra

There are approximately 15 distilleries in Sweden, making it one of the leading countries for new distilleries

JUNIPER TWIG

ORANGE FRUITS

Mackmyra spirit is matured on several sites, including an underground coal mine and the old military armories on an island off the coast near Stockholm

SALTY

M

Sws

SH

Grythyttan

Spirit of Hven

OFTEN PEATY

NB

B

Spirit of Hven is named after the small holiday island near Denmark where it is made

Norrtelje Brenneri

Box

Box is in northern Sweden and is so named because it is in an old, disused timber mill that made boxes for export to England during the reign of Queen Victoria

PEPPERY SPICE

**KEY TO DIAGRAM** | = Tasting notes | = Recommended distillers | = Factoids

# BLENDED WHISKIES

# CHAPTER
# TWO

Blended whisky doesn't get the best press. The view held by many is that single malt whisky is of a high quality and blended whisky isn't. But it's not that simple, and these commonly held positions aren't justified.

There are many very good blended whiskies, and while it may be argued that these are the exceptions that prove the rule, there are an awful lot of exceptions.

Although Scotland leads the way in the production of blended whiskies, it is not the only country producing them. It is, however, the only country that makes Scotch.

A blended whisky is normally, but not always, a combination of single malts from several different distilleries mixed with grain spirit. Single malt whisky is produced in batches using a pot still, while grain whisky is made in a continuous or column still. Grain whisky is less distinctive than single malt whisky and is quicker and cheaper to produce. But grain makes a rounded, softer, and more palatable whisky and initially it was these traits that made it attractive to consumers across the world.

So why the negative view of blended whisky? Simply because there are many poor-quality whiskies in the marketplace, including a large number from Scotland. There the rules state that malt spirit must be matured for a minimum of three years in an oak barrel in Scotland and have a minimum alcoholic strength of 40% ABV. But the rules governing blended whisky don't state how new the cask must be. As a result, tired casks are being used to make whisky destined for the blended market.

Furthermore, there are no rules about the quantities of grain and single malt in the blend. So for all the Scotch Whisky Association's argument about defending the quality of Scotch whisky, chances are that the bottle of "Clan Bagpipe" for under $10 in the local store contains whisky matured for just over three years in tired casks, is comprised of more than 80% grain whisky, and has that beautiful chestnut color not because of the cask but because of an added dollop of caramel. It's basically colored vodka.

This is equally true elsewhere in the world, but that is nowhere near the whole story. It's very difficult indeed to play with lots of whisky styles to create a high-quality blend. Across the world there are skilled master blenders making fine whiskies that are not only the match of single malts, but surpass many of them. The best blends contain a better balance of grain whisky and are works of art, rich in nuance and complexity.

At the premium end of the sector, blends can retail at hundreds of dollars and contain some of the rarest and oldest whiskies in the world.

In this chapter we look at blends across the world. The definition of a blend and how it should be made varies from country to country. Some countries allow foreign whiskies into the mix, while others, among them Ireland, make their blends from different styles of whisky.

We also look at whiskies made with malts from different distilleries but with no grain in them. These are known as blended malt whiskies as opposed to blended whiskies—a subtle difference, but an important one.

**ORIGIN:** Scotland
**ABV:** 40%
**GRAIN:** Malted barley, other grain whisky

# STANDARD SCOTTISH BLENDED WHISKY

There are few drinks better known than Scottish blended whisky, and even with today's big interest in single malt whisky, nine out of ten glasses of Scotch consumed are of blended whisky.

Blended whiskies are a mix of grain whisky and single malt whiskies from various distilleries. In Scotland, big whisky companies swap malts with each other so that they all have a broad selection to choose from. But every company has a different recipe, each of which is fiercely protected. The skill of the master blender is to source whisky casks each time to recreate the flavor of the blend from batch to batch. But he or she is at liberty to change the quantities of a given malt in the blend or to replace a malt with something else.

## THREE TO TRY

| | | |
|---|---|---|
| **Chivas Regal 12 Year Old** | Green and tropical fruits, clean and sweet with some nice woody notes | ★ |
| **Teacher's Highland Cream** | Gutsy, earthy, and grainy version of a blended whisky, reflecting its link with Ardmore; likes to play rough | ★★ |
| **Johnnie Walker Black Label** | Arguably a premium blend, this is excellently made, full of character, and a smoky, fruity delight | ★★★ |

★ LEAST EXPENSIVE/WIDELY AVAILABLE  ★★ MODERATELY PRICED/ HARDER TO SOURCE  ★★★COSTLY/RARE

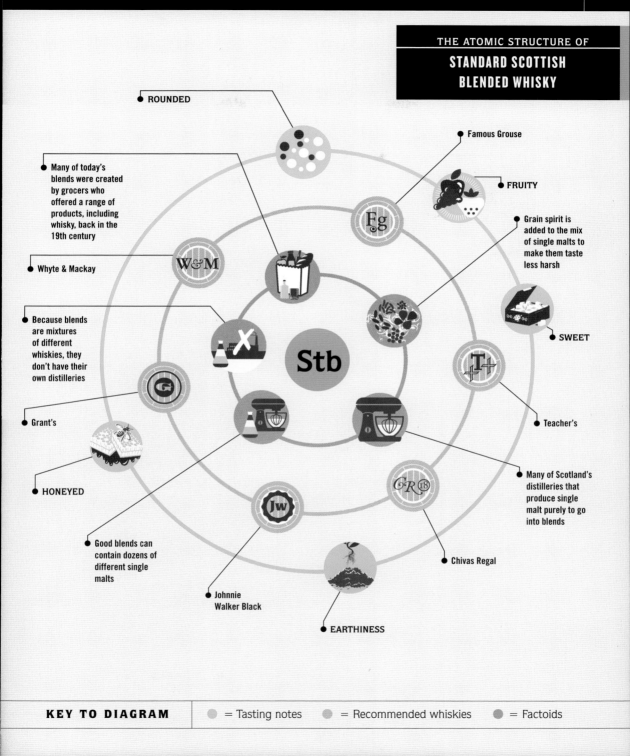

ROUNDED

Many of today's blends were created by grocers who offered a range of products, including whisky, back in the 19th century

Famous Grouse

FRUITY

Grain spirit is added to the mix of single malts to make them taste less harsh

Whyte & Mackay

W&M

Fg

SWEET

Because blends are mixtures of different whiskies, they don't have their own distilleries

Stb

T

Grant's

G

Teacher's

HONEYED

Many of Scotland's distilleries that produce single malt purely to go into blends

CR 18

Jw

Good blends can contain dozens of different single malts

Chivas Regal

Johnnie Walker Black

EARTHINESS

**KEY TO DIAGRAM**   ● = Tasting notes   ● = Recommended whiskies   ● = Factoids

**ORIGIN:** Scotland
**ABV:** 43%–50%
**GRAIN:** Malted barley, other grain whisky

# PREMIUM SCOTTISH BLENDED WHISKY

**Blended whiskies don't always receive the same level of respect as single malts do, but they can be every bit as good.**

Whisky producers face a problem when the spirit is in demand, as it has been in recent years. Distilleries can only make a limited amount of malt whisky and it takes years for it to reach full maturation. But premium blends are a way forward—through clever blending, the whisky makers can swap and change the malts and grains in the recipe without compromising on quality, using lesser-known, but perfectly good malts which would not ordinarily sell in their own right. If a blend bears an age statement it denotes that all whisky in the blend—grain as well as malts—must be at least that age.

## THREE TO TRY

| | | |
|---|---|---|
| **Ballantine's 17 Year Old** | Complex, excellently made, with the perfect balance between barley and oak, sugar and spice, honey and citrus | ★ |
| **Cutty Sark 25 Year Old** | Juicy fat raisins and dates, some almonds and Christmas cake, with oaky and milk chocolate notes | ★★ |
| **Dewar's Signature** | Sweet honey, citrus, and spice combine over a Highland oaky backbone from some very old Aberfeldy malt | ★★★ |

★ LEAST EXPENSIVE/WIDELY AVAILABLE   ★★ MODERATELY PRICED/HARDER TO SOURCE   ★★★ COSTLY/RARE

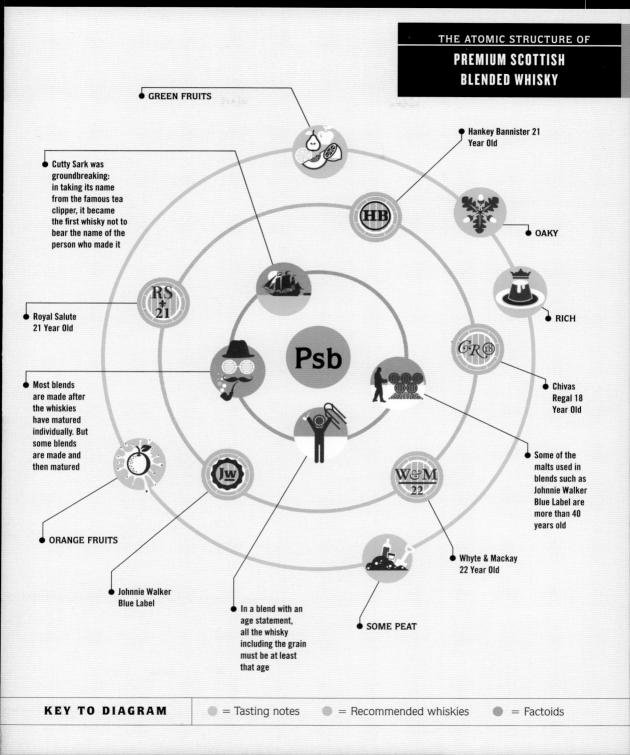

THE ATOMIC STRUCTURE OF
# PREMIUM SCOTTISH BLENDED WHISKY

GREEN FRUITS

Hankey Bannister 21 Year Old

Cutty Sark was groundbreaking: in taking its name from the famous tea clipper, it became the first whisky not to bear the name of the person who made it

OAKY

RICH

Royal Salute 21 Year Old

Psb

Chivas Regal 18 Year Old

Most blends are made after the whiskies have matured individually. But some blends are made and then matured

Some of the malts used in blends such as Johnnie Walker Blue Label are more than 40 years old

ORANGE FRUITS

Whyte & Mackay 22 Year Old

Johnnie Walker Blue Label

In a blend with an age statement, all the whisky including the grain must be at least that age

SOME PEAT

KEY TO DIAGRAM    ● = Tasting notes    ● = Recommended whiskies    ● = Factoids

ORIGIN: Scotland
ABV: 40%–55%
GRAIN: Malted barley, other grain whisky

# RARE AND EXCLUSIVE SCOTTISH BLENDED WHISKY

**Produced only in limited quantities, these blends are now an acknowledged match for some of the finest cognacs and attract connoisseurs in emerging whisky territories such as Taiwan and Russia.**

With Scotch in short supply, the industry is taking two approaches to maximize revenue. The first is to put younger whisky in fancy packaging without an age statement and sell it at inflated prices through the travel retail industry. The other is to take the oldest whiskies and play on their rarity.

Old doesn't always mean good, of course, but before the quality of a whisky flatlines there may be a spectacular late flowering, such as in the licorice rancio taste (a flavor associated with fortified wines), which, for many, is the Holy Grail. This comes at a price, of course, but arguably one worth paying.

## THREE TO TRY

| William Grant's 25 Year Old | Sherry and oak to the fore, honeyed fruits in the center, and a spicy woody finish | ★ |
|---|---|---|
| Ballantine's 30 Year Old | Fresh and juicy, but with all the tell-tale signs of great age; marvelous stuff | ★★ |
| Hankey Bannister 40 Year Old | Rich, complex and citrusy, this is a world beater and can be sipped alongside the very finest single malts | ★★★ |

★ LEAST EXPENSIVE/WIDELY AVAILABLE  ★★ MODERATELY PRICED/ HARDER TO SOURCE  ★★★COSTLY/RARE

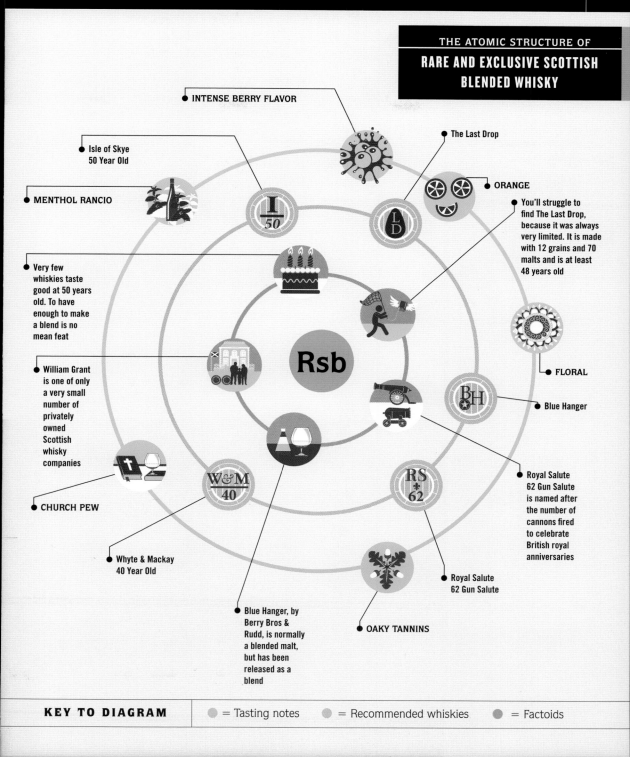

# RARE AND EXCLUSIVE SCOTTISH BLENDED WHISKY

INTENSE BERRY FLAVOR

The Last Drop

Isle of Skye 50 Year Old

ORANGE

MENTHOL RANCIO

You'll struggle to find The Last Drop, because it was always very limited. It is made with 12 grains and 70 malts and is at least 48 years old

Very few whiskies taste good at 50 years old. To have enough to make a blend is no mean feat

**Rsb**

FLORAL

William Grant is one of only a very small number of privately owned Scottish whisky companies

Blue Hanger

CHURCH PEW

Royal Salute 62 Gun Salute is named after the number of cannons fired to celebrate British royal anniversaries

Whyte & Mackay 40 Year Old

Royal Salute 62 Gun Salute

Blue Hanger, by Berry Bros & Rudd, is normally a blended malt, but has been released as a blend

OAKY TANNINS

**ORIGIN:** Ireland, Northern Ireland
**ABV:** 40%
**GRAIN:** Irish pot still, other grain whiskey

# STANDARD IRISH BLENDED WHISKEY

After dominating the finest dining tables of the world, Irish whiskey's fall from grace was spectacular. Its decline was partly self-inflicted, partly due to bad luck, and partly to a vicious assault from the Scottish competition.

In the 1960s, Irish whiskey was in danger of extinction. The surviving producers, including Bushmill's in the North, formed Irish Distillers and defined Irish whiskey as distinct from Scotch: a non-peaty, triple-distilled blend of pot still and grain whiskeys normally bottled at 40% ABV.

For a while this initiative revived the industry's fortunes, but then independent company Cooley started producing single malts and peaty Irish whiskeys. This caused an outcry and was seen as a fresh threat to Irish whiskey's future. In fact, Cooley had the opposite effect. Nowadays, blends are just part of an excitingly diverse Irish whiskey scene.

## THREE TO TRY

| | | |
|---|---|---|
| **Jameson** | The biggest is, arguably, the best. This is definitive Irish whiskey and a must try for anyone who has somehow missed it | ★ |
| **Black Bush** | A sherried Irish delight, with lots of raisins and then sweet and savory spices battling out to the end | ★★ |
| **Locke's** | One for those with a sweet tooth: lots and lots of honey and quite chunky | ★★★ |

★ LEAST EXPENSIVE/WIDELY AVAILABLE   ★★ MODERATELY PRICED/HARDER TO SOURCE   ★★★ COSTLY/RARE

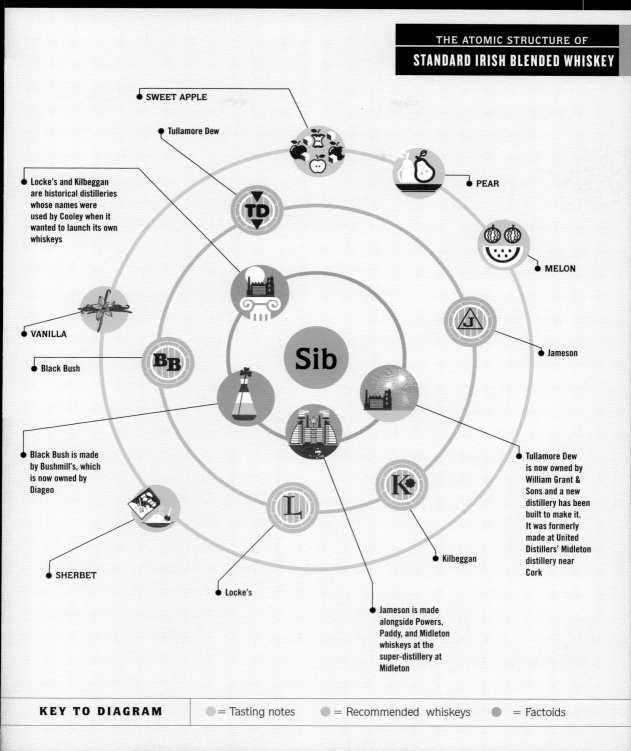

THE ATOMIC STRUCTURE OF
# STANDARD IRISH BLENDED WHISKEY

SWEET APPLE

Tullamore Dew

Locke's and Kilbeggan are historical distilleries whose names were used by Cooley when it wanted to launch its own whiskeys

PEAR

MELON

VANILLA

Black Bush

Jameson

Sib

Black Bush is made by Bushmill's, which is now owned by Diageo

Tullamore Dew is now owned by William Grant & Sons and a new distillery has been built to make it. It was formerly made at United Distillers' Midleton distillery near Cork

SHERBET

Locke's

Kilbeggan

Jameson is made alongside Powers, Paddy, and Midleton whiskeys at the super-distillery at Midleton

**KEY TO DIAGRAM** | ● = Tasting notes | ● = Recommended whiskeys | ● = Factoids

**ORIGIN:** Ireland
**ABV:** 40%–46%
**GRAIN:** Pot still whiskey, other grain whiskeys

# PREMIUM BLENDED IRISH WHISKEY

**When it became apparent that the mavericks at Cooley were winning the hearts and minds of the public with their single malts and peaty Irish whiskeys, Irish Distillers was forced to counter the threat.**

Irish Distillers' response was to crank up their output of pot still whiskeys, a market sector in which they already had a monopoly. They began by offering some truly superb new versions of Jameson. Whiskeys at 43% and 46% ABV started to appear, along with a variety of blends with a higher pot still content and some others from unusual woods. These were premium Irish whiskeys of a type never previously encountered: Cooley had brought about the dawn of a golden period.

Irish whiskey producers tend not to talk about their whiskeys as blends, and they are not directly comparable to Scottish blends. Historically, whiskeys such as Jameson, Paddy, and Powers were made and sold in different regions, much in the same way that Scottish single malts once were.

## THREE TO TRY

| | | |
|---|---|---|
| **Jameson Rarest Vintage Reserve** | Perhaps the most triumphant product of the multi-distillery collaboration | ★ |
| **The Wild Geese Rare Irish** | Perfect straight, but a favorite cocktail ingredient; citrus fruits, gooseberry, and floral notes; honeysuckle with a peppery overtone. | ★★ |
| **Kilbeggan 15 Year Old** | The sweet, honeyed fruit bowl at the heart of this is flipped on its head by toasty cereal and oak notes | ★★★ |

★ LEAST EXPENSIVE/WIDELY AVAILABLE   ★★ MODERATELY PRICED/ HARDER TO SOURCE   ★★★COSTLY/RARE

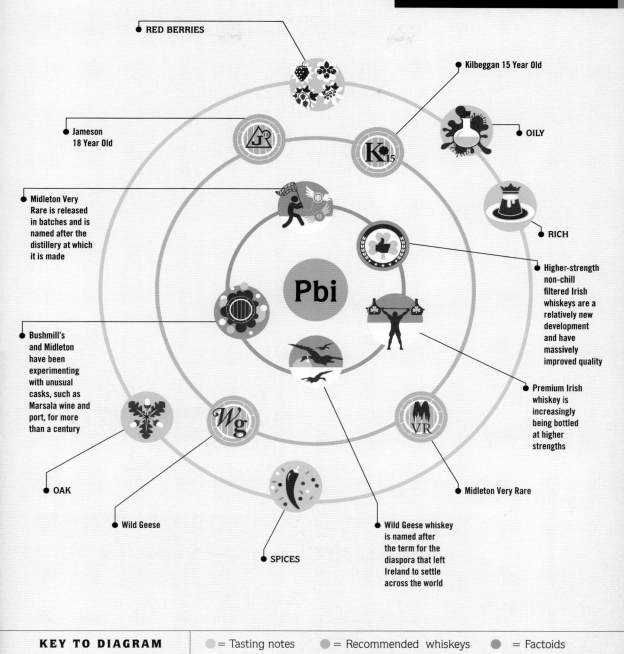

RED BERRIES

Kilbeggan 15 Year Old

OILY

Jameson
18 Year Old

Midleton Very
Rare is released
in batches and is
named after the
distillery at which
it is made

RICH

Pbi

Higher-strength
non-chill
filtered Irish
whiskeys are a
relatively new
development
and have
massively
improved quality

Bushmill's
and Midleton
have been
experimenting
with unusual
casks, such as
Marsala wine and
port, for more
than a century

Premium Irish
whiskey is
increasingly
being bottled
at higher
strengths

OAK

Midleton Very Rare

Wild Geese

Wild Geese whiskey
is named after
the term for the
diaspora that left
Ireland to settle
across the world

SPICES

**KEY TO DIAGRAM** | = Tasting notes | = Recommended whiskeys | = Factoids

**ORIGIN:** Japan, Scotland
**ABV:** 40%–51%
**GRAIN:** Malted barley, other grain whisky

# STANDARD JAPANESE BLENDED WHISKY

**In Scotland, whisky makers have an agreement to share their whiskies so that all of them have the best possible range of malts to use in their blends. This does not happen in Japan.**

In Japan there are only two main players, and they do not supply each other with their malts. So to provide a choice of whiskies for blending, the producers have two options. One is to buy Scottish distilleries and use Scotch whisky for variety. The other is to build complex distilleries with different still shapes and styles, a mix of column and pot stills, and different yeasts and casks.

The Japanese have adopted both options, but the use of malt from Scotland weakens the case for their blends. Pity, because they are exceedingly good and full flavored: Hibiki and Nikka are regular global award winners.

## TWO TO TRY

| Hibiki 12 Year Old | Gentle and sweet, with plum liqueur on the nose and lots of citrus and vanilla on the palate | ★ |
|---|---|---|
| Ginko | Easy drinking, soft, and fruity, with some toffee and chocolate | ★★ |

★ LEAST EXPENSIVE/WIDELY AVAILABLE  ★★ MODERATELY PRICED/ HARDER TO SOURCE

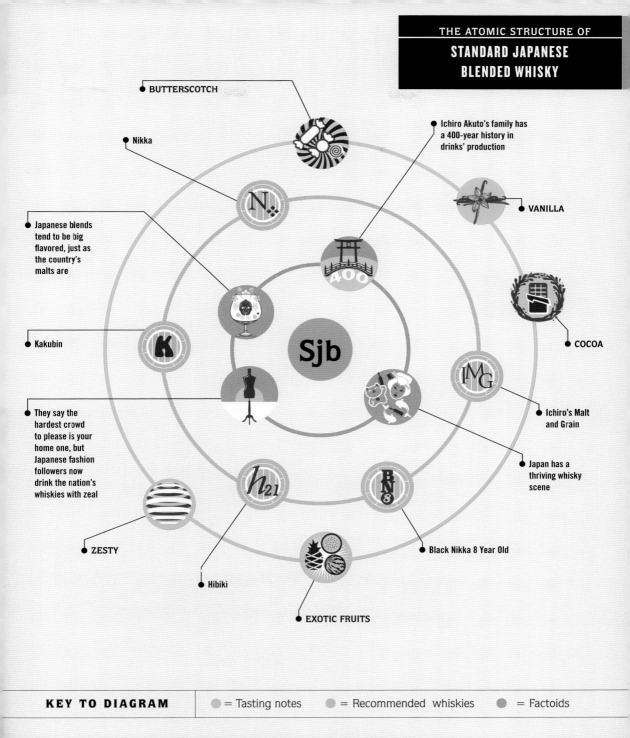

BUTTERSCOTCH

Nikka

Ichiro Akuto's family has a 400-year history in drinks' production

VANILLA

Japanese blends tend to be big flavored, just as the country's malts are

COCOA

Kakubin

Sjb

Ichiro's Malt and Grain

They say the hardest crowd to please is your home one, but Japanese fashion followers now drink the nation's whiskies with zeal

Japan has a thriving whisky scene

ZESTY

Black Nikka 8 Year Old

Hibiki

EXOTIC FRUITS

**KEY TO DIAGRAM** ⬤ = Tasting notes ⬤ = Recommended whiskies ⬤ = Factoids

**ORIGIN:** Japan
**ABV:** 43%–51%
**GRAIN:** Malted barley, other grain whiskies

# PREMIUM JAPANESE BLENDED WHISKY

**The biggest problem facing the Japanese whisky industry today is its own success. As recently as the 1990s, the main producers had no idea that they would sweep all the awards from across the world.**

They didn't lay down anything like as much stock as they would need to meet subsequent demand. As a result, it is now a challenge to find Japanese single malts and grain whiskies aged over 20 years. Particularly rare is the premium blend Hibiki 21 Year Old, which has won countless awards and earned plaudits all round.

This and other Japanese premium blends pull off the remarkable feat of being rounded and gossamer-soft to drink, but absolutely bursting with flavor at the same time. Some of the Nikka bottlings in particular are very reasonably priced, but extremely hard to find.

## THREE TO TRY

| | | |
|---|---|---|
| **Suntory Old** | No age statement, but a delicious mix of sherbet then vanilla ice cream, chocolate sauce, and hazelnuts | ★ |
| **Nikka Rare Old Super** | Among the very best blends; crackles with oak, buzzes with peat, and revels in sharp potpourri | ★★ |
| **Hibiki Aged 21 Year Old** | The daddy of them all, chosen more than once as the best whisky in the world. Orange marmalade, fruitcake, cherries, and raisins | ★★★ |

★ LEAST EXPENSIVE/WIDELY AVAILABLE ★★ MODERATELY PRICED/ HARDER TO SOURCE ★★★COSTLY/RARE

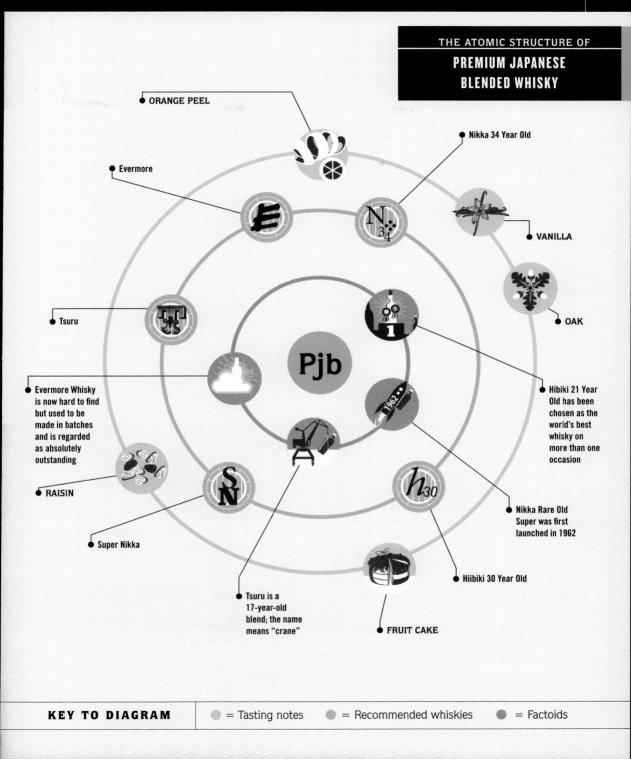

ORANGE PEEL

Nikka 34 Year Old

Evermore

VANILLA

Tsuru

OAK

Pjb

Evermore Whisky
is now hard to find
but used to be
made in batches
and is regarded
as absolutely
outstanding

Hibiki 21 Year
Old has been
chosen as the
world's best
whisky on
more than one
occasion

RAISIN

Super Nikka

Nikka Rare Old
Super was first
launched in 1962

Tsuru is a
17-year-old
blend; the name
means "crane"

Hiibiki 30 Year Old

FRUIT CAKE

**KEY TO DIAGRAM**   = Tasting notes   = Recommended whiskies   = Factoids

ORIGIN: France, Corsica
ABV: 40%–42%
GRAIN: Malted barley, other grain whisky, chestnut, buckwheat

# FRENCH BLENDED WHISKY

**France is a hotbed of whisky consumption, and when it comes to making the drink, there is something distinctively Gallic about the approach: invariably painstaking, but often deliberately unconventional.**

The French are anything but frivolous about producing whisky: they work to the highest standards and take great pride in what they do. But they push the boundaries as far as they can be pushed. One distillery makes its whisky with buckwheat, which most people wouldn't strictly class as a grain but the French government does. Another makes whisky with a beer that includes chestnut in the mix, and that's not usually permitted either.

Purists may object, but there's no denying that these ingredients add taste to the variety and quality of the products.

## THREE TO TRY

| Breizh | With a very high malt content (50%), this is a smooth and sweet whisky with lychee and sweet pear | ★ |
|---|---|---|
| Eddu Grey Rock | Feisty, anarchic whisky with a coastal tang, plenty of fruit, and some smoke | ★★ |
| P&M Supérieur | Less sweet than some of its compatriot whiskies, this has a nutty and spicy theme with some botanical and delicatessen notes | ★★★ |

★ LEAST EXPENSIVE/WIDELY AVAILABLE  ★★ MODERATELY PRICED/ HARDER TO SOURCE  ★★★COSTLY/RARE

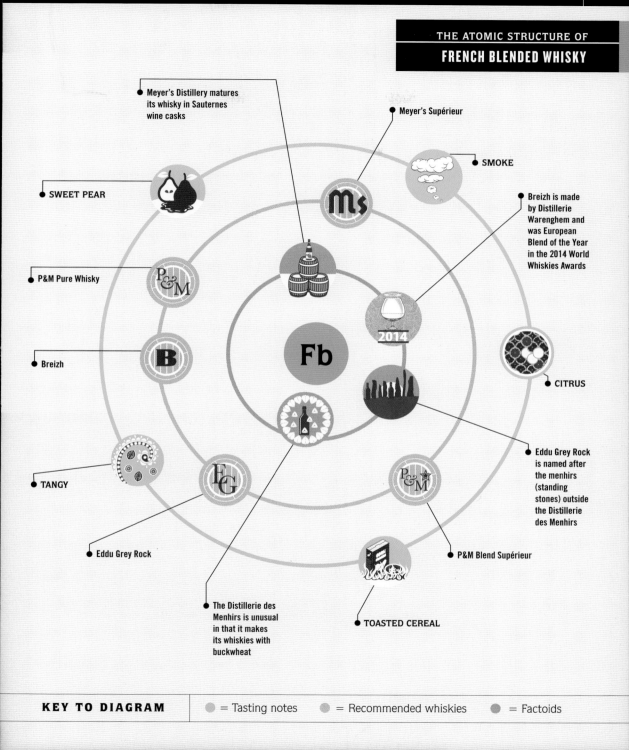

THE ATOMIC STRUCTURE OF
# FRENCH BLENDED WHISKY

Meyer's Distillery matures its whisky in Sauternes wine casks

Meyer's Supérieur

SMOKE

SWEET PEAR

Breizh is made by Distillerie Warenghem and was European Blend of the Year in the 2014 World Whiskies Awards

P&M Pure Whisky

P&M

2014

B

Breizh

Fb

CITRUS

TANGY

E G

P&M

Eddu Grey Rock is named after the menhirs (standing stones) outside the Distillerie des Menhirs

Eddu Grey Rock

P&M Blend Supérieur

The Distillerie des Menhirs is unusual in that it makes its whiskies with buckwheat

TOASTED CEREAL

**KEY TO DIAGRAM**    = Tasting notes    = Recommended whiskies    = Factoids

**ORIGIN:** India, Scotland
**ABV:** NA
**GRAIN:** Malted barley, other grain whisky, molasses

# INDIAN BLENDED WHISKY

**The Indian blended whisky market is difficult to comprehend because it's vast and largely unregulated, and because a good proportion of what is sold on it isn't whisky at all—it would probably be classed as rum if it were exported.**

India has two first-class single malt distilleries and there are more on the way. But the picture on the blended side is altogether more complicated. India's middle classes look to Scotland for whisky. The huge numbers of poor Indian "whisky" drinkers choose between globally owned blends such as McDowell's or Bagpiper, as well as many other blends that are either industrial spirit with whisky flavoring or young spirits made with molasses. Although the Indian market is too big to ignore, many of its blended products are whisky in name only: they are not the real thing.

## WHY YOU SHOULD TRY

India has a thirst for whisky, but Scotch is too expensive for the majority of the population. As a result there is a plethora of cheap, sweet, locally produced whiskies, made with molasses, and with not much going for them. The better Indian whiskies such as Bagpiper and McDowell's are a curio, though—with some containing some Scottish single malt to give them body and depth. They may well appeal if you like easy-drinking and sweet whiskies. All of them tend to be bland, sweet, flabby, and honeyed. Pretty inoffensive and fine to be mixed.

## THE ATOMIC STRUCTURE OF
# INDIAN BLENDED WHISKY

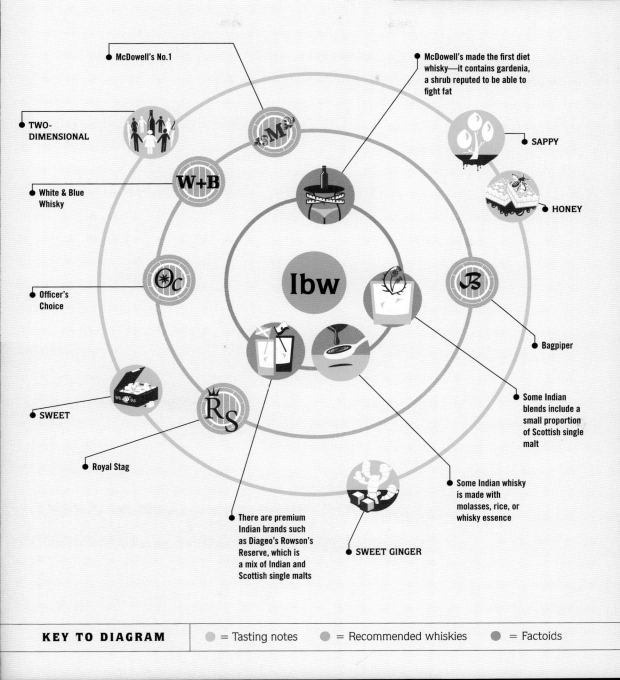

McDowell's No.1

McDowell's made the first diet whisky—it contains gardenia, a shrub reputed to be able to fight fat

TWO-DIMENSIONAL

SAPPY

White & Blue Whisky

HONEY

Officer's Choice

**Ibw**

Bagpiper

SWEET

Some Indian blends include a small proportion of Scottish single malt

Royal Stag

There are premium Indian brands such as Diageo's Rowson's Reserve, which is a mix of Indian and Scottish single malts

SWEET GINGER

Some Indian whisky is made with molasses, rice, or whisky essence

**KEY TO DIAGRAM**   ● = Tasting notes   ● = Recommended whiskies   ● = Factoids

**ORIGIN:** South Africa, Scotland
**ABV:** 43%
**GRAIN:** South African malted barley, Scottish malted barley

# SOUTH AFRICAN BLENDED WHISKY

**The problem facing most nations with only small whisky industries is that of making a blend, because in order to create a good one they need a greater range and diversity than their domestic product can provide.**

What many distilleries do in that situation is buy in whisky from elsewhere, normally Scotland. Now South Africa's drinks giant Distell has followed the big Japanese producers and taken it all a step further by buying its own Scottish distilling group—Burn Stewart, which owns Bunnahabhain, Tobermory, and Deanston distilleries. Following on from the slew of awards the company received for its Three Ships range and Bains grain whisky, it would seem highly likely that the company will soon be expanding into new export markets.

## TWO TO TRY

| | | |
|---|---|---|
| **Three Ships Premium Select 5 Year Old** | The nose is toasted oak, overripe yellow fruit, and smoke. Fresh and fruity on the palate, with traces of sap among the sweet apple. Cumin, paprika, and coriander at the finish | ★ |
| **Three Ships Bourbon Cask Finish** | A dessert whisky oozing with strong candy, the vanilla notes associated with bourbon wood, and a maple syrup and toffee-cream edge | ★★ |

★ LEAST EXPENSIVE/WIDELY AVAILABLE ★★ MODERATELY PRICED/ HARDER TO SOURCE

## THE ATOMIC STRUCTURE OF
# SOUTH AFRICAN BLENDED WHISKY

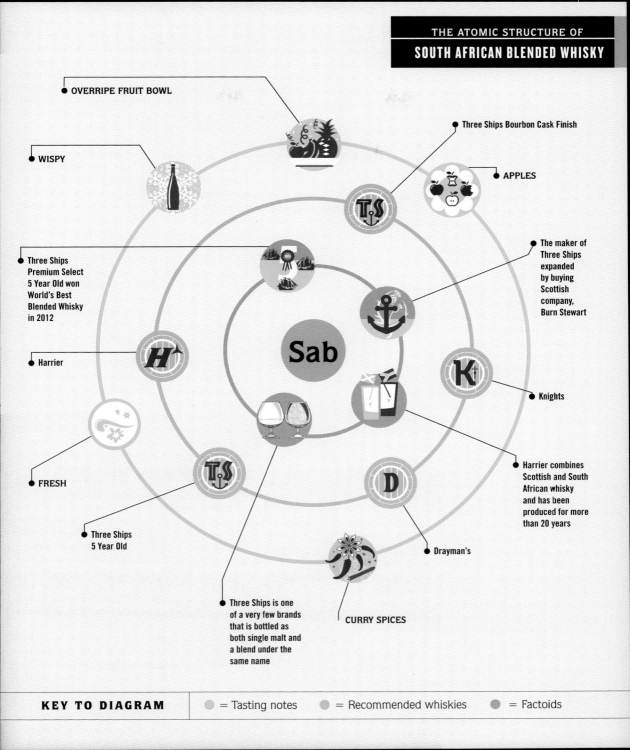

OVERRIPE FRUIT BOWL

WISPY

Three Ships Bourbon Cask Finish

APPLES

Three Ships Premium Select 5 Year Old won World's Best Blended Whisky in 2012

The maker of Three Ships expanded by buying Scottish company, Burn Stewart

Sab

Harrier

Knights

FRESH

Harrier combines Scottish and South African whisky and has been produced for more than 20 years

Three Ships 5 Year Old

Drayman's

Three Ships is one of a very few brands that is bottled as both single malt and a blend under the same name

CURRY SPICES

**KEY TO DIAGRAM**   = Tasting notes   = Recommended whiskies   = Factoids

ORIGIN: Spain, Scotland
ABV: 40%–43%
GRAIN: Malted barley, other grains

# SPANISH BLENDED WHISKY

**The standard of Spanish whisky has improved greatly over recent years and Destilerías y Crianza (DYC) has been at the core of the growth. It is something of a one-stop shop for whisky production.**

The DYC site, about an hour north of Madrid, contains a sizeable pot still distillery, column stills, various smaller stills for making other spirits including a craft gin, a bottling plant, and a packaging area. It even houses a powerful electricity generator.

The operation is owned by Beam Global, which explains why its blends are so rugged. You might expect sweet and fruity, but you get gritty and savory, courtesy of the addition of Scottish malt whiskies Laphroaig and Ardmore, neither of which is a shrinking violet. As a result, DYC produce some of the better non-Scottish blends. Their pure malt is particularly good.

## TWO TO TRY

| DYC Pure Malt | Tastes like a Highland whisky and to a degree it is, with peat smoke at its core, some green salad and apple in the mix and a savory, almost anchovy, undertow | ★ |
| --- | --- | --- |
| DYC 5 Year Old | The addition of grain whisky gives this a smoother, sweeter taste and there are some underlying pear and orange notes. Peat and pepper spice work their way through eventually | ★★ |

★ LEAST EXPENSIVE/WIDELY AVAILABLE ★★ MODERATELY PRICED/ HARDER TO SOURCE

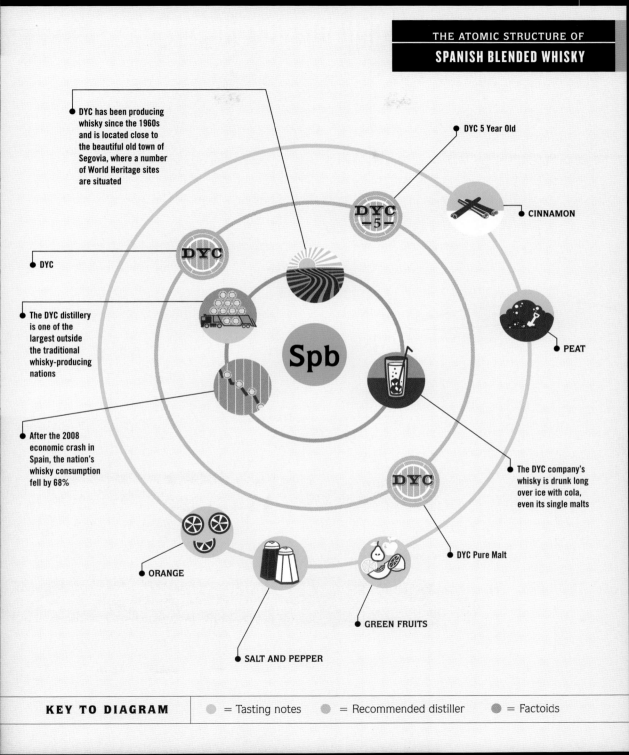

DYC has been producing whisky since the 1960s and is located close to the beautiful old town of Segovia, where a number of World Heritage sites are situated

DYC 5 Year Old

CINNAMON

DYC

The DYC distillery is one of the largest outside the traditional whisky-producing nations

PEAT

Spb

After the 2008 economic crash in Spain, the nation's whisky consumption fell by 68%

The DYC company's whisky is drunk long over ice with cola, even its single malts

DYC Pure Malt

ORANGE

GREEN FRUITS

SALT AND PEPPER

**KEY TO DIAGRAM** ● = Tasting notes ● = Recommended distiller ● = Factoids

**ORIGIN:** Canada, USA
**ABV:** 40%–46%
**GRAIN:** Rye, malted barley, wheat, bourbon

# CANADIAN BLENDED WHISKY

**For a long time, Canadian whisky makers seemed oblivious to their poor global image. Once they realized, however, they set about raising their profile with admirable gusto and are now reaping the benefits of the makeover.**

Canadian Club sold by the bucket-load across the United States, so there was some reluctance to change a winning formula. The first person in Canada to resist this complacency was John Hall at Forty Creek, who began to make use of the wriggle-room in U.S. regulations that permits up to 11% of a whisky to contain something else, such as bourbon or even fruit drinks. Following in Hall's wake came a new wave of distillers who brought innovation to the category and earned Canadian whiskies new respect.

## THREE TO TRY

| | | |
|---|---|---|
| **Alberta Premium** | One of the biggest, fullest, rye spice and rich sweet whiskies you'll find in Canada | ★ |
| **Crown Royal** | Rich, creamy, and soft, with milk chocolate, caramel, and hazelnut whirl, all set on an apricot and peach smoothie | ★★ |
| **Forty Creek Portwood** | Great match-up between the sharp, spicy red berry notes of the port wood and the caramel and banana toffee at the core | ★★★ |

★ LEAST EXPENSIVE/WIDELY AVAILABLE  ★★ MODERATELY PRICED/
HARDER TO SOURCE  ★★★COSTLY/RARE

THE ATOMIC STRUCTURE OF
# CANADIAN BLENDED WHISKY

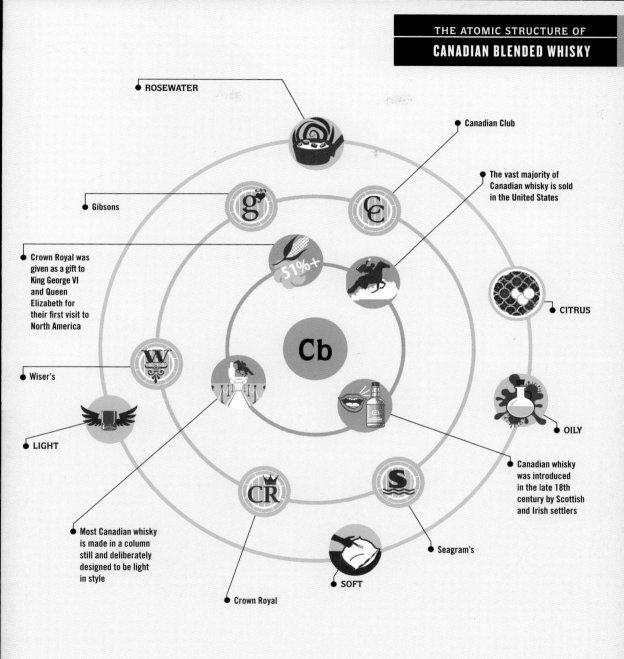

ROSEWATER

Canadian Club

The vast majority of Canadian whisky is sold in the United States

Gibsons

Crown Royal was given as a gift to King George VI and Queen Elizabeth for their first visit to North America

CITRUS

Cb

Wiser's

OILY

LIGHT

Canadian whisky was introduced in the late 18th century by Scottish and Irish settlers

Most Canadian whisky is made in a column still and deliberately designed to be light in style

Seagram's

Crown Royal

SOFT

51%+

**KEY TO DIAGRAM** ● = Tasting notes ● = Recommended whiskies ● = Factoids

# BLENDED MALT WHISKY

# CHAPTER
# THREE

Confusing as it may be, blended whisky and blended malt whisky are not the same thing. Blended malt whisky is made up only of malt whiskies from different distilleries. They provide the perfect platform for experimentation and innovation.

Although they are often bracketed together, particularly in North America, the first thing to note about blended malt whiskies is that they are not the same thing as blended whiskies. The key difference is the word "malt." Blended whiskies are made by adding grain whisky to a mix of malts from different distilleries. Blended malts have no grain whisky component and are just a mix of malt whiskies from different distilleries.

Whiskies made this way have existed from the very earliest days; there is nothing new about them. But the way we describe them is new. We used to call them "vatted malts," and indeed some countries still do. But new rules introduced at the end of the 20th century removed "vatted" and replaced it with the term "blended malts."

It could be argued that, as a result of this change, the vatted malt category stalled because for many consumers the word "blended" is not considered as good as the term "single malt." But it isn't always. When a blended malt is made properly, it can match up to even the finest single malt whiskies.

Blended whiskies are often produced by independent bottlers who pick up a wide range of malt whiskies from a large number of different sources. It may be that by mixing malts of limited quantities together they are able to create one much bigger new drink that is unique and all their own. There is something else, too. Although producing whiskies with no age statements has become more commonplace in recent years, many customers don't feel comfortable buying a single malt whisky without knowing how old it is. Blended malts don't face the same hurdle, and they provide the platform from which other baggage can be stripped away. Descriptive or off-the-wall names may be used.

There is a downside, too. With whisky in short supply, independent bottlers may have some pretty poor casks, and blending them with something else is one way of hiding the shortcomings.

The modern era for the blended malt whisky began as a result of the efforts of whisky innovator and alchemist John Glaser, who produced the Compass Box range, and Jon, Mark, and Robbo, creators of Easy Drinking Whisky. Glaser's approach is to give his creations names that either indicate what you're likely to taste (Spice Tree, Peaty Monster, Oak Cross), or are emotively and aspirationally descriptive (Eleuthera, Hedonism). Jon, Mark, and Robbo meanwhile focus more on descriptors (The Smoky Peaty One, The Smooth Fruity One).

In the last few years, blended malts have been seen as a way of attracting a new, younger clientele who want to buy in to something innovative and original.

It's highly likely that this category will expand in the future, but the sincere hope should be that it is developed for quality rather than for quantity. Some of our very best whiskies are blended malt whiskies. For this reason, the category should be allowed to survive and thrive.

**ORIGIN:** Scotland
**ABV:** 40%–50%
**GRAIN:** A mix of malted barley whiskies

# FRUITY BLENDED MALT WHISKIES

Blended malt whiskies have tended to fall into three distinct categories—fruity and smooth; spicy; and smoky and peaty. There have been attempts to straddle these boundaries in blended malt whisky, but they have largely been awkward.

However, in the fruity category we have some of the best whiskies of all. Clan Denny Speyside and the groundbreaking Monkey Shoulder are a match for many Speyside single malts—which is not surprising when you consider the standard of the single malts that they each contain. Monkey Shoulder shows what can be done to encourage a new generation of whisky drinkers by dumping the traditional baggage and adopting a modern and stylish image. The range of fruits on offer is amazing, with tropical fruit, pineapple, and banana joining the more traditional citrus and berry fruits.

## THREE TO TRY

| | | |
|---|---|---|
| **Monkey Shoulder** | With Glenlivet and Balvenie in the mix, this is just bursting with fresh, clean, fruity loveliness | ★ |
| **Clan Denny Speyside** | Rich, full-flavored, and mouth-coating, this is a comprehensive road trip through the best distilleries of the Speyside region | ★★ |
| **Mackinlay's Rare Old Highland Malt** | The balance between lemon and sweetness makes this a whisky version of homemade lemonade | ★★★ |

★ LEAST EXPENSIVE/WIDELY AVAILABLE  ★★ MODERATELY PRICED/
HARDER TO SOURCE  ★★★ COSTLY/RARE

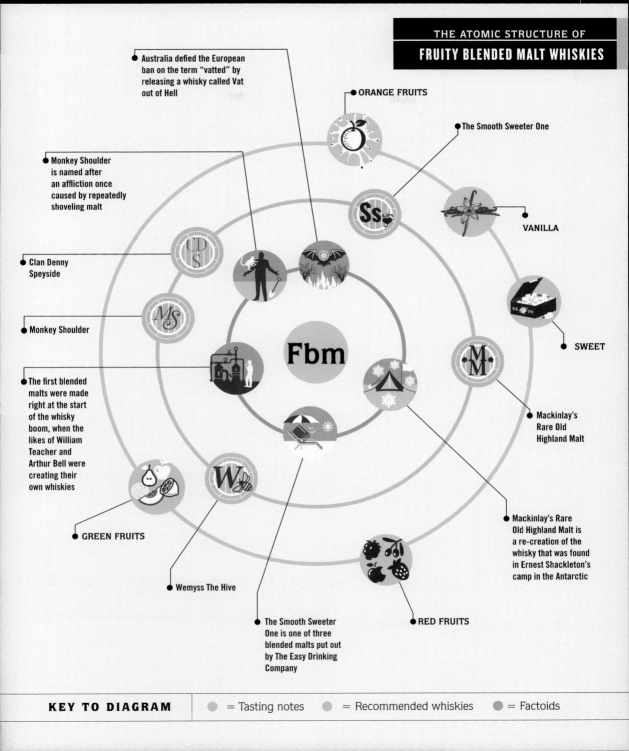

THE ATOMIC STRUCTURE OF
## FRUITY BLENDED MALT WHISKIES

Australia defied the European ban on the term "vatted" by releasing a whisky called Vat out of Hell

ORANGE FRUITS

The Smooth Sweeter One

VANILLA

Monkey Shoulder is named after an affliction once caused by repeatedly shoveling malt

Clan Denny Speyside

Monkey Shoulder

SWEET

Fbm

The first blended malts were made right at the start of the whisky boom, when the likes of William Teacher and Arthur Bell were creating their own whiskies

Mackinlay's Rare Old Highland Malt

Mackinlay's Rare Old Highland Malt is a re-creation of the whisky that was found in Ernest Shackleton's camp in the Antarctic

GREEN FRUITS

Wemyss The Hive

The Smooth Sweeter One is one of three blended malts put out by The Easy Drinking Company

RED FRUITS

KEY TO DIAGRAM    ● = Tasting notes    ● = Recommended whiskies    ● = Factoids

**ORIGIN:** Scotland
**ABV:** 43%–50%
**GRAIN:** A mix of malted barley

# SPICY BLENDED MALT WHISKIES

**With their subtlety and depth, spicy blends comprise one of the most exciting whisky categories, and are especially popular with people who like a drink that is sweet and fruity but not too cloying.**

The spice comes in various forms and may impact on the taste at different stages of the drinking process. It isn't always hot or savory, and is often sweet. The most impactful flavor comes from new oak. Recycled casks are used to subdue this effect.

Limited amounts of spice can be introduced by using virgin oak heads on the cask, or by adding a cask of very spiced whisky to a vatting of casks with no virgin oak. The best spicy blended whiskies—Johnnie Walker Green Label or The Last Vatted Malt—could equally be classified as smoky or fruity blended malts.

## THREE TO TRY

| The Spice Tree | Compass Box excels at this sort of thing: subtle ginger, light chili pepper, just enough oak | ★ |
|---|---|---|
| Wemyss Spice King 8 Year Old | Pepper arrives late and is sprinkled liberally on a mellow butterscotch and cream combo | ★★ |
| The Last Vatted Malt | Another Compass Box whisky with smoke, tropical fruit, and spice finely balanced; if you see it, buy it | ★★★ |

★ LEAST EXPENSIVE/WIDELY AVAILABLE  ★★ MODERATELY PRICED/ HARDER TO SOURCE  ★★★ COSTLY/RARE

THE ATOMIC STRUCTURE OF
# SPICY BLENDED MALT WHISKIES

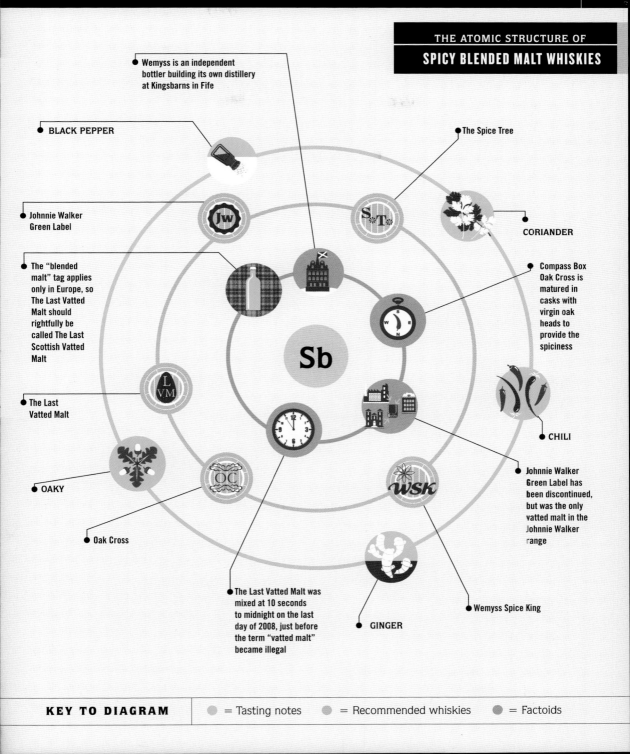

Wemyss is an independent bottler building its own distillery at Kingsbarns in Fife

BLACK PEPPER

The Spice Tree

Johnnie Walker Green Label

CORIANDER

The "blended malt" tag applies only in Europe, so The Last Vatted Malt should rightfully be called The Last Scottish Vatted Malt

Compass Box Oak Cross is matured in casks with virgin oak heads to provide the spiciness

Sb

The Last Vatted Malt

CHILI

OAKY

Oak Cross

Johnnie Walker Green Label has been discontinued, but was the only vatted malt in the Johnnie Walker range

The Last Vatted Malt was mixed at 10 seconds to midnight on the last day of 2008, just before the term "vatted malt" became illegal

GINGER

Wemyss Spice King

KEY TO DIAGRAM        ● = Tasting notes     ● = Recommended whiskies     ● = Factoids

**ORIGIN:** Scotland
**ABV:** 40%–55%
**GRAIN:** Mix of malted barley

# SMOKY AND PEATY BLENDED MALT WHISKIES

**When a blended malt whisky successfully combines smoke and peat, it's a total treat.**

However, with whisky in short supply, the balance is sometimes made up with spirits that are not fit to be bottled as single malts.

Sappy and immature spirit can be hidden by mixing it with peated whisky. Therefore you should tread carefully among blended malts: if you can, try before you buy. On the other hand, there are also some fabulous whiskies out there. The likes of Blue Hanger, The Big Peat, and Flaming Heart are up there with the very best in the world. Each has been created by a whisky alchemist, and it shows. Find your level with peaty blended malts—some are peat lite and designed to tease; others are weighty powerpacks with all the subtlety of a sledgehammer. You decide: Bon Jovi or Metallica?

## THREE TO TRY

| | | |
|---|---|---|
| **The Big Peat** | Each release seems to get better and they are among the best whiskies of the year | ★ |
| **Compass Box Flaming Heart** | Big on flavors throughout, with a fruity center, lots of smoke, and beautiful sweetness | ★★ |
| **Blue Hanger 9th Release** | Made independently by London specialists Berry Bros & Rudd, this is a smoky departure to a fruity, blended malt; it's great | ★★★ |

★ LEAST EXPENSIVE/WIDELY AVAILABLE  ★★ MODERATELY PRICED/ HARDER TO SOURCE  ★★★ COSTLY/RARE

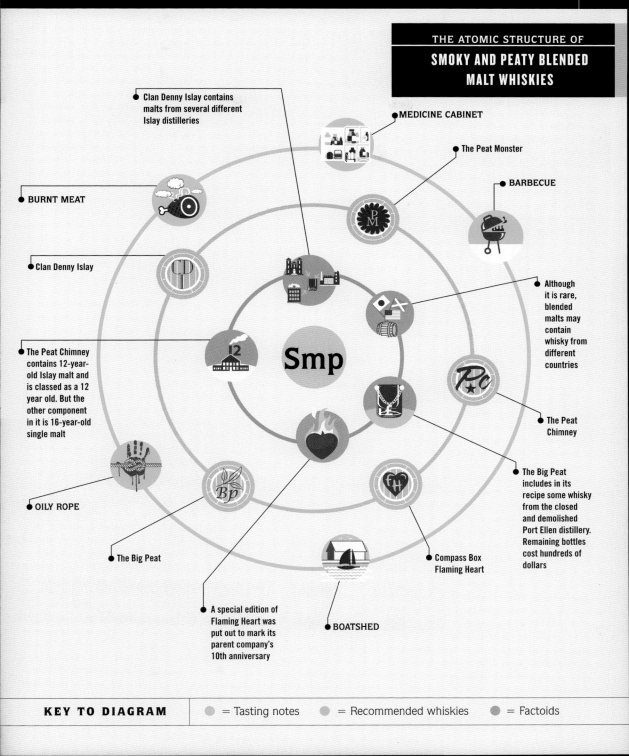

THE ATOMIC STRUCTURE OF
# SMOKY AND PEATY BLENDED MALT WHISKIES

Clan Denny Islay contains malts from several different Islay distilleries

MEDICINE CABINET

The Peat Monster

BARBECUE

BURNT MEAT

Clan Denny Islay

Although it is rare, blended malts may contain whisky from different countries

The Peat Chimney contains 12-year-old Islay malt and is classed as a 12 year old. But the other component in it is 16-year-old single malt

The Peat Chimney

Smp

The Big Peat includes in its recipe some whisky from the closed and demolished Port Ellen distillery. Remaining bottles cost hundreds of dollars

OILY ROPE

The Big Peat

Compass Box Flaming Heart

A special edition of Flaming Heart was put out to mark its parent company's 10th anniversary

BOATSHED

**KEY TO DIAGRAM**   ● = Tasting notes   ● = Recommended whiskies   ● = Factoids

**ORIGIN:** Japan, Scotland
**ABV:** 40%–56%
**GRAIN:** A mix of malted barleys

# JAPANESE BLENDED MALT WHISKIES

**The category of blended malt whiskies from Japan is something of an oddball, because each of the main producers has only two distilleries. Their products are similar to those of Scotland, but with the volume turned up.**

Although the Japanese distilleries make a wide range of different whisky styles, when combined they still form a single malt whisky because the word "single" refers to the distillery, not to the number of styles from that distillery. So both Nikka and Suntory have two single malts each. To add to the variety, Japan uses Scottish single malt whisky in its blended malts. This practice is often frowned on, but no matter: it offers drinkers big, bold, enjoyable whiskies, and the skill of the makers cannot be faulted. These whiskies are not easy to find, but they are well worth hunting for.

## THREE TO TRY

| | | |
|---|---|---|
| **Nikka All Malt Pure & Rich** | Honey, hickory, and red liquorice, a rich and complex potpourri; very enjoyable | ★ |
| **Taketsuru Pure Malt 21 Year Old** | Almost Highland Park-like, with spice, smoke, oak honey, and fruit perfectly weighted | ★★ |
| **Taketsuru Pure Malt 17 Year Old** | Lots going on here, with oak and rich barley coming through an immense and dense fruit compôte | ★★★ |

★ LEAST EXPENSIVE/WIDELY AVAILABLE  ★★ MODERATELY PRICED/ HARDER TO SOURCE  ★★★ COSTLY/RARE

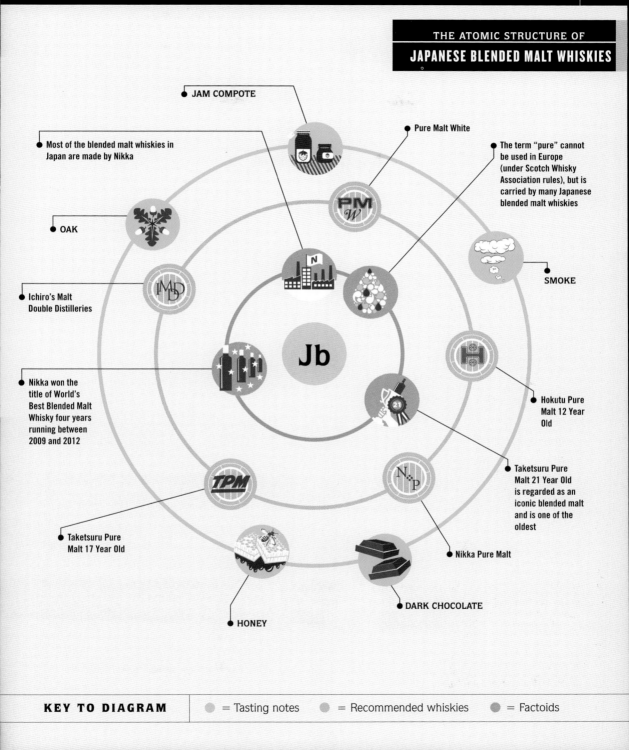

THE ATOMIC STRUCTURE OF
# JAPANESE BLENDED MALT WHISKIES

JAM COMPOTE

Pure Malt White

Most of the blended malt whiskies in Japan are made by Nikka

The term "pure" cannot be used in Europe (under Scotch Whisky Association rules), but is carried by many Japanese blended malt whiskies

OAK

SMOKE

Ichiro's Malt Double Distilleries

Jb

Nikka won the title of World's Best Blended Malt Whisky four years running between 2009 and 2012

Hokutu Pure Malt 12 Year Old

Taketsuru Pure Malt 21 Year Old is regarded as an iconic blended malt and is one of the oldest

Taketsuru Pure Malt 17 Year Old

Nikka Pure Malt

HONEY

DARK CHOCOLATE

**KEY TO DIAGRAM**    = Tasting notes    = Recommended whiskies    = Factoids

**ORIGIN:** Ireland, Spain, Scotland
**ABV:** 40%–48%
**GRAIN:** Various malted barleys

# EUROPEAN HYBRID BLENDED MALT WHISKY

These two whiskies could arguably have been included in the Rebel Whiskies section later in this book, but they are both blended malts and conventional, except for the fact that they are made from whiskies from different countries.

The two listed here have little in common. DYC Pure is made of a rough-and-ready though mild-mannered Spanish malt and two assertive Scottish single malts: Ardmore, a gutsy, citrus-rich Highland single malt with a distinctive peat taste; and peat whisky royalty in the form of Laphroaig.

The other is a mixture of whiskey from Teeling and the Islay distillery Bruichladdich, which provides sweet pear and apple and vanilla up front and grumbling smoke and spice later on. Such hybrid whiskies aren't new; there are examples of experimentation in this area dating back decades.

## TWO TO TRY

| Destilerías y Crianza Pure Malt | This Spanish whisky has evolved; it began as a blend and can now be found as a 10-year-old single malt. But at its hybrid stage, it took a Spanish single malt and mixed it with whisky produced by owner company Beam Global's Scottish distilleries, Laphroaig and Ardmore. This whisky combines light, floral, and fruity notes with earthy smoky ones. Unusual | ★ |
| Teeling Hybrid | Mixing Irish and Scottish whiskies is bound to get up the noses of the Scotch Whisky Association—but the Teelings like being industry mavericks. The Scottish element gives the whisky a savory depth that contrasts with the sweet apple and pear fruits of the Teeling whiskey | ★★ |

★ LEAST EXPENSIVE/WIDELY AVAILABLE   ★★ MODERATELY PRICED/HARDER TO SOURCE

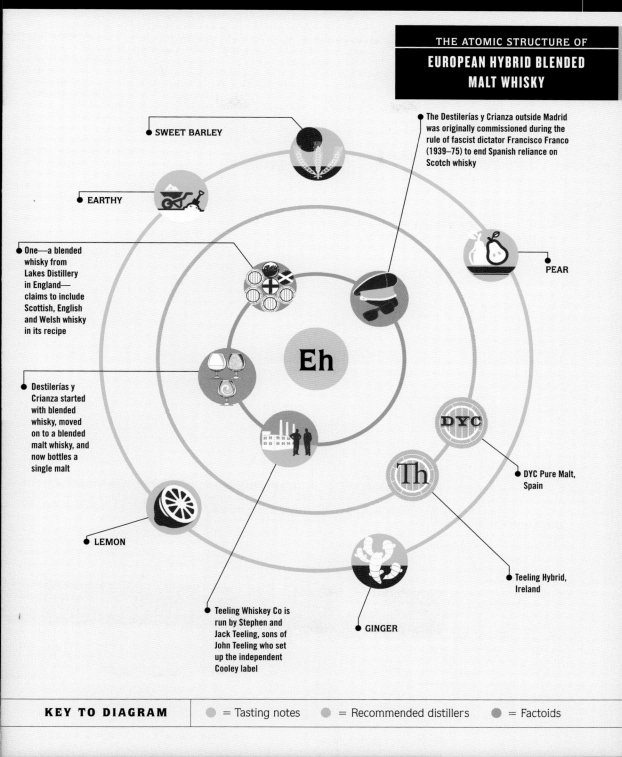

THE ATOMIC STRUCTURE OF
# EUROPEAN HYBRID BLENDED MALT WHISKY

SWEET BARLEY

The Destilerías y Crianza outside Madrid was originally commissioned during the rule of fascist dictator Francisco Franco (1939–75) to end Spanish reliance on Scotch whisky

EARTHY

PEAR

One—a blended whisky from Lakes Distillery in England— claims to include Scottish, English and Welsh whisky in its recipe

**Eh**

Destilerías y Crianza started with blended whisky, moved on to a blended malt whisky, and now bottles a single malt

**DYC**

DYC Pure Malt, Spain

**Th**

LEMON

Teeling Hybrid, Ireland

GINGER

Teeling Whiskey Co is run by Stephen and Jack Teeling, sons of John Teeling who set up the independent Cooley label

**KEY TO DIAGRAM**   ● = Tasting notes   ● = Recommended distillers   ● = Factoids

# BOURBON, CORN, AND

# TENNESSEE WHISKEY

CHAPTER FOUR

These styles are grouped together because they are linked by a common ingredient—corn. Corn is a hard grain to turn into distiller's beer and then to distill, but the rewards are soft and sweet flavors that you'll find in all three whiskey styles.

Corn whiskey tends to be less complex, but it is rarely matured in oak at all or for very long. Tennessee whiskey and bourbon have more in common than some people care to admit. In Louisville, Kentucky, and Lynchburg, Tennessee, there will be folks flinching at the title of this chapter. When it comes to whiskey, the two states just don't get on. A few years ago I attended a competition in Bardstown, Kentucky, spiritual home of bourbon. The atmosphere was great as old distilling friends caught up with each other. Except two.

"Who are they?" I asked. "Oh, they're up from Jack Daniel's," came the nonchalant reply.

It's a common mistake to describe Jack Daniel's as a bourbon, but it's not surprising that it happens because the two whiskey styles have everything in common apart from the charcoal-filtering method called the Lincoln County Process that is carried out in Tennessee before the distilled spirit is put in the cask for maturation. This is done by pouring the spirit through a wall of maple-wood charcoal; they say it mellows the spirit.

Both styles are made under strict rules. Each must contain at least 51 percent corn in the original mash-bill, but the actual percentage is far higher. Both are subject to strict controls on alcoholic strength during distillation and, at the time of writing, both styles must be matured in virgin oak charred barrels, although a legal action has been brought in Tennessee by Diageo, owners of George Dickel Tennessee Whiskey, in an effort to overturn the rule and allow the use of used barrels.

Unlike single malt whisky, American whiskey is normally made using a column or continuous still. After the mash bill is mixed with water, yeast is added to create beer, and the resulting sweet milky wash, complete with husks, is forced up columns where it is met by pressurized steam at very high temperatures. This process forces the alcohol from the water; the former is collected on plates running up the side of the column still. The resulting spirit, known as White Dog, is sweet and robust but not as flavorsome as single malt.

The cask is charred to release the properties in the wood that will give the spirit its distinctive candy stick, polished leather, vanilla, and sweet spice characteristics. Despite what you might be told, even in Kentucky the spirit becomes bourbon the minute it goes into the cask. It becomes straight bourbon after two years' maturation.

The climate of Tennessee and Kentucky is vastly different from that of Scotland, and the extremes of temperature between the short, sharp winters and the scorching summers, which result in temperatures above 120°F (50°C) degrees at the top of a maturation warehouse, make for a faster maturation than the Scots could ever achieve. For this reason, bourbon and American whiskey can taste wonderful at just four years old, and premium ages are anything above six years old.

**ORIGIN:** Kentucky, USA
**ABV:** 40%–72%
**GRAIN:** At least 51% corn, malted barley, either wheat or rye
**CASK:** Virgin white oak

# STANDARD KENTUCKY BOURBON

**Brought to North America by Irish immigrants in the 18th century, bourbon made its principal residence in Kentucky. Since then it has gone in and out of fashion, but it is currently one of the world's most popular distilled spirits.**

Remember the scene in *It's a Wonderful Life* where Clarence takes George Bailey to Nick's bar and Nick throws them out because Clarence asks for a sherry? Those back shelves contained nothing but bourbon. Now it's the whiskey of choice for barmen in the world's most stylish bars. Made in a column still with a mixture of grains dominated by corn, and matured in charred or toasted casks made from white oak, bourbon is to Scotch whisky what ice hockey is to curling. It can be enjoyed straight, with water or over ice, and is often drunk from a tumbler.

## THREE TO TRY

| | | |
|---|---|---|
| **Buffalo Trace** | A classic entry-level bourbon with sweet candy, rich fruit, some tobacco, and spice notes plus a touch of oak | ★ |
| **Woodford Reserve** | With a higher than average rye content, this is less sweet than most bourbons and considerably spicier | ★★ |
| **Baker's 7 Year Old** | Chocolate, coffee, and licorice up against some tropical fruits, with woody and peppery notes to set it all off | ★★★ |

★ LEAST EXPENSIVE/WIDELY AVAILABLE ★★ MODERATELY PRICED/ HARDER TO SOURCE ★★★COSTLY/RARE

THE ATOMIC STRUCTURE OF
# STANDARD KENTUCKY BOURBON

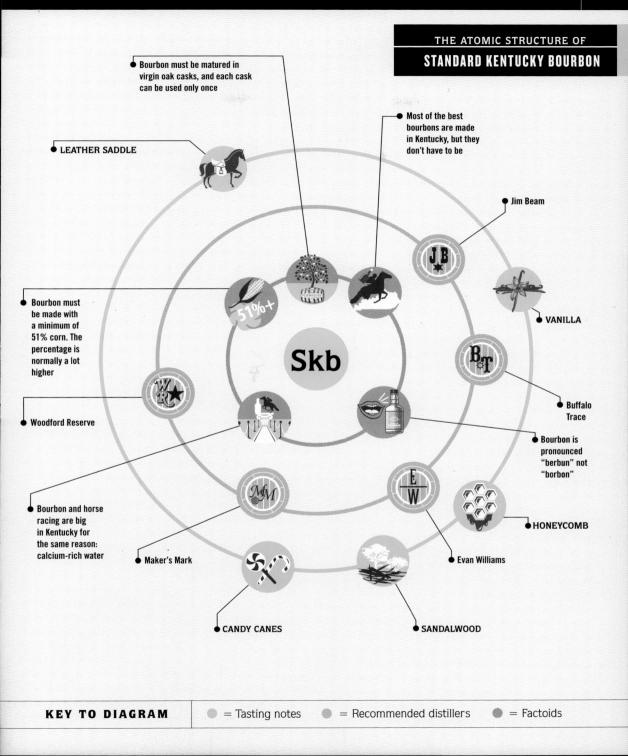

Bourbon must be matured in virgin oak casks, and each cask can be used only once

LEATHER SADDLE

Most of the best bourbons are made in Kentucky, but they don't have to be

Jim Beam

Bourbon must be made with a minimum of 51% corn. The percentage is normally a lot higher

51%+

Skb

VANILLA

Buffalo Trace

Woodford Reserve

Bourbon is pronounced "berbun" not "borbon"

Bourbon and horse racing are big in Kentucky for the same reason: calcium-rich water

Maker's Mark

HONEYCOMB

Evan Williams

CANDY CANES

SANDALWOOD

**KEY TO DIAGRAM**     = Tasting notes     = Recommended distillers     = Factoids

ORIGIN: Kentucky, USA
ABV: 46%–73%
GRAIN: At least 51% corn, malted barley, wheat or rye
CASK: Virgin white oak

# PREMIUM KENTUCKY BOURBON

**There is no set definition as to what constitutes a premium bourbon, but there are a number of limited-release and aged bourbons that are greatly sought after by enthusiasts.**

Every fall, Kentucky's best distillers bring out their oldest and rarest whiskeys for release as limited editions. Some of them are more than 20 years old.

Purists contend that no bourbon warrants maturation beyond eight years, but there can be no dispute that these whiskeys are sensational. George T. Stagg, Eagle Rare, and Evan Williams Special Releases are among the very best whiskeys in the world.

Whether you'll get a hand on any of them is another matter—such is the demand every year that the producers are inundated with complaints from stores and bars that have missed out.

## THREE TO TRY

| | | |
|---|---|---|
| **Blanton's** | Leather saddle, honey, and the most glorious array of sweet spices | ★ |
| **Eagle Rare 17 Year Old** | Big, oily, spicy, in-your-face whiskey that divides opinion but is worth the effort for its rye, licorice, and intense fruits | ★★ |
| **George T. Stagg** | Perhaps the world's best whiskey, bottled at a strength above 67% and packed with the most complex selection of flavors. Drink neat | ★★★ |

★ LEAST EXPENSIVE/WIDELY AVAILABLE  ★★ MODERATELY PRICED/ HARDER TO SOURCE  ★★★ COSTLY/RARE

THE ATOMIC STRUCTURE OF
# PREMIUM KENTUCKY BOURBON

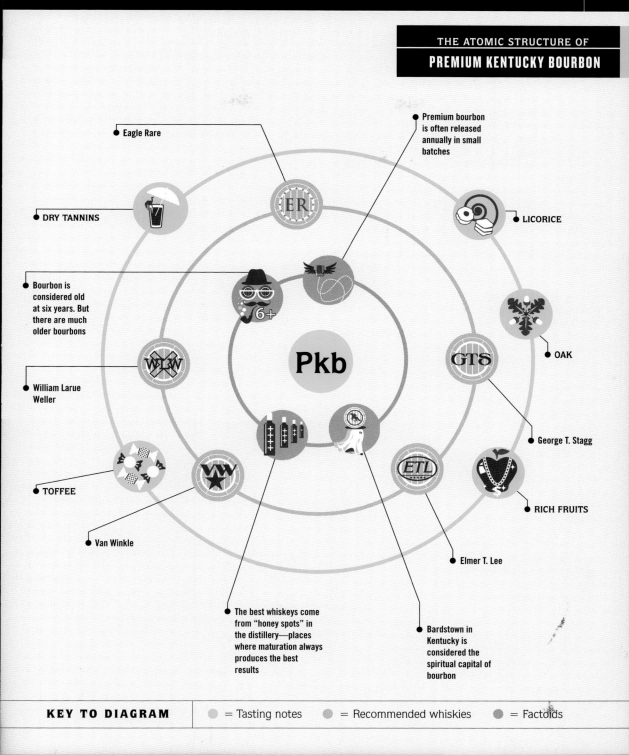

- Eagle Rare

- Premium bourbon is often released annually in small batches

- DRY TANNINS

- LICORICE

- Bourbon is considered old at six years. But there are much older bourbons

**ER**

**6+**

- OAK

**WLW**

- William Larue Weller

**Pkb**

**GTS**

- George T. Stagg

- TOFFEE

**VW**

**ETL**

- RICH FRUITS

- Van Winkle

- Elmer T. Lee

- The best whiskeys come from "honey spots" in the distillery—places where maturation always produces the best results

- Bardstown in Kentucky is considered the spiritual capital of bourbon

**KEY TO DIAGRAM**    ● = Tasting notes    ● = Recommended whiskies    ● = Factoids

**ORIGIN:** USA
**ABV:** 40%–60%
**GRAIN:** At least 51% corn, malted barley, wheat, or rye
**CASK:** Virgin white oak

# NON-KENTUCKY BOURBON

**It's a common mistake to think that bourbon must come from Kentucky. Other U.S. states such as Virginia also have strong bourbon traditions, and the whiskey they produce can be very good indeed.**

Do non-Kentucky bourbons differ much? In many respects, they do. They can be grainier and fruitier, honey and sweetness often play more of a role, and they are lighter, with sweet citrus notes.

Bourbon is a surprisingly subtle drink, but at the lighter end of the spectrum it's like the tide's gone out and you're able to see the rich and diverse life that inhabits the rock pools. There are exceptions, though: Virginia, from which Kentucky became independent in 1792, has a couple of big whiskeys that are every bit a match for those of the neighboring state.

## THREE TO TRY

| | | |
|---|---|---|
| **Peach Street Bourbon** | Raisins, sweet pears, oranges, and tropical fruit make this a delight. Not complex, but a late flurry of pepper and oak provides balance | ★ |
| **Virginia Gentleman** | Milk chocolate and orange, toasted tannins, and wafts of sweet corn combine to full effect | ★★ |
| **John J. Bowman Virginia Straight Bourbon** | Hickory and wood up front, treacle toffee, and then fruits make this a bruiser with licorice sophistication | ★★★ |

★ LEAST EXPENSIVE/WIDELY AVAILABLE  ★★ MODERATELY PRICED/ HARDER TO SOURCE  ★★★ COSTLY/RARE

THE ATOMIC STRUCTURE OF
## NON-KENTUCKY BOURBON

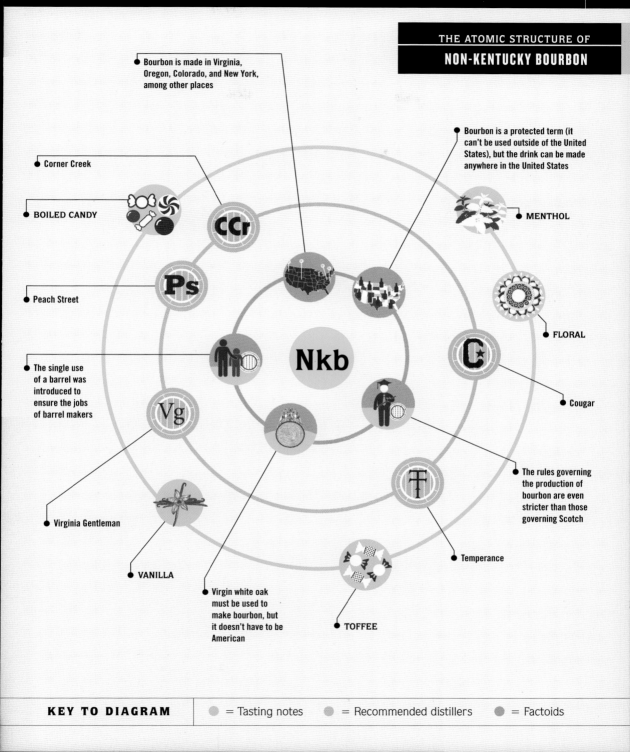

Bourbon is made in Virginia, Oregon, Colorado, and New York, among other places

Bourbon is a protected term (it can't be used outside of the United States), but the drink can be made anywhere in the United States

Corner Creek

BOILED CANDY

CCr

MENTHOL

Ps

Peach Street

FLORAL

The single use of a barrel was introduced to ensure the jobs of barrel makers

Nkb

C

Cougar

Vg

The rules governing the production of bourbon are even stricter than those governing Scotch

Virginia Gentleman

VANILLA

T

Temperance

Virgin white oak must be used to make bourbon, but it doesn't have to be American

TOFFEE

**KEY TO DIAGRAM**   ● = Tasting notes   ● = Recommended distillers   ● = Factoids

**ORIGIN:** USA
**ABV:** 40%–60%
**GRAIN:** Corn, wheat, malted barley, rye
**CASK:** Virgin white oak

# NEW WAVE/CRAFT BOURBON

**The craft distilling revolution is hard to keep tabs on due to the large numbers of distillers operating today in the States. Much of what they are doing is not great, but some of it is very clever.**

Kentucky's distillers, who have generations of experience behind them, are particularly sniffy about the bourbons that the new whiskey makers are producing, describing them as two-dimensional, too young, and unbalanced.

The new distillers, though, say that this misses the point, which is that they are creating baggage-free whiskey with a different taste point to appeal to a younger and less masculine audience.

They may have a point. In the style bars of New York and Los Angeles, some new-wave whiskeys are in great demand.

## THREE TO TRY

| | | |
|---|---|---|
| **Cedar Ridge Reserve** | This bourbon from Iowa's first micro distillery has a corn content of more than 75% and is softer, sweeter, rounder and smoother than many bourbons | ★ |
| **McKenzie** | Aromatic, light, balanced, and complex, with a big reputation | ★★ |
| **Breckenridge** | With a relatively low corn content and nearly as much rye, this is a flavorsome and spicy whiskey with a personality all its own | ★★★ |

★ LEAST EXPENSIVE/WIDELY AVAILABLE   ★★ MODERATELY PRICED/ HARDER TO SOURCE   ★★★ COSTLY/RARE

THE ATOMIC STRUCTURE OF
# NEW WAVE/CRAFT BOURBON

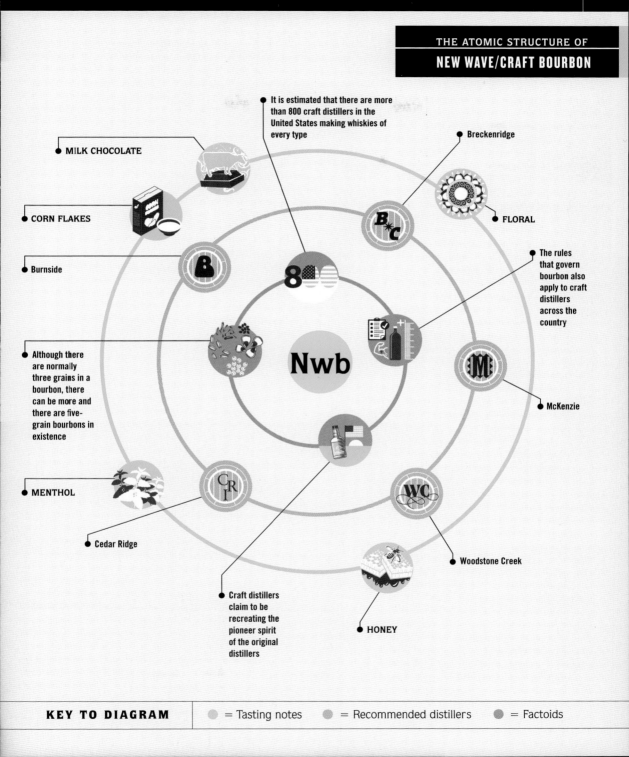

- It is estimated that there are more than 800 craft distillers in the United States making whiskies of every type

- MILK CHOCOLATE

- Breckenridge

- CORN FLAKES

- FLOMAL

**B·C**

- Burnside

**B**

**8**

- The rules that govern bourbon also apply to craft distillers across the country

**Nwb**

- Although there are normally three grains in a bourbon, there can be more and there are five-grain bourbons in existence

**M**

- McKenzie

- MENTHOL

**C R I**

- Cedar Ridge

**WC**

- Woodstone Creek

- Craft distillers claim to be recreating the pioneer spirit of the original distillers

- HONEY

**KEY TO DIAGRAM**    ● = Tasting notes    ● = Recommended distillers    ● = Factoids

**ORIGIN:** USA
**ABV:** 40%–46%
**GRAIN:** Corn, barley, wheat, rye
**CASK:** Virgin white oak

# BABY BOURBON

**There has always been an element of smoke and mirrors about whisky in general, and about American whiskey in particular. The new craft distillers haven't been slow to exploit gray areas. But they have also shone a light into the darkness.**

I know two very senior members of the Kentucky bourbon industry who don't seem to know the definition of what constitutes the whiskey they're making, and this category points a finger directly at them. Baby bourbon is young bourbon, often well under two years old. But it is bourbon. It's bourbon a minute after it goes into the cask.

These whiskeys are sappy, grainy, unsophisticated, and young, but that, say their makers, is the whole point. Unsophisticated whiskey drinkers like these characteristics.

## THREE TO TRY

| | | |
|---|---|---|
| **Lewis Redmond Aged 10 Months** | High corn content and wheat make for a soft, sweet, honey-coated whiskey with distinctive nuttiness | ★ |
| **Balcones Baby Blue** | An acquired taste perhaps more suited to tequila drinkers; sappy, sweet, and fruity | ★★ |
| **Hudson Baby Bourbon** | This successful whiskey is bourbon light, but its mild vanilla, oak, and spice flavor make it the perfect introduction to aged spirits | ★★★ |

★ LEAST EXPENSIVE/WIDELY AVAILABLE   ★★ MODERATELY PRICED/ HARDER TO SOURCE   ★★★ COSTLY/RARE

THE ATOMIC STRUCTURE OF
# BABY BOURBON

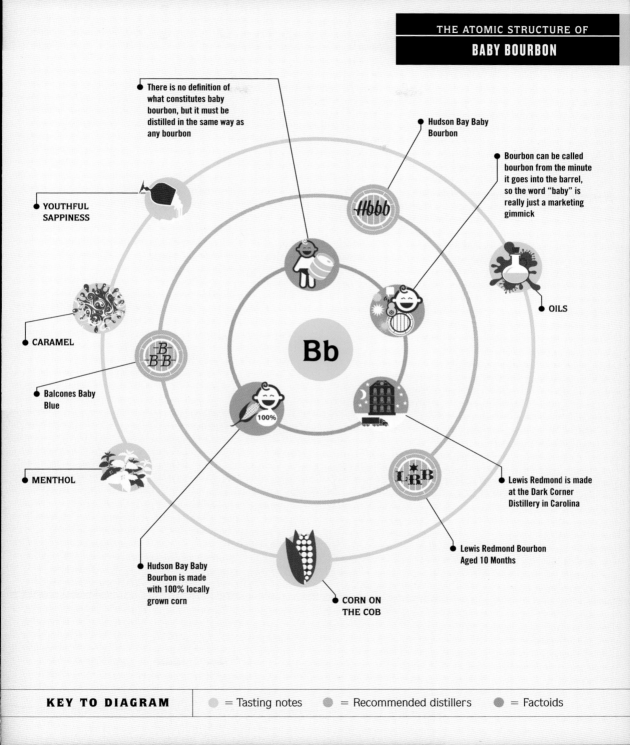

There is no definition of what constitutes baby bourbon, but it must be distilled in the same way as any bourbon

Hudson Bay Baby Bourbon

Bourbon can be called bourbon from the minute it goes into the barrel, so the word "baby" is really just a marketing gimmick

YOUTHFUL SAPPINESS

OILS

CARAMEL

Balcones Baby Blue

MENTHOL

Bb

Lewis Redmond is made at the Dark Corner Distillery in Carolina

Hudson Bay Baby Bourbon is made with 100% locally grown corn

Lewis Redmond Bourbon Aged 10 Months

CORN ON THE COB

**KEY TO DIAGRAM**    ● = Tasting notes    ● = Recommended distillers    ● = Factoids

# TENNESSEE WHISKEY

**ORIGIN:** USA
**ABV:** 40%–45%
**GRAIN:** Corn, malted barley, rye
**CASK:** Virgin white oak

One major production step separates Tennessee whiskey from bourbon—in Tennessee they pour their new spirit through a wall of charcoaled maple wood. This is known as the Lincoln County Process and they claim it has a mellowing effect.

If it does change the character of the spirit, it can't be bourbon—but nobody in Tennessee has any interest in it being so. The big player here is Jack Daniel's, one of the biggest spirits in the world and a brand that has managed to hold a line between good ol' country boy image on the one hand and essential accessory for bad boy rock stars.

Some people are snotty about Jack, but they really shouldn't be. Single Barrel Jack is outstanding and it's no mean feat to sell dark brown hard liquor worldwide. Credit where it's due.

## THREE TO TRY

| | | |
|---|---|---|
| **Jack Daniel's Old No. 7** | Batches with a higher hickory and licorice blast among the vanilla and spices are a treat | ★ |
| **George Dickel Superior No. 12** | Not as sweet as Jack, with a hit of oak, tannin, pepper, and citrus notes | ★★ |
| **Jack Daniel's Single Barrel** | If No. 7 is the Rolling Stones, these single-barrel releases are a Ron Wood solo show—variable, but characteristic of the full ensemble | ★★★ |

★ LEAST EXPENSIVE/WIDELY AVAILABLE  ★★ MODERATELY PRICED/HARDER TO SOURCE  ★★★ COSTLY/RARE

THE ATOMIC STRUCTURE OF
# TENNESSEE WHISKEY

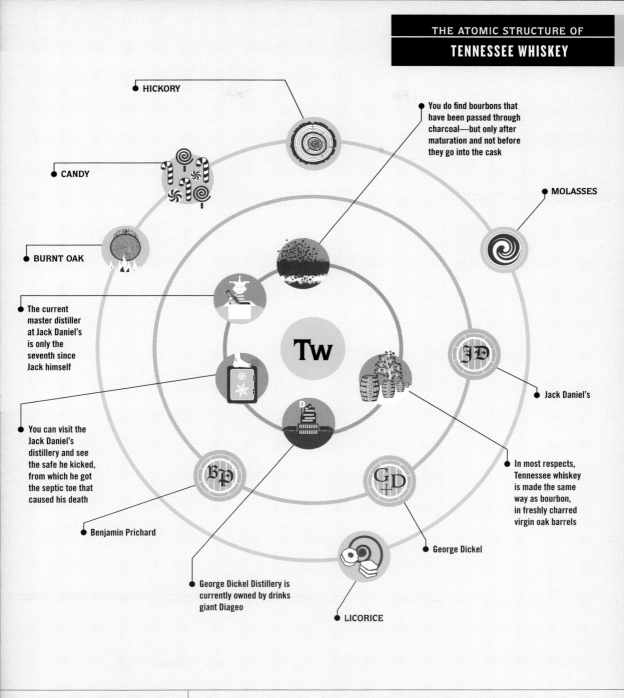

HICKORY

CANDY

BURNT OAK

You do find bourbons that have been passed through charcoal—but only after maturation and not before they go into the cask

MOLASSES

The current master distiller at Jack Daniel's is only the seventh since Jack himself

**Tw**

Jack Daniel's

You can visit the Jack Daniel's distillery and see the safe he kicked, from which he got the septic toe that caused his death

In most respects, Tennessee whiskey is made the same way as bourbon, in freshly charred virgin oak barrels

Benjamin Prichard

George Dickel

George Dickel Distillery is currently owned by drinks giant Diageo

LICORICE

**KEY TO DIAGRAM**    ● = Tasting notes    ● = Recommended distillers    ● = Factoids

**ORIGIN:** USA
**ABV:** 45%–50%
**GRAIN:** Corn, malted barley, wheat, rye
**CASK:** Virgin white oak

# KENTUCKY CORN WHISKEY

**We're out on the margins of whiskey now, in areas where few expressions exist and there's confusion about what belongs in which category. Some of the whiskeys here are made to the same recipe but packaged differently for marketing purposes.**

The principal reason for placing these products in a separate category here is that, although they share the same high corn content—far higher than in the case of bourbon—they have also spent months and often years in oak, and that is normally not the case with other corn whiskeys. The results have all the sweetness and vanilla flavor of corn-based spirits, but they are often cut through with pepper spice and tannin in much the same way as European grain whiskies.

## THREE TO TRY

| | | |
|---|---|---|
| **Dixie Dew** | A surprisingly complex, rich, and fruity version of Kentucky corn; a good introduction to the genre | ★ |
| **J.W. Corn** | Chocolate and vanilla ice cream, with some maple syrup in the mix for good measure | ★★ |
| **Hirsch Selection Special Reserve** | Matured for a weighty four years; the length of time is reflected in the rich, sweet notes that set off the toasted oak | ★★★ |

★ LEAST EXPENSIVE/WIDELY AVAILABLE   ★★ MODERATELY PRICED/HARDER TO SOURCE   ★★★ COSTLY/RARE

THE ATOMIC STRUCTURE OF
## KENTUCKY CORN WHISKEY

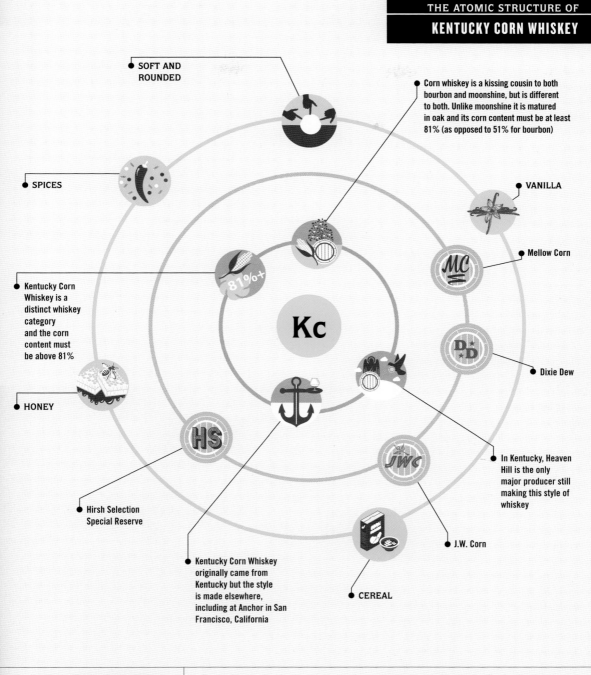

SOFT AND ROUNDED

Corn whiskey is a kissing cousin to both bourbon and moonshine, but is different to both. Unlike moonshine it is matured in oak and its corn content must be at least 81% (as opposed to 51% for bourbon)

SPICES

VANILLA

Mellow Corn

Kc

81%+

Kentucky Corn Whiskey is a distinct whiskey category and the corn content must be above 81%

Dixie Dew

HONEY

In Kentucky, Heaven Hill is the only major producer still making this style of whiskey

HS

Hirsh Selection Special Reserve

J.W. Corn

Kentucky Corn Whiskey originally came from Kentucky but the style is made elsewhere, including at Anchor in San Francisco, California

CEREAL

**KEY TO DIAGRAM**    ● = Tasting notes    ● = Recommended distillers    ● = Factoids

**ORIGIN:** USA
**ABV:** 40%–50%
**GRAIN:** Corn, malted barley, rye, wheat
**CASK:** Virgin white oak

# OTHER CORN WHISKEY/MOONSHINE

**Corn whiskey is enjoying a renaissance among U.S. craft distillers, because it conjures up moonshining, the good ol' boy image of *The Dukes of Hazzard*, and fast cars in which to run for the state border with an illegal cache.**

This marketing executive's dream gave the drink a young image. And because it doesn't need much aging, it's soon ready to drink and hence ideal for the "now" generation. What's not to like? Well, all the hype that surrounds it, for starters: the perfectly incredible recipes from original moonshiners and "premium moonshine."

This drink is meant to be sweet and simple, but at its worst, it can be gut rot. Each to his or her own: young folk buy into this sort of thing. But a product that doesn't meet even the most basic criteria of what whisk(e)y should be? No thanks.

KINGS COUNTY DISTILLERY
moonshine
corn whiskey 200ml
40% alcohol by volume

## THREE TO TRY

| | | |
|---|---|---|
| **Georgia Moon Corn Whiskey** | This is aged for less than 30 days, and it's like drinking alcohol-soaked sweetcorn. Which is what it sort of is. Sweet, enjoyable, and simple. | ★ |
| **Kings County Moonshine Whiskey** | When you make corn whiskey, there is no hiding place. You get one shot and you have to hit the sweet spot. This does so brilliantly, with sweet, oily corn. | ★★ |
| **McMenamins White Dog** | Unaged "White Dog" spirit and a sweet treat, like alcoholic popping corn | ★★★ |

★ LEAST EXPENSIVE/WIDELY AVAILABLE   ★★ MODERATELY PRICED/ HARDER TO SOURCE   ★★★ COSTLY/RARE

THE ATOMIC STRUCTURE OF
# OTHER CORN WHISKEY/MOONSHINE

- Corn whiskey became known as moonshine because it was often made illicitly at night. Moonshiners spoke to each other in code to avoid detection

- CEREAL

- Georgia Moon

- There must be at least 80% corn in corn whiskey, but it doesn't need to be barrel matured

- SAPPY

- Original moonshine or corn whiskey had an extremely high alcohol content

- PEPPER

GM

80%+

Oc

- Hudson Bay

HB

- SWEET

- Moonshine is associated with the poor South and the Appalachian Mountains

- Montana

M

CG

- Colorado Gold

Fl

- Moonshine was often stored in jam jars, a practice that has recently been revived as a marketing gimmick

- Finger Lakes

- CITRUS

**KEY TO DIAGRAM** ● = Tasting notes ● = Recommended distillers ● = Factoids

# RYE WHISKY

**CHAPTER
FIVE**

Rye whisky can take various guises, but the defining style is the full-blooded spicy one associated with America. This is cowboy whisky: in-your-face, big-flavored whisky ingrained in the story of America itself. It's in vogue as a core spirit for a host of cocktails, too.

Whisky can be made with any grain, but some grains are easier to work with than others. Malted barley is included in the grist of most whiskies because it is easy to malt and it is an excellent catalyst for the conversion of starches and sugars to alcohol.

But it is possible to make whisky with 100 percent of another grain and that's the case with rye. Rye, though back in fashion in recent years, is something of an enigma when it comes to the whisky-making process.

For starters, the term covers a broad range of styles and flavors, from the easy drinking and mellow ryes we associate with Canadian whisky to the feisty and spicy rye whiskeys that other parts of North America can produce. As with other grains, rye takes on different characteristics in different parts of the world. Thus, for example, a Dutch rye is very different from an Australian one.

Rye is notoriously difficult to make whisky with. It produces a gloopy, sticking jello that's a bit like wallpaper paste, which clogs and blocks the still. Great bubbles of carbon dioxide escape from the mess, exploding and splattering dollops of rye around the room.

It's an altogether unpredictable beast during distillation, too. Just as you think you're starting to make some progress with it, it turns ugly again, and it's very hard to know what the end product will be like. Dutch distiller Patrick Zuidam describes how he persuaded his father to let him invest in relatively expensive rye. After two years, the maturing spirit was so bad that he didn't know whether to admit defeat and inform his father of the waste, or leave the rye alone for another couple of years. He chose the latter course, which was a good thing because the whisky his distillery now produces is stunning.

And that's the point with rye whisk(e)y. When it works, as it does in all the great American ryes, the results are simply wonderful, and at its best rye can rarely be bettered by any other whisky style.

Once distilled and matured, rye is a highly versatile drink, too. It commands a muscular "big boy" reputation when consumed neat or on the rocks, but it is also highly sought after as an ingredient in cocktails because of its distinctively peppery notes. With a huge surge in the popularity of new takes on traditional cocktails and drinks with heritage and provenance, the demand for American rye has become so great that it's pretty well impossible to get it in many places.

Perhaps the most fascinating use of rye is in the countries of central Europe, especially Germany, Austria, and Switzerland, where there is an abundant supply and distillers have long used it in their distinctive whiskies. Marcel Telser in Liechtenstein has also started working with rye.

**ORIGIN:** USA
**ABV:** 40%–64%
**GRAIN:** Rye, malted barley
**CASK:** Virgin white oak

# STANDARD AMERICAN RYE WHISKEY

**You'll struggle to find rye whiskey, and if you do find it you'll have to pony up, because there is currently a high demand for whisky of all sorts, and rye is especially popular with mixologists and bar managers.**

There are three different styles of rye, but within those broad categories there is considerable diversity, particularly in the United States. Rye can be distilled with 100 percent rye content, but it need only be 51 percent by law, so there are great variations in flavor. There are also wide ranges of alcoholic strength and in time in the barrel, which will affect the taste. The division between standard and premium whiskey is somewhat arbitrary, particularly as some of the rarer ryes come from less distinguished craft distilleries.

## THREE TO TRY

| | | |
|---|---|---|
| **Sazerac Rye 6 Year Old** | A fine age for American whiskey; big and assertive but not too complex—a good starting point | ★ |
| **Templeton Rye** | Less rye-like than many; supposedly based on a Prohibition recipe enjoyed by Al Capone. Sweet and smooth, a little like Canadian rye | ★★ |
| **Rittenhouse 100 Proof** | Fruitier than many ryes, and with a big spiciness that battles with a fruit bowl of flavors | ★★★ |

★ LEAST EXPENSIVE/WIDELY AVAILABLE  ★★ MODERATELY PRICED/ HARDER TO SOURCE  ★★★ COSTLY/RARE

THE ATOMIC STRUCTURE OF
# STANDARD AMERICAN RYE WHISKEY

Hudson Manhattan Rye is from Tuthilltown Spirits, which reignited New York's interest in whiskey and is now owned by Scotland's William Grant & Sons

OAKINESS

Rittenhouse

SYRUP

Rye is very hard to distill, but several new craft distillers are turning their hands to it

Hudson Manhattan Rye

Rye used to be made across the United States but it fell out of fashion and almost disappeared. Now the whiskey makers can't keep up with renewed demand for it

SPICE

Sar

Jim Beam Rye

FLORAL

Pikesville Supreme is named after the town in Maryland where it was originally made. But it has now been made in Kentucky for nearly 40 years

Sazerac 6 Year Old

Russell's Reserve Rye

NUTTINESS

Rittenhouse Rye has picked up several international awards in recent years and is considered an outstanding whiskey

**KEY TO DIAGRAM**     = Tasting notes     = Recommended whiskeys     = Factoids

**ORIGIN:** USA
**ABV:** 45%–65%
**GRAIN:** Rye, malted barley, wheat
**CASK:** Virgin white oak

# PREMIUM AMERICAN RYE WHISKEY

**This category features some of the world's most exciting, innovative, and important whiskeys; unfortunately, they are also some of the hardest to find. But they are well worth searching for.**

Anchor Brewing makes a stunning range of whiskeys under the name Old Potrero. Pappy Van Winkle is a legend among distillers, and Rittenhouse  Thomas Handy, and Sazerac have important roles in the development of the American spirits industry.

   Anchor have brought innovation to the Old Potrero range by going back in time: all three varieties are made from recipes that are 150 years old. They are almost unobtainable, but if you are lucky enough to find any of them, expect a big, bold, and totally unforgettable drinking experience.

## THREE TO TRY

| | | |
|---|---|---|
| **Sazerac Rye 18 Year Old** | A flip-flop whiskey, with tannin and chili; dark at its core, but with floral and honey notes around the edges | ★ |
| **Thomas Handy Sazerac** | Punchy rye, boiled candy, fruits, and a spice line-up of chili, tarragon, nutmeg, and mint | ★★ |
| **Old Potrero 18th Century Style Whiskey** | Oily hickory notes, cloves, pepper, anisette, treacle toffee, and apricot; as complex as it gets | ★★★ |

★ LEAST EXPENSIVE/WIDELY AVAILABLE  ★★ MODERATELY PRICED/ HARDER TO SOURCE  ★★★COSTLY/RARE

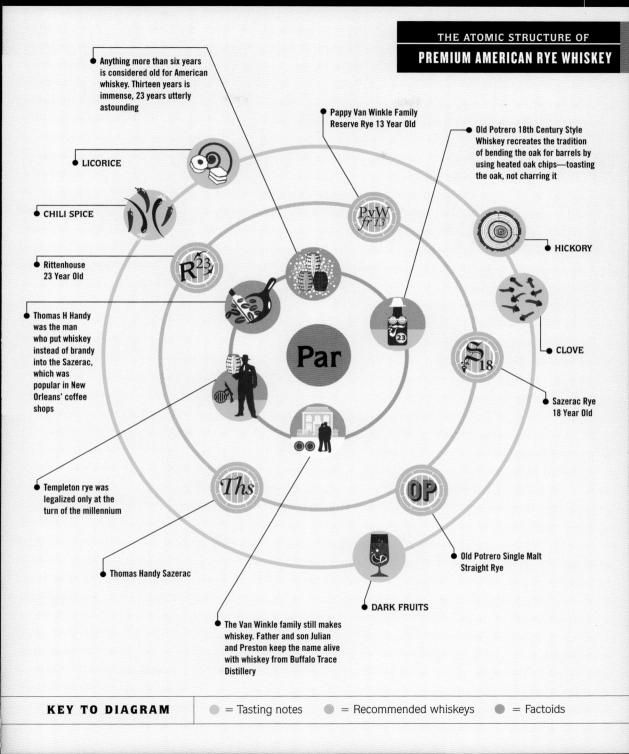

THE ATOMIC STRUCTURE OF
# PREMIUM AMERICAN RYE WHISKEY

Anything more than six years is considered old for American whiskey. Thirteen years is immense, 23 years utterly astounding

LICORICE

CHILI SPICE

Rittenhouse 23 Year Old

Thomas H Handy was the man who put whiskey instead of brandy into the Sazerac, which was popular in New Orleans' coffee shops

Templeton rye was legalized only at the turn of the millennium

Thomas Handy Sazerac

Pappy Van Winkle Family Reserve Rye 13 Year Old

Old Potrero 18th Century Style Whiskey recreates the tradition of bending the oak for barrels by using heated oak chips—toasting the oak, not charring it

HICKORY

CLOVE

Sazerac Rye 18 Year Old

Old Potrero Single Malt Straight Rye

DARK FRUITS

The Van Winkle family still makes whiskey. Father and son Julian and Preston keep the name alive with whiskey from Buffalo Trace Distillery

Par

R23

PvW fr13

S18

Ths

OP

**KEY TO DIAGRAM**    = Tasting notes    = Recommended whiskeys    = Factoids

# CANADIAN BLENDED RYE WHISKY

**ORIGIN:** Canada with a touch of Kentucky
**ABV:** 40%–45%
**GRAIN:** Rye, wheat, barley
**CASK:** Virgin white oak

Most Canadian whisky is blended and so could have been included in the relevant section of this book. However, that would be to do a huge disservice to one of the world's most distinctive, regionalized, and unfairly maligned whisky styles.

As in many other parts of the world, a new interest among smaller producers is reviving the reputation of Canada's whisky, but it has been a struggle. The most commercial brands, many of them owned by U.S. companies, focused on bland drinks suited to the North American market. Canadian whisky rules even allowed 11 percent of the liquid to be from non-Canadian sources—including Kentucky and its bourbons. These days, we're seeing the emergence of some delightful and exciting new whiskies from Canada. And when Canadian whisky is good, it's great.

## THREE TO TRY

| | | |
|---|---|---|
| **Alberta Premium** | Subtle yet hard hitting, complex and meaty; a lesson in Canadian whisky in a glass | ★ |
| **Crown Royal Special Reserve** | Another big whisky, but this one bursts with rich tropical fruits and dollops of oily rye | ★★ |
| **Forty Creek Port Wood Reserve** | Pretty much anything from Forty Creek is great, but the curious spat here between wine and rye grows on you with time; irresistible | ★★★ |

★ LEAST EXPENSIVE/WIDELY AVAILABLE  ★★ MODERATELY PRICED/
HARDER TO SOURCE  ★★★ COSTLY/RARE

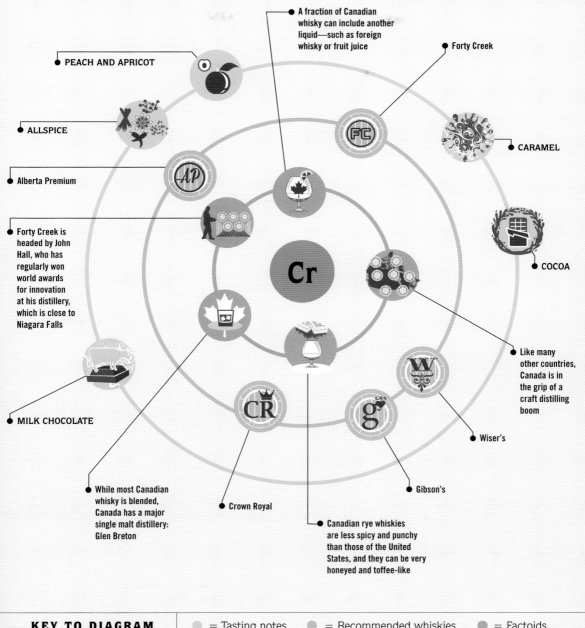

PEACH AND APRICOT

A fraction of Canadian whisky can include another liquid—such as foreign whisky or fruit juice

Forty Creek

ALLSPICE

CARAMEL

Alberta Premium

Forty Creek is headed by John Hall, who has regularly won world awards for innovation at his distillery, which is close to Niagara Falls

Cr

COCOA

Like many other countries, Canada is in the grip of a craft distilling boom

MILK CHOCOLATE

Wiser's

Gibson's

While most Canadian whisky is blended, Canada has a major single malt distillery: Glen Breton

Crown Royal

Canadian rye whiskies are less spicy and punchy than those of the United States, and they can be very honeyed and toffee-like

**KEY TO DIAGRAM** | = Tasting notes | = Recommended whiskies | = Factoids

**ORIGIN:** USA, Germany, Holland
**ABV:** 40%–60%
**GRAIN:** Rye
**CASK:** Virgin white oak

# SINGLE MALT RYE WHISKY

**Some say it's impossible to have a 100 percent rye whiskey. They argue that malted rye cannot perform the same role as malted barley, which acts as a catalyst that allows the conversion of sugars and starches into alcohol.**

Nevertheless, some distillers do produce whisky purporting to be from 100 percent malted rye, although this description does not exclude the possibility that, although all the rye used has been malted, not all the ingredients are necessarily rye.

Does that matter? Not really, when you realize that the whiskies listed here are the most complex, exciting, and tasty you'll find anywhere. Once you acquire a taste for them, they will become a lifelong obsession.

Although it is very difficult to produce whisky from just rye, the results, from Canada to Kentucky and over to the Netherlands, are highly impressive.

## THREE TO TRY

| | | |
|---|---|---|
| **Zuidam Millstone 100 Rye** | The spice is muted by lashings of butterscotch, toffee, and vanilla | ★ |
| **Alberta Premium** | A big bang whisky that kicks off in lots of directions as it fills the mouth and pumps out a rainbow of flavors | ★★ |
| **Old Potrero Hotaling's** | A smorgasbord of offal and sweetmeats; ostensibly unappealing but, if you're brave enough to dive in, overflowing with flavor | ★★★ |

★ LEAST EXPENSIVE/WIDELY AVAILABLE  ★★ MODERATELY PRICED/ HARDER TO SOURCE  ★★★ COSTLY/RARE

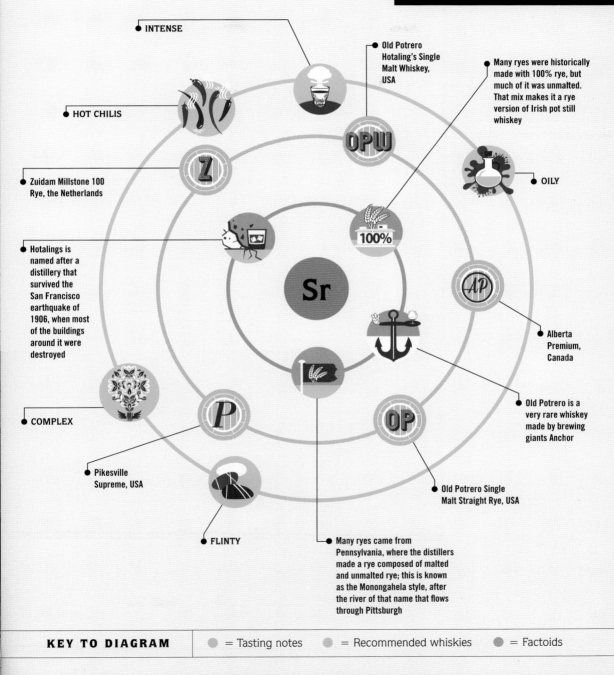

INTENSE

Old Potrero
Hotaling's Single
Malt Whiskey,
USA

Many ryes were historically
made with 100% rye, but
much of it was unmalted.
That mix makes it a rye
version of Irish pot still
whiskey

HOT CHILIS

OILY

Zuidam Millstone 100
Rye, the Netherlands

Hotalings is
named after a
distillery that
survived the
San Francisco
earthquake of
1906, when most
of the buildings
around it were
destroyed

**Sr**

Alberta
Premium,
Canada

COMPLEX

Old Potrero is a
very rare whiskey
made by brewing
giants Anchor

Pikesville
Supreme, USA

Old Potrero Single
Malt Straight Rye, USA

FLINTY

Many ryes came from
Pennsylvania, where the distillers
made a rye composed of malted
and unmalted rye; this is known
as the Monongahela style, after
the river of that name that flows
through Pittsburgh

**KEY TO DIAGRAM** | ● = Tasting notes  ● = Recommended whiskies  ● = Factoids

**ORIGIN:** Austria
**ABV:** 41%–45%
**GRAIN:** Rye, malted barley, wheat
**CASK:** Virgin white oak

# AUSTRIAN RYE WHISKY

**American rye whiskey is all about intensity and big fruit and spice flavors; Dutch rye whisky is about soft toffee, vanilla, and butterscotch. Austrian rye swings between the two, making it a surprisingly diverse whisky style.**

You'll find rye whiskies in other parts of central Europe, especially in Germany, a nation that exports its rye to other countries, including the United States. But it's in Austria that the best are to be found. Their ryes swing between sweet and savory, starter and dessert, hard spiky pepper spice and soft chocolate-and-nut-covered ice cream. As in other Germanic countries, much Austrian whisky is produced almost as a lark, an annual scene-changer for local consumption only. This may make them hard to find, but they are well worth the effort.

## THREE TO TRY

| | | |
|---|---|---|
| **Roggenhof Waldviertler J.H. Rye Whisky** | Oily, intense, nutty, and sharp, with a distinctive, slightly burnt taste | ★ |
| **Whisky Alpin Single Malt Rye** | Starts slowly, with indistinct fruit and oak notes, then leaps into life with big fruit and spices. Like a rocket firework with a lengthy tail | ★★ |
| **Haider Original Rye Whisky** ° | One of the most approachable ryes ever. Honeyed, with tinned fruit, hickory, and licorice | ★★★ |

★ LEAST EXPENSIVE/WIDELY AVAILABLE  ★★ MODERATELY PRICED/HARDER TO SOURCE  ★★★COSTLY/RARE

THE ATOMIC STRUCTURE OF
# AUSTRIAN RYE WHISKY

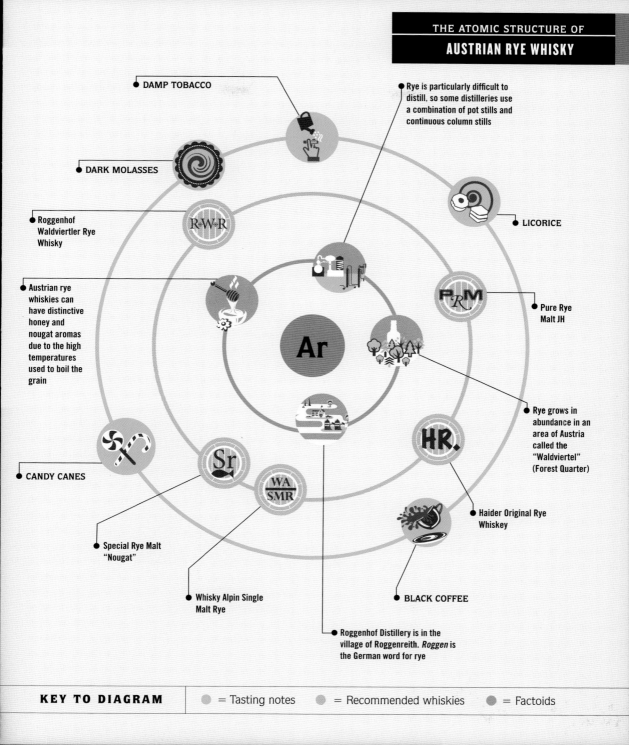

DAMP TOBACCO

Rye is particularly difficult to distill, so some distilleries use a combination of pot stills and continuous column stills

DARK MOLASSES

R•W•R

LICORICE

Roggenhof Waldviertler Rye Whisky

Ar

P•R•M

Pure Rye Malt JH

Austrian rye whiskies can have distinctive honey and nougat aromas due to the high temperatures used to boil the grain

Rye grows in abundance in an area of Austria called the "Waldviertel" (Forest Quarter)

CANDY CANES

Sr

WA SMR

HR.

Haider Original Rye Whiskey

Special Rye Malt "Nougat"

BLACK COFFEE

Whisky Alpin Single Malt Rye

Roggenhof Distillery is in the village of Roggenreith. *Roggen* is the German word for rye

**KEY TO DIAGRAM**   ● = Tasting notes   ● = Recommended whiskies   ● = Factoids

**ORIGIN:** Holland
**ABV:** 40%–50%
**GRAIN:** Rye
**CASK:** Virgin white oak

# DUTCH RYE WHISKY

**Dutch rye—and by that we mean rye from the Zuidam distillery that is the creation of the gifted whisky maker Patrick Zuidam—is different from other ryes, and falls somewhere between Canadian rye and the spicier, fruitier American ones.**

Some of the flavor that Zuidam gets is from virgin oak, but rather than bring even more spice to an already spicy grain, the distillery has pulled off the remarkable feat of bringing maple syrup, caramel, vanilla ice cream, and overripe fruits into the equation. This is a whisky style that can appeal to younger drinkers and to people who think they don't like whisky because they had blended Scotch after a heavy night of beer and wine just after they hit the legal drinking age and it disagreed with them. Zuidam is as distinctive from Scotch as bourbon is.

## TWO TO TRY

| Zuidam Dutch Rye Aged Five Years | Twists and turns unpredictably, but the hickory heart and sweet, gloopy body make it a treat | ★ |
|---|---|---|
| Discovery Road Smile | Sweet caramel and toffee over a soft puréed fruit underlayer; the ultimate dessert whisky | ★★ |

★ LEAST EXPENSIVE/WIDELY AVAILABLE    ★★ MODERATELY PRICED/ HARDER TO SOURCE

THE ATOMIC STRUCTURE OF
# DUTCH RYE WHISKY

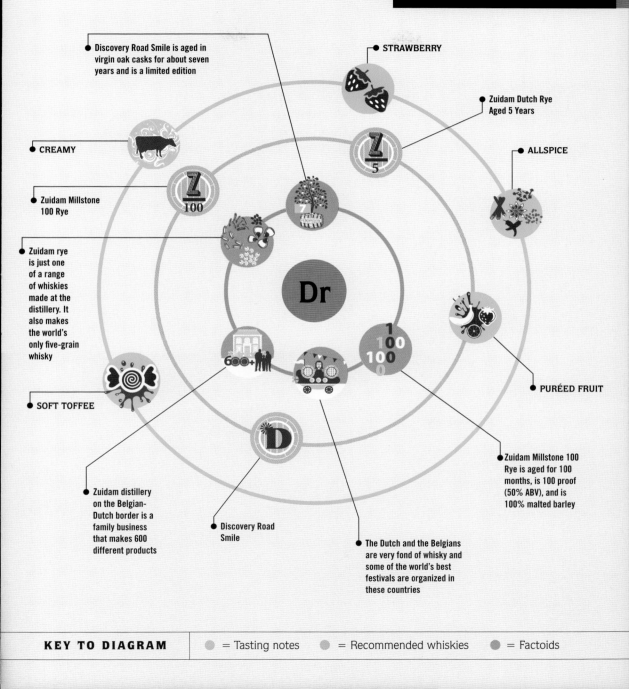

Discovery Road Smile is aged in virgin oak casks for about seven years and is a limited edition

STRAWBERRY

Zuidam Dutch Rye Aged 5 Years

CREAMY

ALLSPICE

Zuidam Millstone 100 Rye

Zuidam rye is just one of a range of whiskies made at the distillery. It also makes the world's only five-grain whisky

Dr

SOFT TOFFEE

PURÉED FRUIT

Zuidam distillery on the Belgian-Dutch border is a family business that makes 600 different products

Discovery Road Smile

Zuidam Millstone 100 Rye is aged for 100 months, is 100 proof (50% ABV), and is 100% malted barley

The Dutch and the Belgians are very fond of whisky and some of the world's best festivals are organized in these countries

KEY TO DIAGRAM   ● = Tasting notes   ● = Recommended whiskies   ● = Factoids

**ORIGIN:** Germany, Liechtenstein
**ABV:** 45%–55%
**GRAIN:** Malted rye, malted barley, wheat, oats
**CASK:** Virgin white oak

# OTHER EUROPEAN RYE WHISKIES

Traditionally, whisky has been made anywhere grain is grown. It was the logical way to use excess grain and extend its longevity, and in most cases local whiskies reflected the grains that were grown locally.

Germany is one of the best places in the world to grow rye, and the nation has used the grain for whisky production for generations, exporting the distilling knowledge and the grain to North America somewhere along the line. Often, though, German whisky is stored in casks that have been used for other brewery and distillery products and they don't always work. For rye, there are now a couple of very promising new products. Marcel Telser, in particular, seems to be a distiller growing in stature year by year.

## TWO TO TRY

| | | |
|---|---|---|
| **Telser Single Cask Pure Rye, Liechtenstein** | Very young still and a work in progress, but sweet, with as much fruit as pepper and a nice sweet finish | ★ |
| **Fränkischer Rye Whisky, Germany** | A fairground whisky, with lots of noise and business, but almost too much to take in; altogether a little bit crazy. | ★★ |

★ LEAST EXPENSIVE/WIDELY AVAILABLE ★★ MODERATELY PRICED/ HARDER TO SOURCE

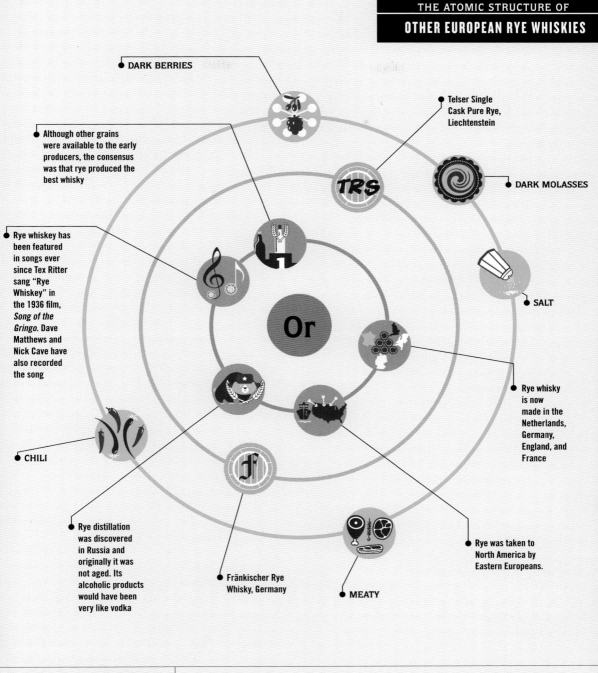

THE ATOMIC STRUCTURE OF
## OTHER EUROPEAN RYE WHISKIES

DARK BERRIES

Although other grains were available to the early producers, the consensus was that rye produced the best whisky

Telser Single Cask Pure Rye, Liechtenstein

TRS

DARK MOLASSES

Rye whiskey has been featured in songs ever since Tex Ritter sang "Rye Whiskey" in the 1936 film, *Song of the Gringo*. Dave Matthews and Nick Cave have also recorded the song

Or

SALT

CHILI

Rye whisky is now made in the Netherlands, Germany, England, and France

Rye distillation was discovered in Russia and originally it was not aged. Its alcoholic products would have been very like vodka

Fränkischer Rye Whisky, Germany

Rye was taken to North America by Eastern Europeans.

MEATY

**KEY TO DIAGRAM** ● = Tasting notes ● = Recommended whiskies ● = Factoids

# OTHER GRAIN WHISKIES

**CHAPTER**
**SIX**

Over the last 160 or so pages, most of the world's whiskies have been covered. How then, is it proportionate to dedicate some 50 pages—a quarter of the entire book—to obscure and esoteric whiskies?

It's a fair question, and there are three parts to the answer. But first it's necessary to get a sense of proportion: there are more than 60 distilleries in Speyside and countless whiskies, and yet the region gets only four pages of its own, and can claim some shared ownership of another 14. That's because, in a book based on flavor, the characteristics of those hundreds of whiskies can be summarized in less than 20 pages. Over the next 50 pages we are dealing with whiskies that are either unique or in very elite company.

So the three reasons these more obscure whiskies are included are as follows.

First, these are the varieties that are taking whisky into new and uncharted territory. Although it might seem strange to give one grain whiskey from a small U.S. state half as much space as the whole of Speyside, it merits such extensive treatment because it adds so much to the overall patchwork quilt of whisky flavors.

Second, it's highly likely that, as more and more craft distillers turn their hands to innovating in whisky, these will be the areas that will attract the greatest interest among whisky fans, who have been bombarded in recent years with books covering the standard territories.

And third, and linked to the last point, this is where we can gaze into a crystal ball and see where whisky might go next. It presents the rare opportunity to see whisky as an evolving and progressive spirit and not one hog-tied by tradition and stuffiness, as it has so often been portrayed in the past.

The final chapter of this book looks at the whiskies that are pushing their feet onto the boundary line of acceptability and perhaps straying across it. This section is more conventional, taking whisky styles that play completely by the rules but are not commonly seen. The most obvious of these is grain whisky, which is produced in several countries and is usually used as an addition to blended Scotch whisky but which can be quite fantastic in its own right.

But there are also some whisky styles, such as wheat whiskey, that are left-field but nevertheless important to whisky history, and others, such as Irish pot still whiskey, that are making a comeback as new whiskey makers look to the past for inspiration. An Irish friend of mine has just opened a craft distillery where he intends to make small batches of whiskey based on recipes hundreds of years old, much of it within the pot still category. A generation ago, such an undertaking would have seemed quixotic and doomed to failure; in the modern context, it seems a shrewd commercial move: whisky is more than a drink; it's a fast-moving business.

ORIGIN: USA
ABV: 42.5%–45.5%
GRAIN: Wheat, corn, malted barley
CASK: Virgin white oak

# AMERICAN WHEAT WHISKEY

**It says much about the difficulty of making a worthwhile whiskey from wheat that so few attempts have been made to do it, and so few craft distillers have chanced their arm in the category.**

Wheat whiskey is a distinct category and is not the same as "wheated whiskey," a term applied to bourbons in which relatively high levels of wheat are used to produce a softer, sweeter drink. The wheat content in a wheat whiskey must be at least 51 percent, but is normally considerably higher.

Wheat whiskeys tend to have a soft, sweet, toasty taste. At their best they are a delight. Berrnheim has been a huge success for Heaven Hill, bringing a new audience to the whiskey category.

## THREE TO TRY

| | | |
|---|---|---|
| **Heaven Hill Bernheim Original** | The most commercially successful wheat whiskey and an utter delight from start to finish; sweet, fruity, easy drinking | ★ |
| **McKenzie Wheat Whiskey** | Has some sappiness, but the honeycomb heart is a delight; a notably short finish | ★★ |
| **Dry Fly** | Honey and some orange marmalade on brown buttered toast before late spice | ★★★ |

★ LEAST EXPENSIVE/WIDELY AVAILABLE  ★★ MODERATELY PRICED/ HARDER TO SOURCE  ★★★COSTLY/RARE

THE ATOMIC STRUCTURE OF
## AMERICAN WHEAT WHISKEY

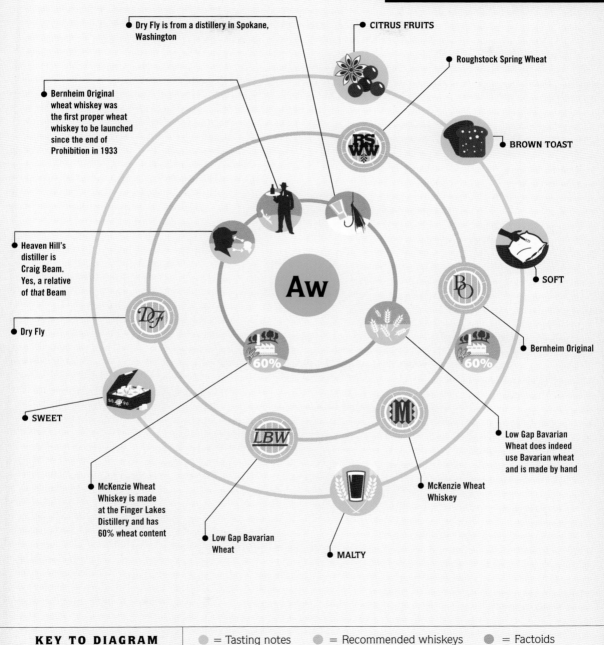

Dry Fly is from a distillery in Spokane, Washington

CITRUS FRUITS

Roughstock Spring Wheat

Bernheim Original wheat whiskey was the first proper wheat whiskey to be launched since the end of Prohibition in 1933

BROWN TOAST

**Aw**

Heaven Hill's distiller is Craig Beam. Yes, a relative of *that* Beam

SOFT

Dry Fly

Bernheim Original

60%

60%

SWEET

Low Gap Bavarian Wheat does indeed use Bavarian wheat and is made by hand

McKenzie Wheat Whiskey is made at the Finger Lakes Distillery and has 60% wheat content

McKenzie Wheat Whiskey

Low Gap Bavarian Wheat

MALTY

**KEY TO DIAGRAM**    = Tasting notes    = Recommended whiskeys    = Factoids

**ORIGIN:** Scotland
**ABV:** 40%–75%
**GRAIN:** Wheat, maize, rye
**CASK:** Ex-bourbon

# SCOTTISH GRAIN WHISKY

**Grain whisky is whisky made from a grain other than malted barley. It is created by a method that is totally different from that used to make single malt whisky.**

Instead of being boiled in pot stills, the distiller's beer is put into columns where high-pressure steam at extreme temperatures separates the alcohol and the water to produce a spirit that has less flavor than single malt whisky. Grain is what is added to single malt whisky to make blended whisky, but it can be sold separately, and often is. There are some astounding grain whiskies aged 40 years or more that have picked up distinctive bourbon notes. And there are plenty of industry voices who think that the category is due to take its place in the sun.

## THREE TO TRY

| Berry's Own Selection North British 2000 | A younger grain whisky, with grape, pepper, and apples | ★ |
|---|---|---|
| Clan Denny Port Dundas 33 Year Old | Sugar, spice, milk, and dark chocolate; the whisky equivalent of chili chocolate | ★★ |
| Duncan Taylor Octave series | Beautiful selection of candied, sugary, and oaky grain whiskies with soft fruits and licorice | ★★★ |

★ LEAST EXPENSIVE/WIDELY AVAILABLE  ★★ MODERATELY PRICED/ HARDER TO SOURCE  ★★★ COSTLY/RARE

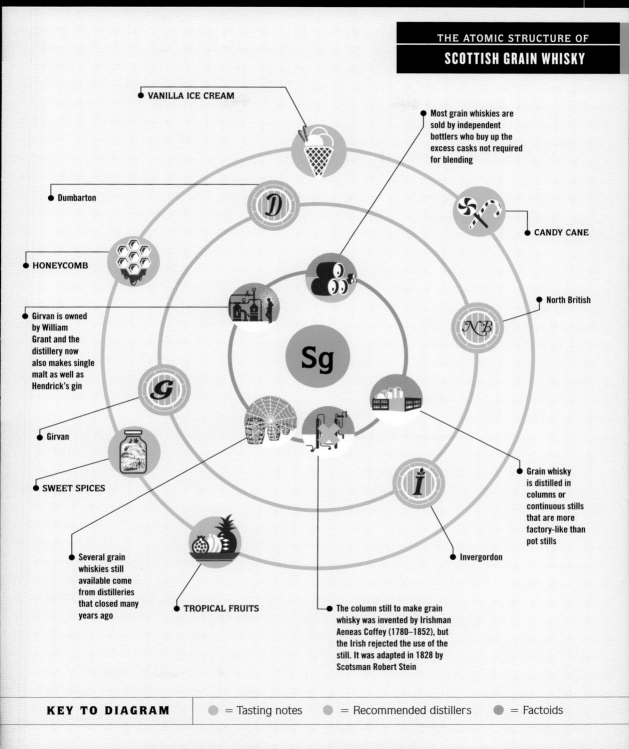

THE ATOMIC STRUCTURE OF
## SCOTTISH GRAIN WHISKY

VANILLA ICE CREAM

Most grain whiskies are sold by independent bottlers who buy up the excess casks not required for blending

Dumbarton

CANDY CANE

HONEYCOMB

North British

Girvan is owned by William Grant and the distillery now also makes single malt as well as Hendrick's gin

Sg

Girvan

SWEET SPICES

Grain whisky is distilled in columns or continuous stills that are more factory-like than pot stills

Several grain whiskies still available come from distilleries that closed many years ago

Invergordon

TROPICAL FRUITS

The column still to make grain whisky was invented by Irishman Aeneas Coffey (1780–1852), but the Irish rejected the use of the still. It was adapted in 1828 by Scotsman Robert Stein

**KEY TO DIAGRAM**    ● = Tasting notes    ● = Recommended distillers    ● = Factoids

**ORIGIN:** Ireland
**ABV:** 43%–58%
**GRAIN:** Malted barley, unmalted other grains
**CASK:** Ex-bourbon, ex-sherry, ex-Marsala

# IRISH SINGLE POT STILL WHISKEY

**You might think that the name "single pot still whiskey" would have something to do with the production method and the copper pot still. But this is Ireland, and they do things differently there.**

In Ireland, the term excludes all single malt whisky and some other whisky styles that are made in pot stills. Irish pot still whiskey is all about the grain—a mixture of malted barley and other unmalted grain mixed at the flour (grist) stage of the production process. Note that we say "other unmalted grain" and not "unmalted barley," which is how it is often defined. The term has been defined by law to include other grains. Whiskey distilled this way is heavy in phenols, flavorsome, and oily. The best pot still whiskeys are a total joy.

## THREE TO TRY

| | | |
|---|---|---|
| **Green Spot** | Easy drinking, refreshing; summery green apple and pears, with enough spice and body to give it assertiveness | ★ |
| **Redbreast 12 Year Old Cask Strength** | A perfect example of great pot still whiskey; characterful, complex, intense, and challenging | ★★ |
| **Midleton Barry Crockett Legacy** | Bold, bright, and beautiful, with sublime vanilla notes holding off the paprika and cinnamon notes | ★★★ |

★ LEAST EXPENSIVE/WIDELY AVAILABLE  ★★ MODERATELY PRICED/ HARDER TO SOURCE  ★★★ COSTLY/RARE

THE ATOMIC STRUCTURE OF
# IRISH SINGLE POT STILL WHISKEY

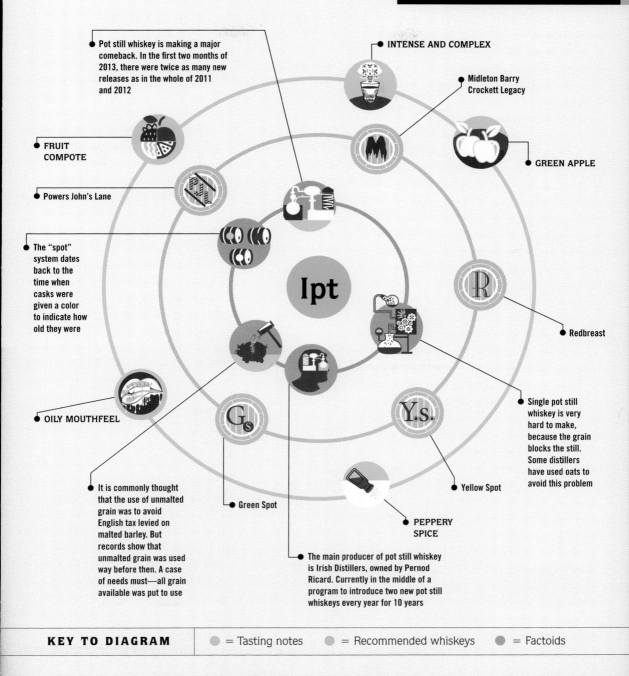

Pot still whiskey is making a major comeback. In the first two months of 2013, there were twice as many new releases as in the whole of 2011 and 2012

INTENSE AND COMPLEX

Midleton Barry Crockett Legacy

FRUIT COMPOTE

GREEN APPLE

Powers John's Lane

The "spot" system dates back to the time when casks were given a color to indicate how old they were

Ipt

Redbreast

OILY MOUTHFEEL

Single pot still whiskey is very hard to make, because the grain blocks the still. Some distillers have used oats to avoid this problem

It is commonly thought that the use of unmalted grain was to avoid English tax levied on malted barley. But records show that unmalted grain was used way before then. A case of needs must—all grain available was put to use

Green Spot

Yellow Spot

PEPPERY SPICE

The main producer of pot still whiskey is Irish Distillers, owned by Pernod Ricard. Currently in the middle of a program to introduce two new pot still whiskeys every year for 10 years

**KEY TO DIAGRAM**    ● = Tasting notes    ● = Recommended whiskeys    ● = Factoids

ORIGIN: Ireland
ABV: 40%–46%
GRAIN: Wheat, maize, rye, oats
CASK: Ex-bourbon

# IRISH GRAIN WHISKEY

**The difference between the earthy, peaty, and savory Scottish single malts and the country's sweet grain whiskies can be a big one. In Ireland, where single malts tend to be triple distilled, the gap between the two types is smaller.**

But the limited number of grain whiskeys that the Teeling family released first at Cooley under the name Greenore and then under their own name are worth seeking out because they show how grain from the same source may change when matured in wood. Arguably the best of the range on offer is the 15 Year Old, because its sweetness has been reined in by tannin and spice but, unlike older versions, it has not taken on Scotch bonnet proportions.

## THREE TO TRY

| | | |
|---|---|---|
| Greenore 8 Year Old | Sweet, with honey and vanilla dominant; a great summer drink and entry-level whiskey | ★ |
| Greenore 15 Year Old | Apple, vanilla, and pear held in check by oak notes and some rapier-like late spice | ★★ |
| Greenore 18 Year Old | Chewy, fruity notes up front, then bang! Chili pepper and oaky tannins slash your mouth and toss the taste from sweet to dry | ★★★ |

★ LEAST EXPENSIVE/WIDELY AVAILABLE  ★★ MODERATELY PRICED/HARDER TO SOURCE  ★★★ COSTLY/RARE

THE ATOMIC STRUCTURE OF
# IRISH GRAIN WHISKEY

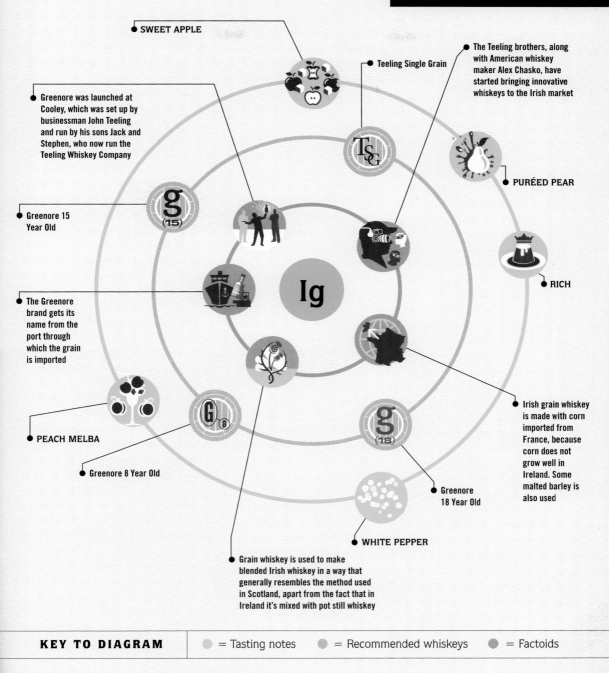

SWEET APPLE

Teeling Single Grain

The Teeling brothers, along with American whiskey maker Alex Chasko, have started bringing innovative whiskeys to the Irish market

Greenore was launched at Cooley, which was set up by businessman John Teeling and run by his sons Jack and Stephen, who now run the Teeling Whiskey Company

PURÉED PEAR

Greenore 15 Year Old

RICH

The Greenore brand gets its name from the port through which the grain is imported

Irish grain whiskey is made with corn imported from France, because corn does not grow well in Ireland. Some malted barley is also used

PEACH MELBA

Greenore 8 Year Old

Greenore 18 Year Old

WHITE PEPPER

Grain whiskey is used to make blended Irish whiskey in a way that generally resembles the method used in Scotland, apart from the fact that in Ireland it's mixed with pot still whiskey

Ig

**KEY TO DIAGRAM**    ● = Tasting notes    ● = Recommended whiskeys    ● = Factoids

# IRISH POT STILL AND MALT WHISKEY

**ORIGIN:** Ireland
**ABV:** 40%–53%
**GRAIN:** Malted barley and unmalted barley
**CASK:** Ex-bourbon

**When is a blend not a blend? When it's one of these whiskeys. Some people may disagree with this judgement, but they will struggle to find a definition of the term "blend" that encompasses Irish pot still and malt whiskey.**

A blended Irish whiskey is a mix of pot still whiskey and grain whiskey. So a mix of pot still whiskey and single malt whiskey is something else again. And it gets even more confusing when you consider that pot still can include other unmalted grains such as maize or wheat. The whiskeys mixed here come from two distilleries, too, so this is arguably a blended malt. Except that it can't be, because it has an unmalted component.

Whatever they are, these creations by Bernard Walsh are fantastic examples of Irish whiskey.

## TWO TO TRY

| The Irishman Rare Cask Strength | Despite its great strength, this is an easy-drinking and highly palatable mix of honey and vanilla, licorice, and green fruits | ★ |
| --- | --- | --- |
| Writer's Tears | Pot still rich, with citrus, mouth-coating oils, and a complex bitter-sweet spice combination | ★★ |

★ LEAST EXPENSIVE/WIDELY AVAILABLE  ★★ MODERATELY PRICED/ HARDER TO SOURCE

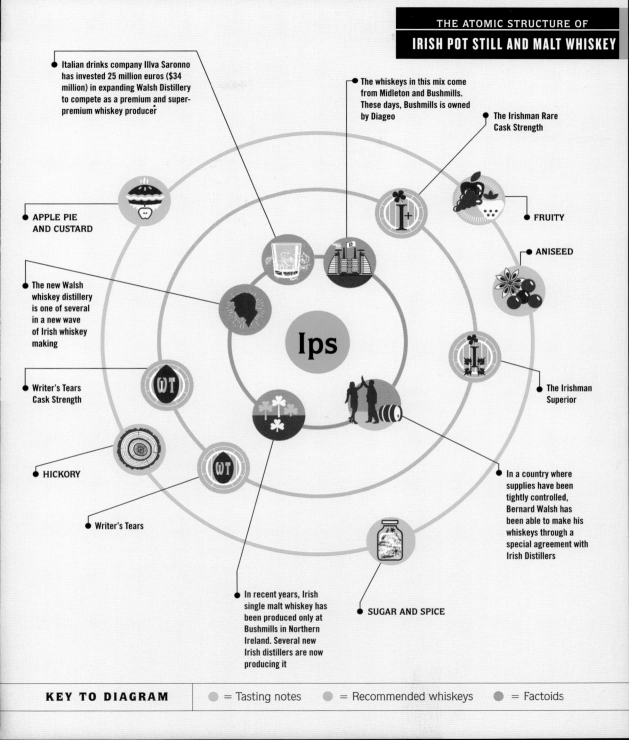

Italian drinks company Illva Saronno has invested 25 million euros ($34 million) in expanding Walsh Distillery to compete as a premium and super-premium whiskey producer

The whiskeys in this mix come from Midleton and Bushmills. These days, Bushmills is owned by Diageo

The Irishman Rare Cask Strength

**APPLE PIE AND CUSTARD**

**FRUITY**

**ANISEED**

The new Walsh whiskey distillery is one of several in a new wave of Irish whiskey making

**Ips**

The Irishman Superior

**Writer's Tears Cask Strength**

**HICKORY**

**Writer's Tears**

In a country where supplies have been tightly controlled, Bernard Walsh has been able to make his whiskeys through a special agreement with Irish Distillers

In recent years, Irish single malt whiskey has been produced only at Bushmills in Northern Ireland. Several new Irish distillers are now producing it

**SUGAR AND SPICE**

**KEY TO DIAGRAM**   ● = Tasting notes   ● = Recommended whiskeys   ● = Factoids

**ORIGIN:** Japan
**ABV:** 45%–65.5%
**GRAIN:** Maize, wheat, malted barley
**CASK:** Ex-bourbon

# JAPANESE GRAIN WHISKY

**If you've been paying close attention thus far, you may have noticed that there seems to be a contradiction in the list of grains used in single grain whisky.**

There is an argument that one of the whiskies listed here should be in the last chapter of the book, because it defies categorization. Nikka Coffey Grain is made using malted barley but in a column still. So it's a single malt whisky in one sense, but under Scotch Whisky Association rules (which Japanese distillers aren't bound by) it can't be a single malt if it's made in a Coffey still. That makes it a grain whisky.

Both these whiskies marry sherry malt with flavors normally associated with American whiskeys. They straddle categories, just as Nikka Coffey Grain straddles definitions.

## TWO TO TRY

| Nikka Coffey Grain | Rich, full, and mouth coating, this is a sweet, honeyed whisky with a soft nuttiness and vanilla side to it | ★ |
|---|---|---|
| Kawasaki Single Grain | A big, full-flavored, heavily sherried whisky with clean and sweet notes, including strawberry or blackcurrant jam | ★★ |

NIKKA COFFEY GRAIN WHISKY

★ LEAST EXPENSIVE/WIDELY AVAILABLE  ★★ MODERATELY PRICED/ HARDER TO SOURCE

THE ATOMIC STRUCTURE OF
# JAPANESE GRAIN WHISKY

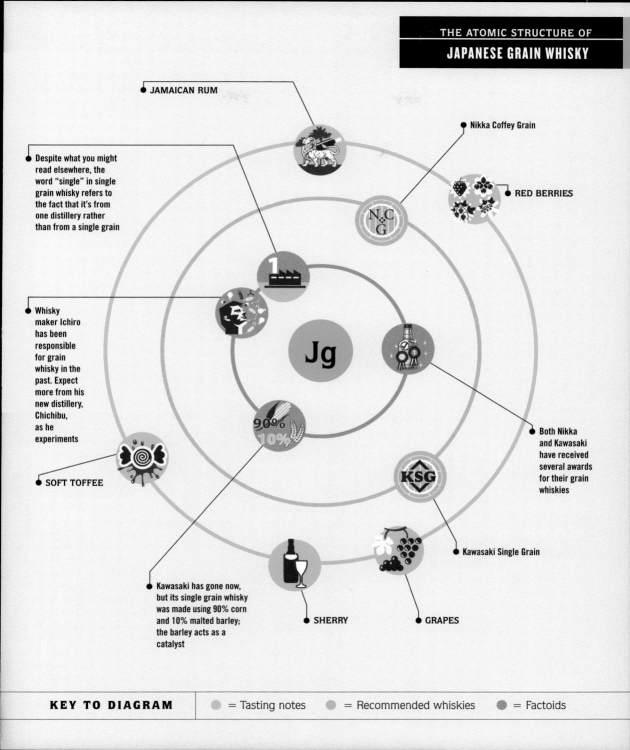

JAMAICAN RUM

Nikka Coffey Grain

Despite what you might read elsewhere, the word "single" in single grain whisky refers to the fact that it's from one distillery rather than from a single grain

RED BERRIES

N C G

1

Whisky maker Ichiro has been responsible for grain whisky in the past. Expect more from his new distillery, Chichibu, as he experiments

Jg

Both Nikka and Kawasaki have received several awards for their grain whiskies

90% 10%

SOFT TOFFEE

KSG

Kawasaki Single Grain

Kawasaki has gone now, but its single grain whisky was made using 90% corn and 10% malted barley; the barley acts as a catalyst

SHERRY

GRAPES

**KEY TO DIAGRAM** ● = Tasting notes ● = Recommended whiskies ● = Factoids

**ORIGIN:** South Africa
**ABV:** 43%
**GRAIN:** Maize, wheat
**CASK:** Ex-bourbon

# SOUTH AFRICAN GRAIN WHISKY

**Bain's deserves its own entry because it is a multiple award winner. If ever there were a whisky that provided evidence that grain whiskies can have their own character and personality, it's this one.**

Grain whiskies have less natural flavor than single malts, and the wood plays a much more dominant role in their final taste profile. Does that mean that if grain whiskies in South Africa and, say, Australia are both matured in Jim Beam barrels, there are significant differences between them? Oh yes! Bain's Cape Mountain Single Grain Whisky uses water from the Cape Mountain and its makers have come up with a grain mash that produces a honeyed and soft whisky. It's impressive stuff, and thankfully it's becoming easier to find.

## WHY YOU SHOULD TRY

A whisky has to be pretty special to be voted the top grain whisky by leading whisky experts, but Bains is just that. And the 2013 accolade is just one in a long line of awards and critical acclaim. For much of its life, the whisky existed in the shadow of the distillery's single malt. But Bain's offers something special to the grain whisky sector, with the typically soft, sweet, and oily characteristics set off by some very attractive sharper, weightier flavors. Classy stuff.

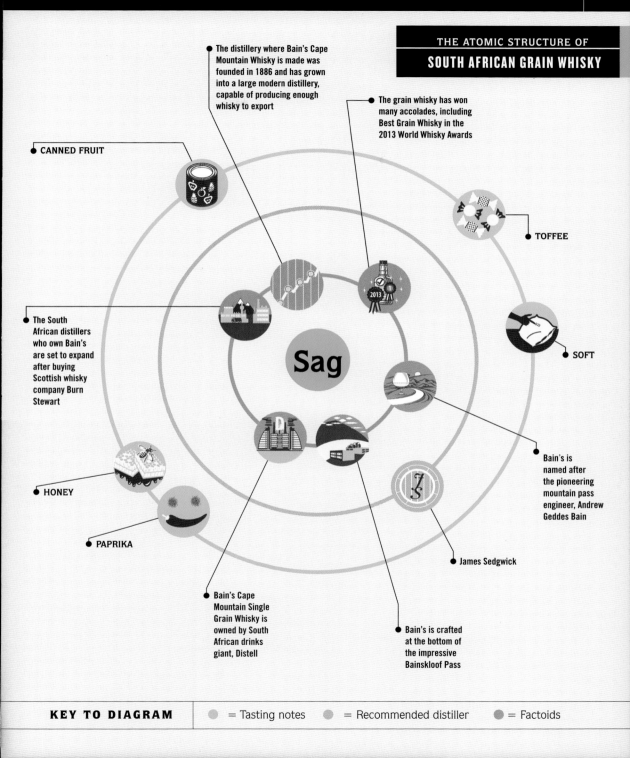

The distillery where Bain's Cape Mountain Whisky is made was founded in 1886 and has grown into a large modern distillery, capable of producing enough whisky to export

The grain whisky has won many accolades, including Best Grain Whisky in the 2013 World Whisky Awards

CANNED FRUIT

TOFFEE

The South African distillers who own Bain's are set to expand after buying Scottish whisky company Burn Stewart

Sag

SOFT

Bain's is named after the pioneering mountain pass engineer, Andrew Geddes Bain

HONEY

PAPRIKA

James Sedgwick

Bain's Cape Mountain Single Grain Whisky is owned by South African drinks giant, Distell

Bain's is crafted at the bottom of the impressive Bainskloof Pass

**KEY TO DIAGRAM** ● = Tasting notes ● = Recommended distiller ● = Factoids

**ORIGIN:** Germany, Austria, Switzerland
**ABV:** 40%–43%
**GRAIN:** Oats, wheat, maize
**CASK:** Ex-bourbon

# EUROPEAN OAT AND OTHER GRAIN WHISKIES

**Although we're calling this "other grain whiskies," barley and rye have been dealt with elsewhere, so here we're really looking only at whiskies made on small column stills, often in very small quantities, and often just for local consumption.**

Oats, wheat, and maize can be classed together because they all make whisky that is sweet and candy styled and, with the exception of the maize/corn variety, softer than usual, too. That's not to say they're easy drinking. Some are heavy on oils due to the distillation process and some have been matured in wine or other unusual casks, making them something of an acquired taste. Should you be traveling through any of the regions in which these are produced, it's well worth stopping off for a tasting.

## TWO TO TRY

| | | |
|---|---|---|
| **Waldviertler Hafer** | Soft and sweet, and with an easy-going rounded flavor, but not cloying because of the savory and oak note in the mix | ★ |
| **Schwarzwälder Roggenmalz** | Almost a tropical fruit and honey combo with a gentle soft sand finish | ★★ |

★ LEAST EXPENSIVE/WIDELY AVAILABLE  ★★ MODERATELY PRICED/ HARDER TO SOURCE

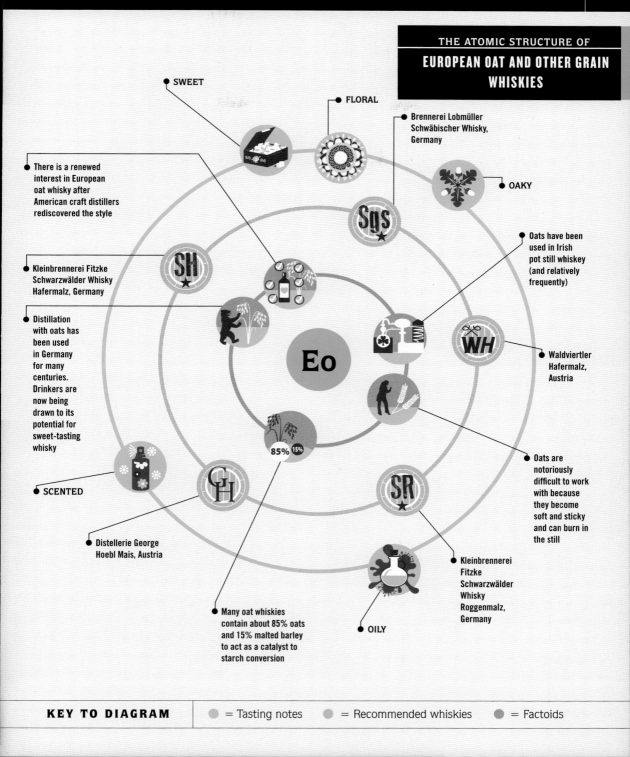

THE ATOMIC STRUCTURE OF
# EUROPEAN OAT AND OTHER GRAIN WHISKIES

SWEET

FLORAL

Brennerei Lobmüller
Schwäbischer Whisky,
Germany

OAKY

There is a renewed
interest in European
oat whisky after
American craft distillers
rediscovered the style

Oats have been
used in Irish
pot still whiskey
(and relatively
frequently)

Kleinbrennerei Fitzke
Schwarzwälder Whisky
Hafermalz, Germany

Distillation
with oats has
been used
in Germany
for many
centuries.
Drinkers are
now being
drawn to its
potential for
sweet-tasting
whisky

Eo

Waldviertler
Hafermalz,
Austria

85% 15%

SCENTED

Oats are
notoriously
difficult to work
with because
they become
soft and sticky
and can burn in
the still

Distellerie George
Hoebl Mais, Austria

Kleinbrennerei
Fitzke
Schwarzwälder
Whisky
Roggenmalz,
Germany

Many oat whiskies
contain about 85% oats
and 15% malted barley
to act as a catalyst to
starch conversion

OILY

**KEY TO DIAGRAM** ● = Tasting notes ● = Recommended whiskies ● = Factoids

# REBEL WHISKY

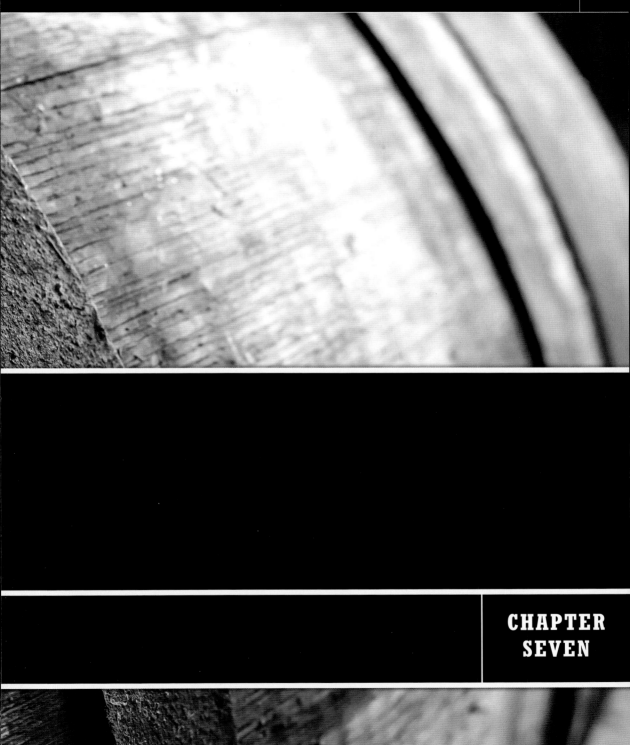

# CHAPTER
# SEVEN

Whisky may only be made with grain, yeast, and water and wouldn't seem to offer much room for maneuver when it comes to plowing a lone furrow. And yet, some whisky makers have managed to create whiskies that have a style all of their own. They're nonconformist and don't fit in anywhere else. So we've dubbed them "rebel whiskies."

The whisky landscape is changing beyond all recognition. New emerging markets are demanding affordable luxuries such as Scotch whisky and their vast economies are sucking in the big drinks' companies, which are meeting the demand by pouring their malts into blends or holding them back for use as super-premium luxuries for the future. In turn this leads to shortages in many mature markets across the world and the gap is being filled by a new wave of distillers in domestic markets.

Go back 20 years and, apart from some farm and craft distilleries across Europe, there were only about 150 distilleries across the world, with more than 100 of them in Scotland. The rest, in Japan, Ireland, Canada, and Kentucky, either accepted the Scottish way of producing whisky or went in their own direction while paying lip service to Scotland.

Today there are about 1,000 distilleries, with just over 100 in Scotland. While no one in the business can fail to acknowledge the vast contribution Scotland has made to whisky's global reputation, that hasn't prevented many people from challenging the nation's preeminence. The Australian and French producers and many of the American craft distillers aren't averse to iconoclasm.

Often they skirt perilously close to the very boundaries of what is legal. Some clearly step beyond them. If Scotch whisky is a fortress protected by the Scotch Whisky Association, the new distillers are operating a sort of whisky Wild West, out on the frontiers, and sometimes drawing new whisky boundaries.

This can be a bad thing, but it can be a very good thing, too. Some of the new distillers are exploring and innovating, using unusual casks and different grain-drying materials, working with unusual grains, or combining different styles of whisky to provide something new.

It brings into focus what exactly whisky is. There are many who state that whisky should taste like whisky, but what does that really mean? Nine times out of ten, the answer is that they mean it should taste like Scotch. And that begs the question, why should it? If it's made with grain, yeast, and water, but it uses regional peat and wood and an unusual cask, isn't that what innovation and progress are all about?

So this chapter is about whisky's equivalent of punk rock. We've called them rebel whiskies because they're nonconformists, not so much tearing up the rule book as fiddling with its covers.

None of the whisky styles included in the following pages is likely to challenge the dominance of single malt whisky, and in particular Scottish single malt whisky. But they do have the potential to attract new drinkers to the whisky category, and ultimately that will benefit Scotland, because if you find whisky you'll eventually find Scotland and/or Kentucky.

ORIGIN: England
ABV: 43%
GRAIN: Wheat, malted barley, oats
CASK: Virgin oak, East European oak

# ENGLISH THREE-GRAIN WHISKY

**At the dawn of the millennium, the idea of English whisky was considered ridiculous. Since then distilleries have appeared all over the country, and with some of the new boys bringing innovation to the drink, experts now take the product very seriously.**

Adnams, a long-established beer maker, became the first English company to brew and distil on the same site. So far it has released two whiskies, each three years old—the minimum age.

No. 2 is the more interesting. Wheat, barley and, unusually, oats are malted and mixed to form the flour used for brewing beer. The beer, with a strength of about 6%, is put into a beer stripping column and then pot stills. The new spirit is then matured in virgin oak casks (casks that have not previously been used for anything else) to create a surprisingly accomplished and full-flavored whisky.

## WHY YOU SHOULD TRY

Adnams is a beer brewer on the east coast of England with an enviable reputation for not cutting corners. It prides itself on mapping the journey from grain to glass, so when it built a distillery and started producing vodkas and gin, two things were always likely: that it would innovate and that it would excel. Both have happened. Adnams thought carefully about what it wanted to do—and this is different enough from standard whiskies to warrant investigation. The brewery-turned-distillery promises surprises in the years to come.

THE ATOMIC STRUCTURE OF

# ENGLISH THREE-GRAIN WHISKY

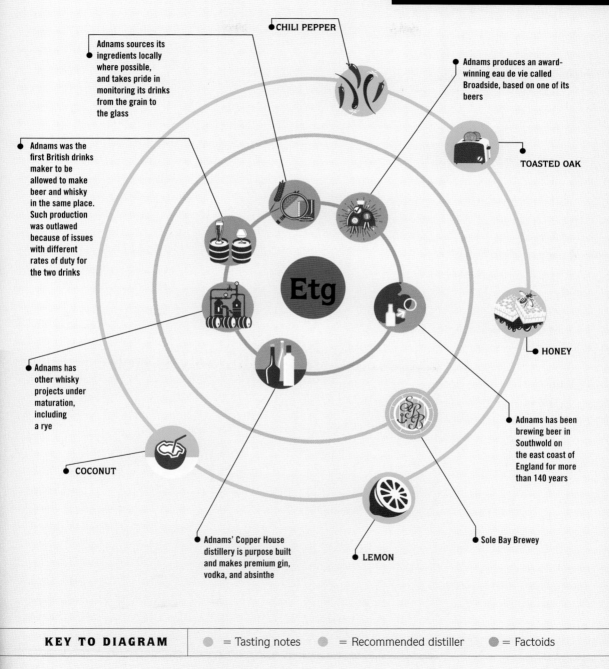

CHILI PEPPER

Adnams sources its ingredients locally where possible, and takes pride in monitoring its drinks from the grain to the glass

Adnams produces an award-winning eau de vie called Broadside, based on one of its beers

TOASTED OAK

Adnams was the first British drinks maker to be allowed to make beer and whisky in the same place. Such production was outlawed because of issues with different rates of duty for the two drinks

Etg

HONEY

Adnams has other whisky projects under maturation, including a rye

Adnams has been brewing beer in Southwold on the east coast of England for more than 140 years

COCONUT

Adnams' Copper House distillery is purpose built and makes premium gin, vodka, and absinthe

LEMON

Sole Bay Brewey

**KEY TO DIAGRAM**    ● = Tasting notes    ● = Recommended distiller    ● = Factoids

**ORIGIN:** Italy
**ABV:** 43%–59%
**GRAIN:** Wheat, barley, rye
**CASK:** Ex-wine, ex-sherry

# ITALIAN THREE-GRAIN WHISKY

**When Puni started using three grains, it thought it was the only distillery in Italy that was doing so. But so great was the sudden surge of new distilleries trying to do something innovative that in fact there were several.**

Italy is not normally associated with whisky, but the north of the country, near the Alps, has plentiful supplies of the two essential ingredients: water and grain.

Puni bottled its first whisky proper in early 2015 but in 2013 it released a one-year-old spirit and a new-make spirit, and in 2014 it celebrated its second birthday with Alba 2, a spirit drink. What makes Puni special is the amount of flavor in even its very young spirits, which were good to go at only two years old.

The distillery's maturation process uses U.S. bourbon barrels, Sicilian marsala casks, and Austrian wine casks.

## WHY YOU SHOULD TRY

On first glance this would seem to be an oddball because when you think of Italy you tend to think of sun, sea, and sand with some nice wines and pretty ruins thrown in for good measure. But that's not the whole story, and the number of world-class skiers from the country provides the clue. Northern Italy backs onto the Alps, and the lakes suggest that rainfall is plentiful. The people behind Puni know what they're doing, as they demonstrated in their new make and young spirit. This whisky will deliver even at three years old.

## THE ATOMIC STRUCTURE OF
# ITALIAN THREE-GRAIN WHISKY

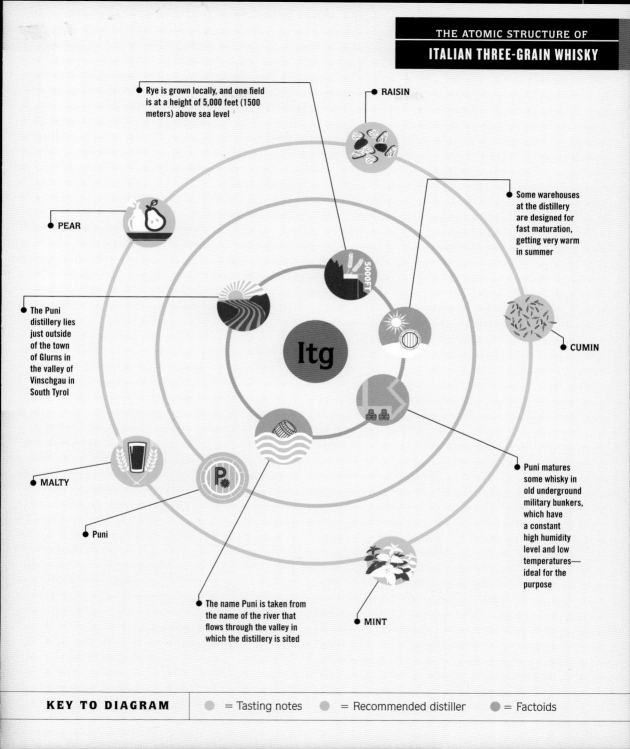

Rye is grown locally, and one field is at a height of 5,000 feet (1500 meters) above sea level

RAISIN

Some warehouses at the distillery are designed for fast maturation, getting very warm in summer

PEAR

The Puni distillery lies just outside of the town of Glurns in the valley of Vinschgau in South Tyrol

Itg

CUMIN

MALTY

Puni

Puni matures some whisky in old underground military bunkers, which have a constant high humidity level and low temperatures— ideal for the purpose

The name Puni is taken from the name of the river that flows through the valley in which the distillery is sited

MINT

**KEY TO DIAGRAM** | = Tasting notes ● = Recommended distiller ● = Factoids

**ORIGIN:** USA
**ABV:** 46.2%
**GRAIN:** Corn, barley, wheat, and rye
**CASK:** Virgin white oak

# AMERICAN FOUR-GRAIN WHISKEY

**Kentucky distiller Chris Morris is all for experimenting. Four Grains was one of his earliest efforts at Woodford Reserve, the pretty distillery where much of the technique to create what we now know as bourbon was originally devised.**

The Master's Collection—Morris's experimental annual release—challenges preconceptions of bourbon. What happens if you use a wood other than oak? What if you mature spirit in a wine cask? Would a sweet mash bourbon be much different from a sour mash one? What happens if you use an extra grain?

Woodford Reserve Four Grain was the first experimental release from 2005, and although it was strictly limited it was so successful that it was rolled out extensively. The extra grain is wheat, which adds softness and nuttiness to a spicy rye-tinged bourbon. It's still a bourbon because it contains more than 51 percent corn.

## WHY YOU SHOULD TRY

Woodford Reserve's master distiller is fascinated by the history and provenance of bourbon. He reads historical documents, questions some of the long-held legends about the evolution of American whiskey, and he has released a series of whiskeys exploring the whiskey-making process. This is one of those, and it's one of his better ones. This offers a departure from standard bourbons and variety is always good for this category.

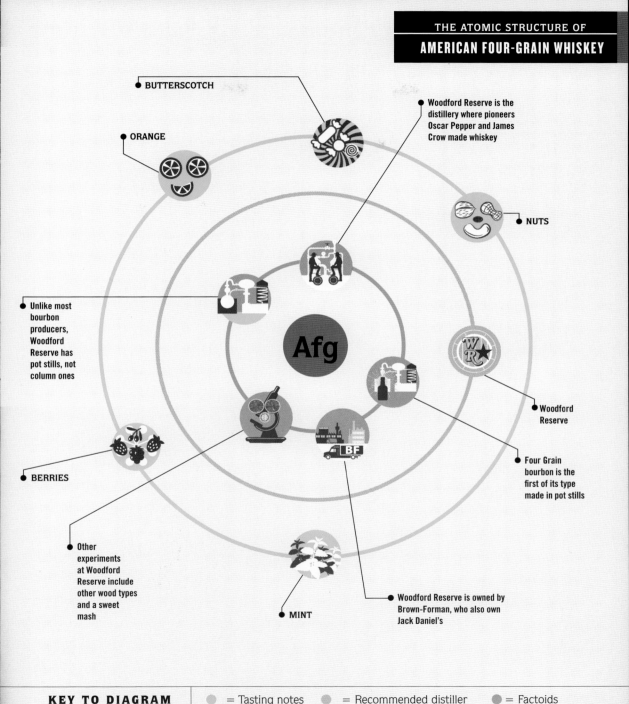

BUTTERSCOTCH

ORANGE

Woodford Reserve is the distillery where pioneers Oscar Pepper and James Crow made whiskey

NUTS

Unlike most bourbon producers, Woodford Reserve has pot stills, not column ones

**Afg**

Woodford Reserve

BERRIES

Four Grain bourbon is the first of its type made in pot stills

Other experiments at Woodford Reserve include other wood types and a sweet mash

MINT

Woodford Reserve is owned by Brown-Forman, who also own Jack Daniel's

**KEY TO DIAGRAM**  ● = Tasting notes  ● = Recommended distiller  ● = Factoids

**ORIGIN:** Holland
**ABV:** 40%
**GRAIN:** Barley, wheat, rye, oats, spelt
**CASK:** Ex-bourbon

# DUTCH FIVE-GRAIN MALT SPIRIT

**Is this oak-matured genever a whisky? It could well be. But we're erring on the side of caution and calling it a malt spirit. Grain is the whisky equivalent of the twin-bladed razor: once a luxury, now the norm.**

Here the addition of spelt, a relative of wheat, makes this, to our knowledge, the only five-grain malt spirit in the world. It's the creation of Patrick Zuidam, who oversees a distillery that produces all sorts of creative and unusual drinks products. Ask him about his five-grain spirit and he is disarmingly honest. Spelt, he says, is pretty useless and its presence doesn't have any real value for the finished drink. So why do it then? "Because," he says, "I wanted a five-grain spirit matured in oak. Simple as that."

## WHY YOU SHOULD TRY

This is from Zuidam, home of the Millstone range of whiskies, and you should try this for the same reason you should taste all Zuidam products; no corners are cut, only the finest ingredients are used and they're extremely well made. The additional grains don't particularly offer anything special, but this is almost certainly the only five-grain whisky in the world and few have tried it.

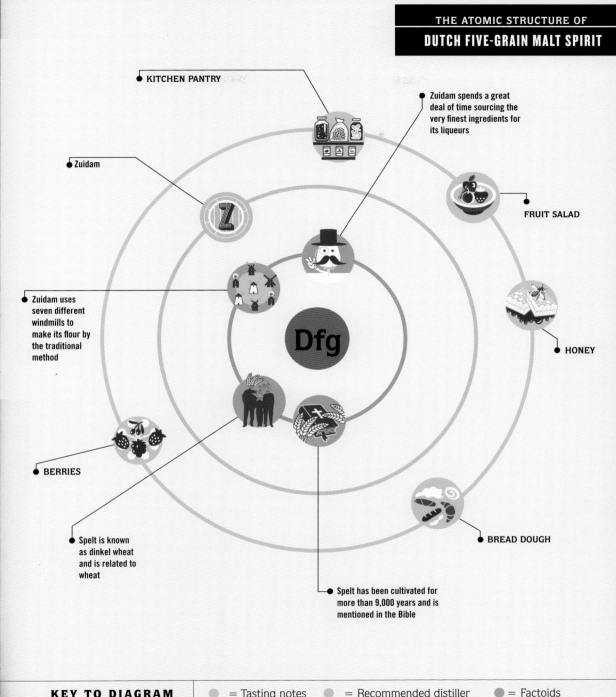

THE ATOMIC STRUCTURE OF
# DUTCH FIVE-GRAIN MALT SPIRIT

KITCHEN PANTRY

Zuidam spends a great deal of time sourcing the very finest ingredients for its liqueurs

Zuidam

FRUIT SALAD

Zuidam uses seven different windmills to make its flour by the traditional method

**Dfg**

HONEY

BERRIES

Spelt is known as dinkel wheat and is related to wheat

BREAD DOUGH

Spelt has been cultivated for more than 9,000 years and is mentioned in the Bible

**KEY TO DIAGRAM**     = Tasting notes     = Recommended distiller     = Factoids

# OAT WHISK(E)Y

**ORIGIN:** USA, Austria
**ABV:** 40%–43%
**GRAIN:** Oats, barley
**CASK:** Virgin white oak, ex-bourbon

**Oats are often overlooked when it comes to making whisky, but in recent years the growth of craft brewing has seen an increase in their use to make richer, creamier beer. Stout and porter, in particular, benefit from their presence.**

Oats make whisky sweet and somewhat flabby, closer to wheat whiskey than rye. They are most commonly used in the German-speaking countries, particularly Austria, but in recent years several whiskeys have come out of North America, the most significant of which are from Kentucky distiller Buffalo Trace, which experiments with a variety of grains in the mashbill, different wood types, and various aging periods.

Their success increases the chances that we will see more grain whisky in the future. Some American oak whiskeys are not aged in wood at all or for a very short time; these are sold as white whiskeys.

## WHY YOU SHOULD TRY

Oats make for a very different style of whisky (or whiskey, now that the drink has been revived in America). There are big differences between European and American versions of this, because in Europe the whisky must be aged for at least three years in oak. Oat whisky is sweet and delicate, and can be overpowered by oak. The Americans tend to prefer it as it's distilled, or when it's matured for a very short period. When it's right, though, this is a soft, creamy, sweet style of whisk(e)y and a pleasant alternative to Scotch or bourbon.

**KOVAL**

SINGLE BARREL
WHISKEY

*Oat*

DISTILLED IN CHICAGO
40% Alc. by Vol. 750ML

THE ATOMIC STRUCTURE OF
# OAT WHISK(E)Y

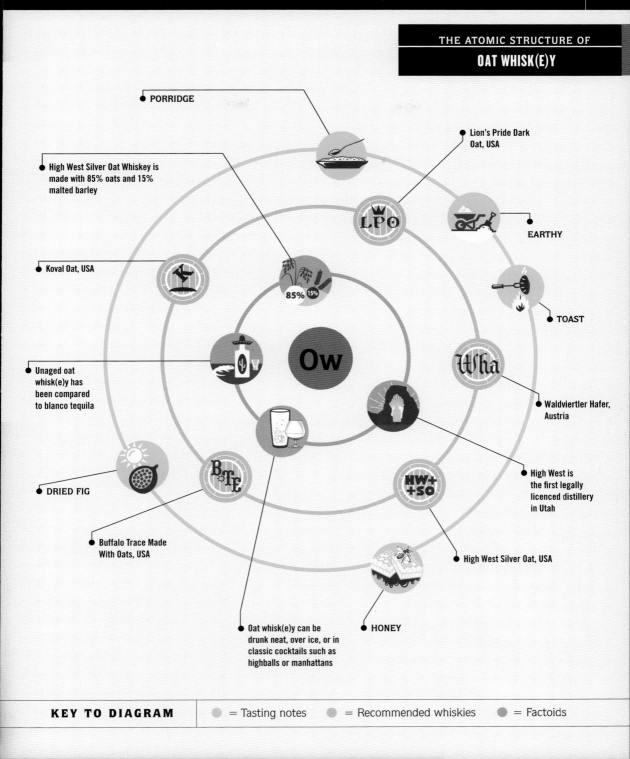

PORRIDGE

Lion's Pride Dark Oat, USA

High West Silver Oat Whiskey is made with 85% oats and 15% malted barley

LPO

EARTHY

Koval Oat, USA

85% 15%

TOAST

Wha

Ow

Unaged oat whisk(e)y has been compared to blanco tequila

Waldviertler Hafer, Austria

High West is the first legally licenced distillery in Utah

DRIED FIG

B.T.E

HW+ +SO

High West Silver Oat, USA

Buffalo Trace Made With Oats, USA

Oat whisk(e)y can be drunk neat, over ice, or in classic cocktails such as highballs or manhattans

HONEY

**KEY TO DIAGRAM**    ● = Tasting notes    ● = Recommended whiskies    ● = Factoids

# QUINOA WHISKEY

**ORIGIN:** USA
**ABV:** 46%
**GRAIN:** Quinoa, barley
**CASK:** Virgin white oak

**Corsair, in Nashville, Tennessee, is one of the leading craft distillers in the United States. It not only makes some very high-quality spirits, it is also happy to experiment with every aspect of whiskey production.**

Since we haven't had a quinoa whiskey before, we must assume that this is a good example of it. And if that's the case, you can't imagine that many more will appear.

On the plus side, it's inoffensive enough, and easy drinking. But is there a market for it? Yes, according to distillery owner Darek Bell, who says that the sort of people who are attracted to Corsair whiskey are young, health-conscious, and fashionable sorts who know all about quinoa and would expect it to feature in whiskey.

You've got to admire Corsair for trying, but this is a difficult whiskey to love.

## WHY YOU SHOULD TRY

Given that quinoa is the super-healthy grain of choice for many people these days, it's tempting to say that you should try it because it's good for you. But, of course, it isn't. The reason you should taste this is because this is the face of whisky's future, a liquid example of innovation and freethinking. These are not traits you see often with whisky.

## THE ATOMIC STRUCTURE OF
## QUINOA WHISKEY

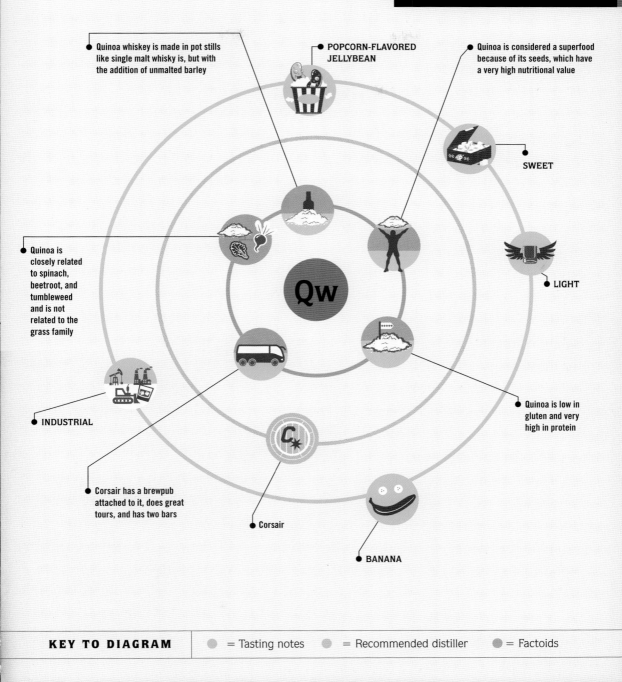

Quinoa whiskey is made in pot stills like single malt whisky is, but with the addition of unmalted barley

POPCORN-FLAVORED JELLYBEAN

Quinoa is considered a superfood because of its seeds, which have a very high nutritional value

SWEET

Quinoa is closely related to spinach, beetroot, and tumbleweed and is not related to the grass family

**Qw**

LIGHT

INDUSTRIAL

Quinoa is low in gluten and very high in protein

Corsair has a brewpub attached to it, does great tours, and has two bars

Corsair

BANANA

**KEY TO DIAGRAM**  ● = Tasting notes  ● = Recommended distiller  ● = Factoids

ORIGIN: USA, Sweden
ABV: 40%–55%
GRAIN: Various
CASK: Virgin white oak

# SMOKED WHISK(E)Y

**Of all the whisky styles to stir the blood, smoked whisky is potentially the most exciting. It is distinct from smoky or peaty whisky, and its style offers numerous possibilities for variations on the basic theme.**

The five whiskies mentioned opposite are all made by distilleries that know what they're doing, and the flavors they are producing are very different and unforgettable.

Brimstone is perfectly named, a charcoal and ashy delight, and different woods offer a range of distinctive characteristics, making these whiskies more than any other a category that might capture a whole new market.

In the vanguard of this movement is the United States, where Corsair is particularly active in this area. But Mackmyra in Sweden dries some of its barley over juniper twigs, giving its whiskies a distinctive Nordic character.

## WHY YOU SHOULD TRY

In the coming years, it's very possible that we'll see the development of whiskies with more distinctive nationalistic flavors, because of the use of different materials to dry the barley at the start of the production process. Peat is traditionally used, and peat is made up the flora and fauna of the place in which it is found. It follows, then, that peat will be different in different parts of the world, and if you replace peat with wood for smoking the barley, you open up even more avenues for regional variations. Already we are getting Swedish whisky made with barley dried with juniper twigs in the way that Sweden dries its food. This is where the future of whisky flavor may lie, and it's a very exciting category as a result.

MACKMYRA
41.4% ALC. BY VOL. • VOLUME 70 cl
THE SWEDISH WHISKY

## THE ATOMIC STRUCTURE OF
# SMOKED WHISK(E)Y

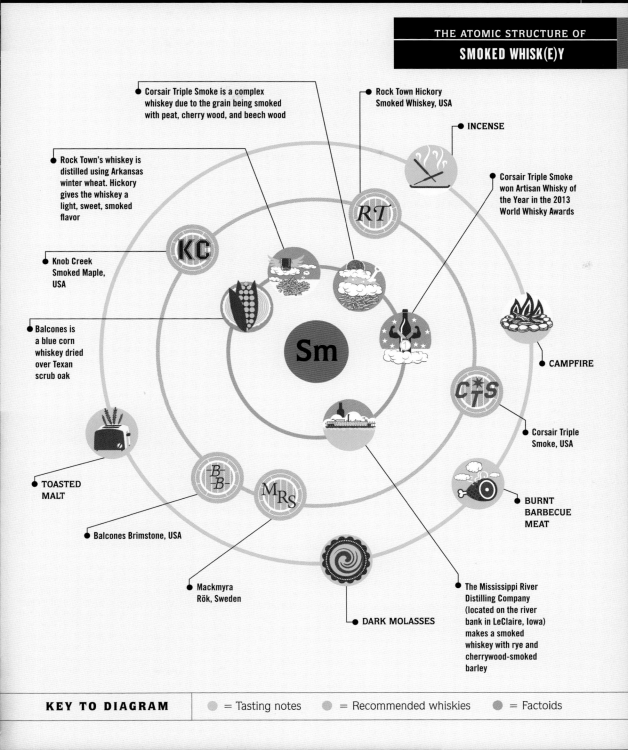

Corsair Triple Smoke is a complex whiskey due to the grain being smoked with peat, cherry wood, and beech wood

Rock Town Hickory Smoked Whiskey, USA

INCENSE

Rock Town's whiskey is distilled using Arkansas winter wheat. Hickory gives the whiskey a light, sweet, smoked flavor

Corsair Triple Smoke won Artisan Whisky of the Year in the 2013 World Whisky Awards

Knob Creek Smoked Maple, USA

Balcones is a blue corn whiskey dried over Texan scrub oak

CAMPFIRE

Corsair Triple Smoke, USA

TOASTED MALT

BURNT BARBECUE MEAT

Balcones Brimstone, USA

Mackmyra Rök, Sweden

DARK MOLASSES

The Mississippi River Distilling Company (located on the river bank in LeClaire, Iowa) makes a smoked whiskey with rye and cherrywood-smoked barley

**KEY TO DIAGRAM** | = Tasting notes | = Recommended whiskies | = Factoids

**ORIGIN:** USA
**ABV:** 35%–40%
**GRAIN:** Corn, wheat, barley, rye
**CASK:** Virgin white oak

# FLAVORED WHISKEYS—USA

**Quite why the market for flavored whiskeys exploded the way it did, when it did, isn't easy to explain. It was perhaps because some marketing person at one of the major companies decided to ignore potential ridicule.**

Wild Turkey had had American Honey for years, and promoted it with skimpily clad women and claimed it tasted good on ice cream. It wasn't taken seriously.

But then bang! Red Stag from Jim Beam and Tennessee Honey from Jack Daniel's blew the lid off the category and it hasn't looked back since. The sweetness was seen as a way of bringing women into the whiskey category, but research shows that men are just as likely to be drawn to it. It certainly appeals to younger drinkers, but whether it's a stepping-stone to "real" whiskey is a moot point.

## WHY YOU SHOULD TRY IT

You have to be careful which flavored drinks you go for, but Wild Turkey American Honey has been around for some years now and if you have it with ice cream it makes for a really pleasant dessert drink. The more well-made drinks in this category are not overly cloying or sickly sweet, and bring an added dimension to American whiskey-based drinks. They are certainly no less desirable than many cocktails.

THE ATOMIC STRUCTURE OF
# FLAVORED WHISKEYS—USA

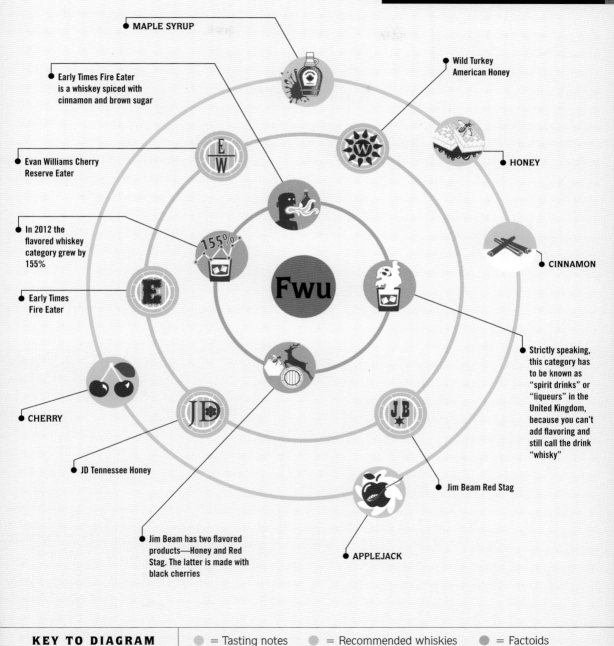

MAPLE SYRUP

Early Times Fire Eater
is a whiskey spiced with
cinnamon and brown sugar

Wild Turkey
American Honey

Evan Williams Cherry
Reserve Eater

HONEY

In 2012 the
flavored whiskey
category grew by
155%

CINNAMON

155%

Fwu

Early Times
Fire Eater

Strictly speaking,
this category has
to be known as
"spirit drinks" or
"liqueurs" in the
United Kingdom,
because you can't
add flavoring and
still call the drink
"whisky"

CHERRY

JD Tennessee Honey

Jim Beam Red Stag

Jim Beam has two flavored
products—Honey and Red
Stag. The latter is made with
black cherries

APPLEJACK

**KEY TO DIAGRAM**    ● = Tasting notes    ● = Recommended whiskies    ● = Factoids

**ORIGIN:** Scotland and Ireland
**ABV:** 40%
**GRAIN:** Barley, wheat, corn
**CASK:** Ex-bourbon, ex-sherry

# FLAVORED WHISKIES— SCOTLAND AND IRELAND

**After years of snobbish aversion to the idea of adding flavoring to Scotch, the commercial temptations grew too great for distillers to resist. Those who held their noses and took the plunge were handsomely rewarded.**

And we're not talking obscure fringe players—we're talking Diageo, Pernod Ricard, and Bacardi, three of the biggest drinks companies in the world. In their defense, they have mainly tended to stick with honey, which has been associated with whisky from the very earliest days of rough single malt. There is a whole tradition of Scottish liqueurs featuring whisky and honey. The hot toddy is based on the combination. Nevertheless, many people regard this latest bout of flavoring whisky as the not particularly thin end of a very large wedge. One of the most objectionable products was a mixture of blended Scotch and chilis.

## WHY YOU SHOULD TRY

This category isn't without controversy, because for years Scotland resisted the temptation to mess around with the fundamentals of whisky making, and adding flavorings is not the done thing. Nevertheless once the American flavored whiskeys became successful perhaps it was inevitable. Honey is a natural partner to Scotch anyway and now we have a ready-made hot toddy. Just add water. The best of these is Ballantine's Brasil: the lime adds a delicious and refreshing twist on quality Scotch.

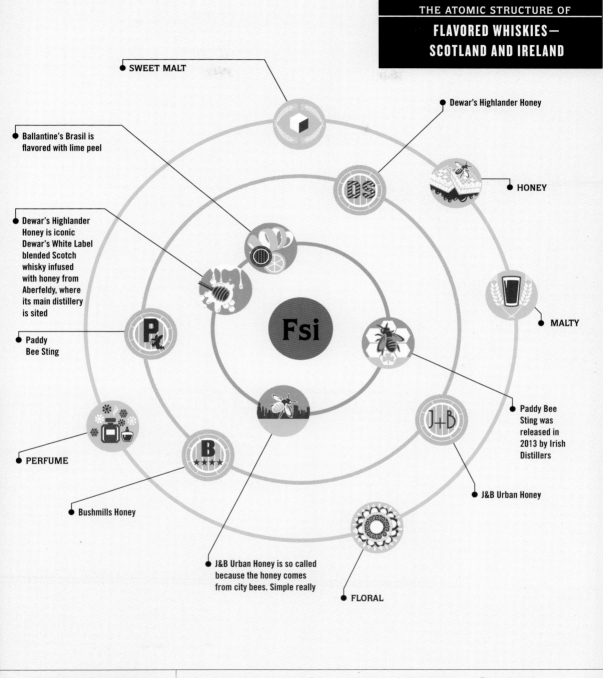

SWEET MALT

Dewar's Highlander Honey

Ballantine's Brasil is flavored with lime peel

HONEY

Dewar's Highlander Honey is iconic Dewar's White Label blended Scotch whisky infused with honey from Aberfeldy, where its main distillery is sited

MALTY

Paddy Bee Sting

**Fsi**

Paddy Bee Sting was released in 2013 by Irish Distillers

PERFUME

J&B Urban Honey

Bushmills Honey

J&B Urban Honey is so called because the honey comes from city bees. Simple really

FLORAL

**KEY TO DIAGRAM**   ● = Tasting notes   ● = Recommended whiskies   ● = Factoids

**ORIGIN:** USA, England
**ABV:** 40%–46%
**GRAIN:** Barley, corn, wheat, rye

# FRUIT-INFUSED WHISKIES

**The Scotch Whisky Association has clear rules about what can be called whisky. It must contain only grain, yeast and water, although caramel is permitted for coloring. Flavored "spirits drinks" must make it clear that they are not whiskies.**

A few years ago, Compass Box released Orangerie and described it as a "whisky infusion." It was widely believed that the company would have run into trouble if it had described the drink as an "infused whisky." That's how fine the margins are.

Unlike infused whisky, however, fruit-infused whisky is crafted, and the products with which it's infused don't necessarily contribute to an over-sweet product. Its progress toward general acceptance is currently being accelerated by North American craft distillers, increasing numbers of whom are now producing it.

## WHY YOU SHOULD TRY

Again this is a category that doesn't just bend the rules, it pretty much snaps them in half. You can't call a product whisky if it has hops or orange peel in it. Compass Box Orangerie was described on its label as a "whisky infusion," but almost certainly couldn't have been called an "infused whisky." But these spirits drinks are often excellent, carefully crafted, and packed with new and exciting flavors. This category looks set to grow and grow.

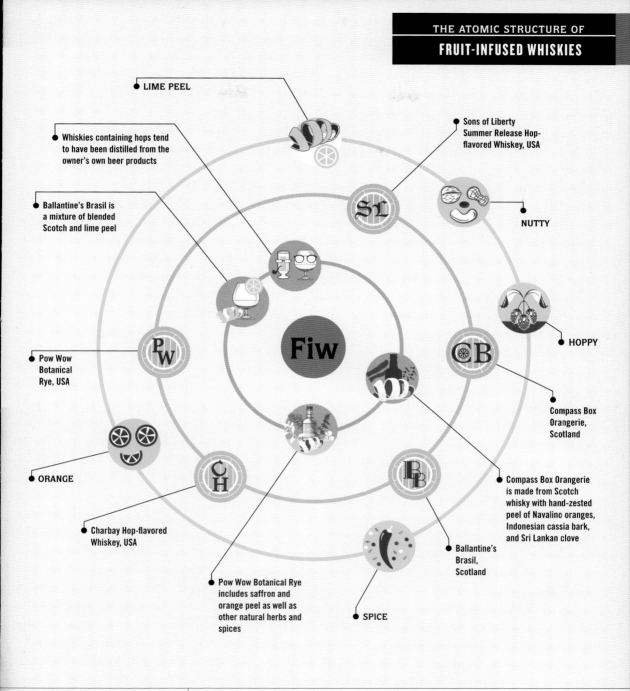

LIME PEEL

Whiskies containing hops tend
to have been distilled from the
owner's own beer products

Sons of Liberty
Summer Release Hop-
flavored Whiskey, USA

NUTTY

Ballantine's Brasil is
a mixture of blended
Scotch and lime peel

SL

Fiw

PW

CB

HOPPY

Pow Wow
Botanical
Rye, USA

Compass Box
Orangerie,
Scotland

ORANGE

CH

BB

Compass Box Orangerie
is made from Scotch
whisky with hand-zested
peel of Navalino oranges,
Indonesian cassia bark,
and Sri Lankan clove

Charbay Hop-flavored
Whiskey, USA

Ballantine's
Brasil,
Scotland

Pow Wow Botanical Rye
includes saffron and
orange peel as well as
other natural herbs and
spices

SPICE

**KEY TO DIAGRAM** | ● = Tasting notes ● = Recommended whiskies ● = Factoids

**ORIGIN:** Ireland, Wales
**ABV:** 40%–90%
**GRAIN:** Any

# IRISH POITÍN

**Poitín or poteen is Ireland's fiery and strong spirit that has more in common with vodka or moonshine than it does with genuine whisky. It has been produced in many forms, from vicious firewater to a toffee-and-mint-flavored commercial drink.**

Poitín was illegal for years. It can have an alcoholic strength of more than 90 percent—enough to make you blind or kill you. It was often made from potatoes, which were a staple of the Irish diet and an obvious choice. But it could equally be made with almost any grain that came to hand. It flourished in periods of austerity, because it's a quick and cheap alternative to whisky.

Legal and commercial versions of poitín are matured in the same sort of casks as those used for whisky. There is something faintly amusing about attempts to market it as a premium spirit.

## WHY YOU SHOULD TRY

Only moonshine matches poitín when it comes to conjuring up images of rebelliousness, lawlessness, and adventure—and with good reason. Poitín is effectively Irish moonshine, a distillate traditionally created from whatever the distiller could get his hands on, and as rough as old boots. Today there are several commercial poitíns which vary enormously in taste (there is a London bar specializing in them) and there is an attempt to build the category. Go for something like Teeling, which is basically a new-make malt spirit. It's fun and feisty.

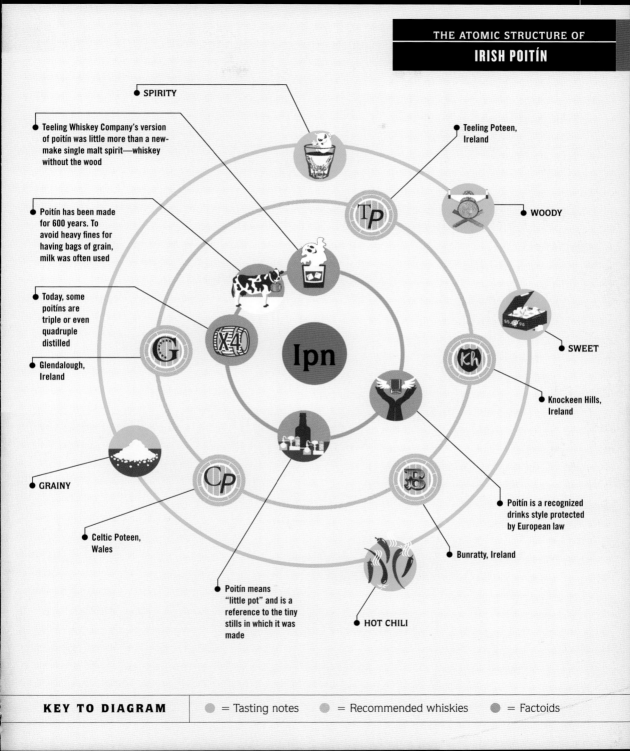

SPIRITY

Teeling Whiskey Company's version of poitín was little more than a new-make single malt spirit—whiskey without the wood

Teeling Poteen, Ireland

TP

WOODY

Poitín has been made for 600 years. To avoid heavy fines for having bags of grain, milk was often used

Today, some poitíns are triple or even quadruple distilled

SWEET

G

X4

Ipn

Kh

Glendalough, Ireland

Knockeen Hills, Ireland

GRAINY

CP

B

Poitín is a recognized drinks style protected by European law

Celtic Poteen, Wales

Bunratty, Ireland

Poitín means "little pot" and is a reference to the tiny stills in which it was made

HOT CHILI

**KEY TO DIAGRAM**    ● = Tasting notes    ● = Recommended whiskies    ● = Factoids

# TRITICALE WHISKY

**ORIGIN:** USA, Wales
**ABV:** 40%–46%
**GRAIN:** Triticale
**CASK:** Ex-bourbon, virgin white oak

**Until very recently the grain triticale had not been used at all for whisky production, but now it is being adopted by a number of distilleries. It is a cross between wheat and rye, and was created in a laboratory and grown in Sweden and Scotland. It combines the relatively high yield and quality of wheat with rye's resistance to disease and can be grown in light soil.**

Triticale has caught the attention of new distillers for two main reasons: one, because some craft distillers use only local products and triticale is often available when rye isn't; and two, because the softness and sweetness of the wheat component mixed with rye makes for a distinct and tasty whisky.

Note that the countries of origin include Wales. Dà Mhìle has started making organic spirits of all sorts, including whisky, and triticale is one of the grains in use there. American craft distillers are also trying triticale: the hybrid is rapidly establishing itself as a source of whisky.

## WHY YOU SHOULD TRY IT

Making whisky with a grain that has never been used for the purpose before, particularly a laboratory-created hybrid grain, could be seen as gimmicky, and to an extent it is. But triticale combines properties of wheat and rye, and these grains produce two very different types of whisky: the former has soft, sweet notes; the latter, sharp and spicy ones. This impacts on different parts of the tongue, making for an intriguing whisky-drinking experience.

CORSAIR
TRITICALE
WHISKEY

AMERICAN WHISKEY POT DISTILLED
FROM TRITICALE AND BARLEY
46% ALC/VOL (92 PROOF)

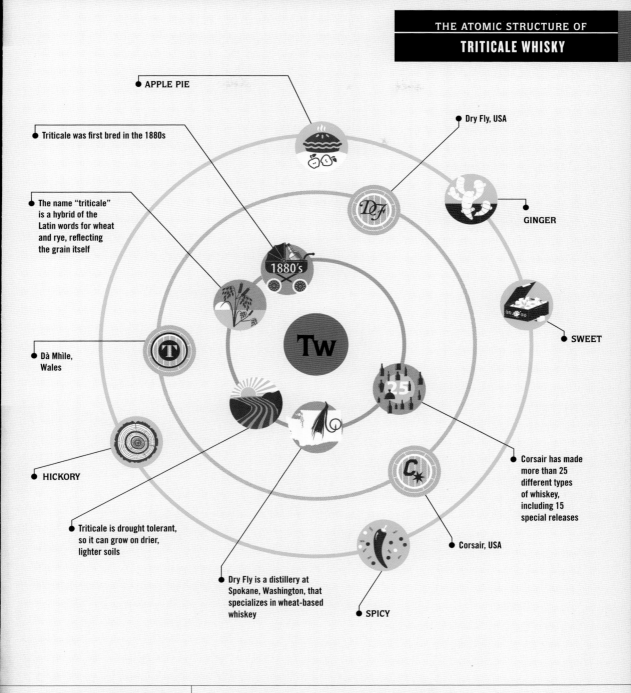

APPLE PIE

Dry Fly, USA

Triticale was first bred in the 1880s

GINGER

The name "triticale" is a hybrid of the Latin words for wheat and rye, reflecting the grain itself

SWEET

Dà Mhìle, Wales

HICKORY

Corsair has made more than 25 different types of whiskey, including 15 special releases

Triticale is drought tolerant, so it can grow on drier, lighter soils

Corsair, USA

Dry Fly is a distillery at Spokane, Washington, that specializes in wheat-based whiskey

SPICY

**KEY TO DIAGRAM** ● = Tasting notes ● = Recommended distillers ● = Factoids

ORIGIN: France
ABV: 40%–43%
GRAIN: Buckwheat, barley
CASK: Ex-bourbon,
ex-wine, ex-Cognac

# FRENCH ROGUE WHISKY

**There is a definite rogue element to French whisky that is strangely endearing. It is hard not to admire the sheer chutzpah of the distillers and their overwhelming passion when it comes to their products.**

Distillerie des Menhirs makes whisky with buckwheat, which is technically a pseudocereal, not a grain. In France, though, it is called blé noir (black wheat), and the French government has ruled that it may be classed as a grain, so that's all right then. Then there's Brenne, made in Cognac barrels and with a taste, gorgeous though it is, which suggests that not all the Cognac has come out. Meanwhile, over in French Corsica, the whisky is made from a beer containing chestnuts. To great effect. Does any of this matter if the drinks taste great? Probably not.

## THREE TO TRY

| Eddu Gold | Fluffy, fruity, and with a touch of Horlicks in the mix, this is a big, proud, and slightly naughty whisky, as the "grain" flavoring comes courtesy of buckwheat | ★ |
|---|---|---|
| P&M | A real oddball flavor: intensely savory and nutty, with some soured fruits around the edge. It shouldn't work, but it does. And it's certainly different | ★★ |
| Brenne Single Cask | Made in very small quantities in Cognac and then imported directly to New York, this has a sweet, floral, winey, and delicate taste | ★★★ |

★ LEAST EXPENSIVE/WIDELY AVAILABLE ★★ MODERATELY PRICED/
HARDER TO SOURCE ★★★ COSTLY/RARE

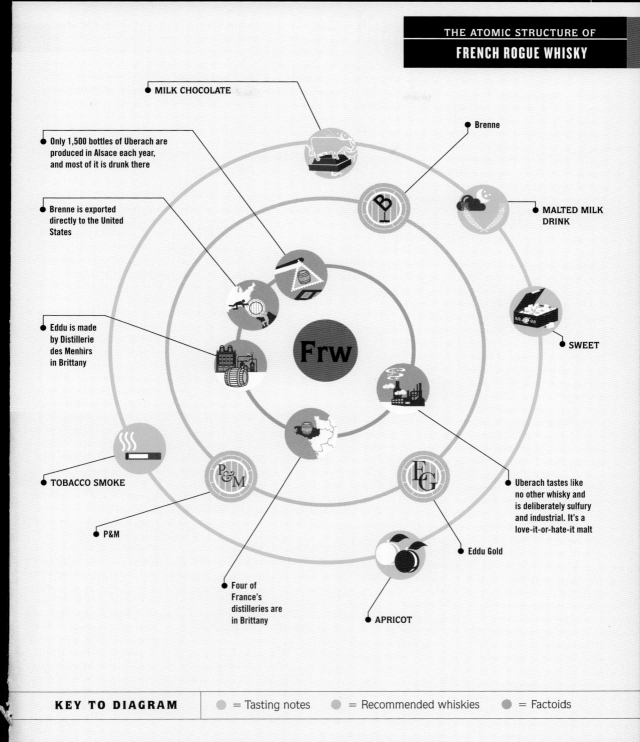

THE ATOMIC STRUCTURE OF
# FRENCH ROGUE WHISKY

MILK CHOCOLATE

Only 1,500 bottles of Uberach are produced in Alsace each year, and most of it is drunk there

Brenne is exported directly to the United States

Brenne

MALTED MILK DRINK

Eddu is made by Distillerie des Menhirs in Brittany

Frw

SWEET

TOBACCO SMOKE

P&M

Uberach tastes like no other whisky and is deliberately sulfury and industrial. It's a love-it-or-hate-it malt

Four of France's distilleries are in Brittany

Eddu Gold

APRICOT

**KEY TO DIAGRAM**     ● = Tasting notes     ● = Recommended whiskies     ● = Factoids

**ORIGIN:** South Africa
**ABV:** 43%
**GRAIN:** Barley, wheat, corn
**CASK:** Virgin oak, malt spirit, whisky

# SOLERA WHISKY

The definition of whisky—a spirits drink distilled using just grain, yeast, and water—is perfectly simple but can be construed in a wide variety of ways. Moritz Kallmeyer's interpretation is one of the most unusual.

A craft beer producer at Drayman's, Kallmeyer turned his hand to making whisky via the solera system of fractional blending, a method that is also used by Glenfiddich and by Loch Fyne Whiskies in its shop at Inveraray, Scotland.

At Drayman's, you fill a small cask with the blend and take it home. As it empties, you refuel it with whatever takes your fancy.

It's hard to describe the flavor, because it changes every time a new bottle is added. But what a fun way to enjoy your whisky. Kallmeyer's DIY concept is now being adopted in bars worldwide.

## WHY YOU SHOULD TRY

It's not likely that you'll be popping over to the Drayman's Brewery and Distillery any time soon, so chances are you won't get to try the South African version of this. If you're in Scotland you might check out Loch Fyne Whiskies at Inverary, which has what it calls a living cask. And failing that, you can always make your own. All you need to do is purchase a little cask and fill it with a mixture of your favorite whiskies. Then as you drink your DIY blended malt, you refill the cask with something different. Why bother? Because it offers you the chance to sample an ever-changing whisky often punching above its weight in terms of depth and taste, and because it's a fun thing to do. If you like one whisky, then that's fine. But if you want to explore different tastes and styles, you can.

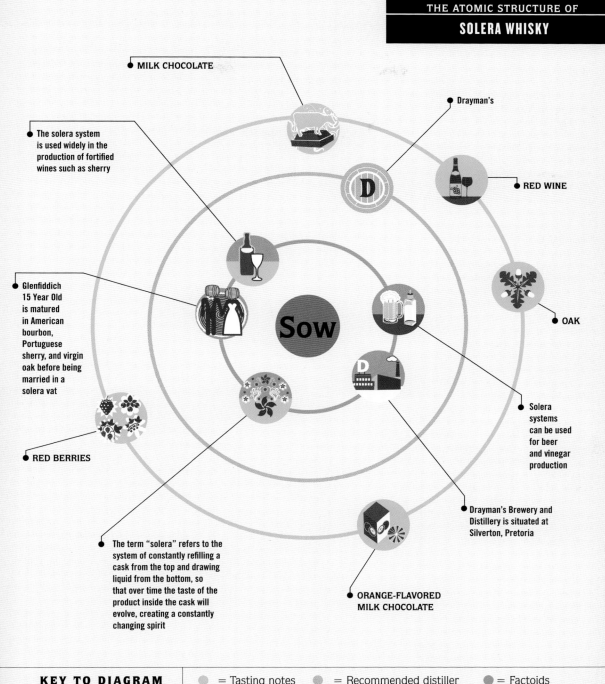

MILK CHOCOLATE

Drayman's

The solera system is used widely in the production of fortified wines such as sherry

RED WINE

Glenfiddich 15 Year Old is matured in American bourbon, Portuguese sherry, and virgin oak before being married in a solera vat

**Sow**

OAK

Solera systems can be used for beer and vinegar production

RED BERRIES

Drayman's Brewery and Distillery is situated at Silverton, Pretoria

The term "solera" refers to the system of constantly refilling a cask from the top and drawing liquid from the bottom, so that over time the taste of the product inside the cask will evolve, creating a constantly changing spirit

ORANGE-FLAVORED MILK CHOCOLATE

**KEY TO DIAGRAM**   ● = Tasting notes   ● = Recommended distiller   ● = Factoids

**ORIGIN:** Across the world
**ABV:** 40%–70%
**GRAIN:** Barley, wheat, corn, rye
**CASK:** Ex-bourbon, ex-sherry

# YOUNG MALT SPIRIT DRINKS

**You have opened a distillery. You have staff and overheads. But you must wait at least three years before you can sell whisky, and even then it will probably be too young and will harm your reputation. What to do?**

You can make vodka and gin, or you can buy in ingredients to make liqueur with your spirit. Alternatively, you can do what an increasing number of distillers do: sell clear new-make spirit or "works in progress."

This is what Glenmorangie did when it bought Ardbeg and wanted to reassure existing customers that it would not dumb down the big peaty whiskies for which its new acquisition was renowned.

The same approach may also work for start-up distilleries in countries such as Italy or England, where there is a genuine interest in the sort of whisky they will eventually produce.

## THREE TO TRY

| | | |
|---|---|---|
| **Mackmyra Withund** | Big, strong, new-make spirit from one of the more intense and flavor-rich European distilleries | ★★ |
| **Buffalo Trace** | American whiskey spirit without wood is like the emperor without his clothes. Intriguing to see the difference between this and BT bourbon, though | ★★ |
| **Puni Pure and Alba** | The Italians like their spirits young, but these are outstanding examples of young spirits and are worth drinking in their own right | ★★ |

★ LEAST EXPENSIVE/WIDELY AVAILABLE  ★★ MODERATELY PRICED/ HARDER TO SOURCE  ★★★ COSTLY/RARE

THE ATOMIC STRUCTURE OF
# YOUNG MALT SPIRIT DRINKS

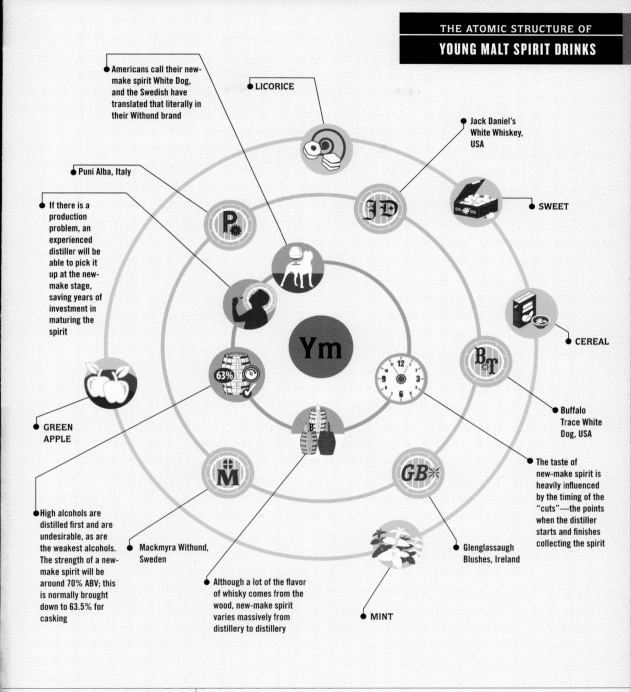

Americans call their new-make spirit White Dog, and the Swedish have translated that literally in their Withund brand

LICORICE

Jack Daniel's White Whiskey, USA

Puni Alba, Italy

If there is a production problem, an experienced distiller will be able to pick it up at the new-make stage, saving years of investment in maturing the spirit

SWEET

Ym

CEREAL

63%

GREEN APPLE

Buffalo Trace White Dog, USA

High alcohols are distilled first and are undesirable, as are the weakest alcohols. The strength of a new-make spirit will be around 70% ABV; this is normally brought down to 63.5% for casking

Mackmyra Withund, Sweden

Although a lot of the flavor of whisky comes from the wood, new-make spirit varies massively from distillery to distillery

The taste of new-make spirit is heavily influenced by the timing of the "cuts"—the points when the distiller starts and finishes collecting the spirit

Glenglassaugh Blushes, Ireland

MINT

**KEY TO DIAGRAM** ● = Tasting notes  ● = Recommended whiskies  ● = Factoids

## Author Acknowledgments

I'd like to dedicate this book to my father Keith, who died in December 2013.

A special thank you to my long-suffering family: my wife Sally and three children Jules, Louie, and Maddy, who are no longer so sure that drinking lots of whisky counts as a real job. Also to my brother Ben, his wife Tracy, and family.

As always a big thank you to distillers and whisky makers around the world for friendship, education and lots of great whisky. Particular thanks go to the following folk who have gone beyond the call of duty:

Tony Bagnall, Michelle Bagnall, Rachel Barrie, Pat Barrow, Bex Barrow, Jefferson Boss, Ronnie Cox, John Craft, Stephen Davies, Christian Davis, Andrew Davison, Paul Davison, Ray Davison, Scott Davison, Joy Elliott, David Fitt, John Glaser, Alwynne Gwilt, Chris Higgins, Ian Logan, Johanne McInnis, Jessica Mason, Doug McIvor, Annabel Meikle, Marcin Miller, Andrew Naylor, Andrew Nelstrop, Richard Paterson, Greg Ramsay, Chris Rodden, David Robertson, Jason Standing, Marcel Telser, Andrew Torrance, Patrick Zuidam.

## Credits

Marshall Editions would like to thank the following distilleries and agencies for supplying images for inclusion in this book:

Kowalczyk, Pawel, Shutterstock.com, p.6w • Liu, Lora, Shutterstock.com, p.9b • Corbis, p.10, 11 • Auchentoshan, www.auchentoshan.com, p.16 • © 2008 Springbank Distillers Ltd, www.springbankwhisky.com, p.18 • Dalwhinnie, Diageo, www.malts.com, p.20 • Glengoyne Distillery, www.glengoyne.com, p.22 • Whyte and Mackay Limited, www.thedalmore.com, p.24 • The Glenlivet Distillery, Pernod Ricard, www.theglenlivet.com, p.26 • Glendronach Distillery, BenRiach Distillery Company, www.glendronachdistillery.com, p.28 • Talisker Whisky Distillery, Diageo, www.malts.com, p.30 • Ardbeg Distillery, Louis Vuitton Moët Hennessy, www.ardbeg.com, p.32 • Laphroaig distillery, Beam Suntory, www.laphroaig.com, p.34 •Jura Distillery, United Breweries Group, www.jurawhisky.com, p.36 • Aberlour Distillery, www.aberlour.com, p.38 •

Glenmorangie Distillery, Louis Vuitton Moët Hennessy, www.glenmorangie.com, p.40, 46 • BenRiach Distillery, BenRiach Distillery Company, www.benriachdistillery.co.uk, p.42 • Balvenie Distillery, William Grant & Sons, www.thebalvenie.com, p.44 • Old Bushmills Distillery, Diageo, www.bushmills.com, p.48 • Cooley Distillery, Beam Suntory, www.kilbeggandistillingcompany.com, p.50 • Balcones Distillery, www.balconesdistilling.com, p.52 • Chichibu Distillery, Venture Whisky, p.54 • Hakushu Distillery, Suntory, p.56 • Limeburners, www.limeburners.com, p.58 • Amrut Distilleries, www.amrutdistilleries.com, p.60 • The New Zealand Whisky Company Distillery, www.thenzwhisky.com, p.62 • Three Ships Whisky, www.threeshipswhisky.co.za, p.64, 108 • Kavalan, King Car Whisky Distillery, www.kavalanwhisky.com, p.66 • The Owl Distillery, www.belgianwhisky.com, p.68 • Stauning Whisky, www.stauningwhisky.dk, p.70 • Zuidam Distillery, www.zuidam.eu, p.72, 196 • St Georges Distillery, www.englishwhisky.co.uk, p.74 • Penderyn Distillery, Welsh Whisky Company, www.welsh-whisky.co.uk, p.76 • Anchor Distilling Company, www.anchordistilling.com, p.78 • Telser Distillery, www.telserdistillery.com, p.80 • Destilerías y Crianza del Whisky S.A., www.dyc.es, p.82, 110 • Mackmyra Svensk Whisky, www.mackmyra.com, p.84, 202 • Chivas Brothers Limited, www.chivas.com, p.90 • © 2013 DEWAR'S, Bacardi, www.livetrue.dewars.com, p.92 • Ballantine's, Pernod Ricard, www.ballantines.com, p.94, 208 • Jameson, Pernod Richard, www.jamesonwhiskey.com, p.96 • The Wild Geese Collection, www.thewildgeesecollection.com, p.98 • Suntory, www.suntory.com, p.100 • Nikka, www.nikka.com, p.102, 124 • Distillerie des Menhirs, www.distillerie.fr, p.104 • McDowell's, United Spirits Limited, www.unitedspirits.in, p.106 • The Crown Royal Company, www.crownroyal.com, p.112 • Monkey Shoulder Company Limited, William Grant & Sons Group, www.monkeyshoulder.com, p.118 • Compass Box Whisky Company, www.compassboxwhisky.com, p.120, 122 • Teeling Whiskey Company, www.teelingwhiskey.com, p.126 • Kings County Distillery, www.kingscountydistillery.com, p.146 • Buffalo Trace Distillery,

www.buffalotracedistillery.com, p.132 • Sazerac Company, www.sazerac.com, p.134 • A. Smith Bowman Distillery, www.asmithbowman.com, p.136 • Breckenridge Distillery, www.breckenridgedistillery.com, p.138 • Balcones Distilling, www.balconesdistilling.com, p.140 • GEORGE A. DICKEL & CO., www.georgedickel.com, p.142 • Anchor Distilling, www.anchordistilling.com, p.144 • Heaven Hill Distilleries, Inc., www.heavenhill.com, p.152, 170 • Sazerac Co., www.sazerac.com, p.154 • Forty Creek Distillery, www.fortycreekwhisky.com, p.156 • Zuidam Distillery, www.zuidam.eu, p.158 • Waldviertler Roggenhof, www.roggenhof.at, p.160 • Discovery Road Smile, www.worldwhisky.co.uk, p.162 • Brennerei Telser, www.telserdistillery.com, p.164 • DOUGLAS LAING & CO LTD, www.douglaslaing.com, p.172 • Redbreast, Pernod Richard, www.singlepotstill.com, p.174 • Greenore, www.greenorewhiskey.com, p.176 • Writers Tears Whiskey Ltd, www.writerstears.com, p.178 • La Maison du Whisky, Nikka Whisky, www.nikkawhisky.eu, p.180 • Bain's Cape Mountain Whisky, www.bains.co.za, p.182 • Waldviertler Hafer, www.weidenauer.at, p.184 • Adnams PLC, www.adnams.co.uk, p.190 • PUNI Destillerie, www.puni.com, Photo: Lukas Ebensperger, p.192, 218 • The Woodford Reserve Distillery, www.woodfordreserve.com, p.194 • KOVAL INC, www.koval-distillery.com, p.198 • CORSAIR ARTISAN, LLC, www.corsairartisan.com, p.200, 212 • James B. Beam Distilling Co., www.jimbeam.com, p.204 • Paddy, Pernod Ricard, www.paddy.ie, p.206 • Glendalough Distillery, www.glendaloughdistillery.com, p.210 • Brenne, www.drinkbrenne.com, p.214 • Drayman's, www.draymans.com, p.216

While every effort has been made to credit contributors, Marshall Editions would like to apologize should there have been any omissions or errors and would be pleased to make the appropriate correction to future editions of the book.